MATERNAL FICTIONS

MATERNAL FICTIONS

Stendhal, Sand, Rachilde, and Bataille

Maryline Lukacher

Duke University Press   Durham and London

1994

© 1994 Duke University Press

All rights reserved

Printed in the United States of America on acid-free paper ∞

Designed by Cherie Holma Westmoreland

Typeset in Weiss by Keystone Typesetting, Inc.

Library of Congress Cataloging-in-Publication Data appear
on the last printed page of this book.

Excerpts from George Sand, *Story of My Life,* a group
translation, ed. Thelma Jurgrau (Albany: State University of New
York Press, 1991), are reprinted in this volume by permission of
the State University of New York Press.

Frontispiece illustration: *Madame la Mort* by Paul Gauguin.

Frontispiece to Rachilde's *Le Théâtre* (Paris, 1891). Courtesy Musée
du Louvre, Département des Arts Graphiques, Paris.

© Photo R. M. N.

FOR LUCE

CONTENTS

CONTENTS

ACKNOWLEDGMENTS

Many people have helped me in preparing this book. I was first introduced to the study of nineteenth- and twentieth-century French literature by Fredric Jameson, Louis Marin, Alain Cohen, and Jean-François Lyotard, who were my teachers at the University of California, San Diego. I am grateful to them for having opened the way to the intellectual project on which I have been embarked ever since.

More recently, I have incurred a large debt to Ross Chambers, who introduced me to the work of Rachilde. His support and encouragement have been immensely valuable over the past few years.

Isabelle Naginski, Mary Lydon, David Powell, and Rima Drell Reck have provided extremely helpful comments on my work over the past three years. I would also like to thank my colleague Johanna Van Lente and my former colleague Marilyn Skinner for their support for this and other projects.

Earlier versions of parts of this book have appeared in various publications. Part of chapter 1, "Stendhal and the Oedipal Palimpsest," appeared under the title of "L'Impossible dire dans le texte stendhalien," *Nineteenth-Century French Studies* 17 (1989). A section of chapter 2, "Sand: Double Identity," appeared as "La Communauté à venir: la fiction sandienne entre 1832–1845," *Romanic Review* 4 (November 1990). Parts of chapter 3, "Mademoiselle Baudelaire: Rachilde and the Sexual Difference," appeared as "Mademoiselle Baudelaire: Rachilde ou le féminin au masculin," *Nineteenth-Century French Studies* 20 (1992). Finally, part of my last chapter, "*Divinus Deus:* Bataille's Erotic Education," appeared as "Writing the Abject: Bataille's *Ma Mère*," in *Literature and the Body,* ed. Anthony Purdy (Amsterdam and Atlanta: Rodopi, 1992). I would like to thank the editors of these publications, Thomas Goetz, Michael Riffaterre, and Anthony Purdy, for their interest in my work. These articles have been completely revised and reworked for inclusion in *Maternal Fictions*.

I would also like to thank Reynolds Smith, my editor at Duke University Press, for his support at all stages of this project. The two readers of my manuscript for Duke University Press offered many helpful suggestions for which I am very grateful. The interlibrary loan staff of Founder's Library at Northern Illinois University was instrumental in the completion of this project.

I thank particularly Ned Lukacher for helping me prepare *Maternal Fictions* for publication.

M.L.
De Kalb, Illinois

ACKNOWLEDGMENTS

Introduction

PSEUDONYMOUS IDENTITIES

His love for his mother was excessive, if indeed excess is
possible in the case of an emotion which, however intense, will
never wear the name of passion because in it there is none of
that imperfection which mars the passions.

HORACE DE SAINT-AUBIN, *The Centenarian*

Horace de Saint-Aubin was one of Honoré de Balzac's pseudonyms. Between 1822 and 1829 Balzac signed his earliest publications with the pseudonyms de Viellerglé, Lord R'Hoone, and
Horace de Saint-Aubin. When his literary apprenticeship ended
in 1829, Balzac decided henceforth to publish under his own
name. It would appear that he began to use his paternal name
only when he felt a certain confidence in his literary talents. The
abandonment of pseudonyms marks the passage from his juve-
nilia to his more mature writing. The return to the father's name
signals Balzac's attachment to legitimacy and the reinscription of
patriarchal values within his own work. Before 1829 Balzac regarded his work as somehow unworthy of his proper name. After
1829 he was able to embrace the patronymic and with it the
legal, aesthetic, and moral legitimacy that the name affords.
Legitimacy thus truly becomes a question of a biological, legal
birthright. For Balzac, becoming a writer literalizes in every sense
the ascendancy of the phallic signifier.

Because Balzac fully recognized what is at stake in assuming a pseudonym, we can see in his commitment to a legitimist mode of thought (in all its dimensions) a highly revealing contrast against which we will be better able to measure the use of pseudonyms by the authors who stand at the center of *Maternal Fictions*. Stendhal, Sand, Rachilde, and Bataille never made the turn toward legitimacy that was constitutive for Balzac's career. Quite to the contrary, they chose precisely *not* to inscribe their writing under the aegis of the father's name. As we will see, the use of pseudonyms by these writers was part of a subversive effort to challenge patriarchal authority and to reinscribe the suppressed relation to the mother.

Eighteen twenty-nine was also the year in which Balzac's father died. Now assuming the place of the father, Balzac went a step further in 1830 by adding the aristocratic "de" to the name Balzac. By signing his name "de Balzac," Honoré inscribed his own singular idiom within the proper name. In a sense, then, the particle "de" situates Balzac in a curious position between pseudonymity and his own name, for "de Balzac" is at once proper and pseudonymous. The particle indicates the distance between the plebeian father and the aristocratic son. More important, I believe, is that rather than challenging the proper name, the aristocratic pseudonym serves only to reinforce its fundamental drift. The particle is pseudonymous, but it remains in the service of the father's name. The whole point of this study is that the pseudonym need not remain in such service; there is no naming without the possibility of copying, forging, masking. The father's name seeks to contain the potential instability of the pseudonym which it always carries with it. Unlike Stendhal, Sand, Rachilde, and Bataille, Balzac managed to contain the conflicting forces at work in the authorial signature; he managed to shore up the proper name against its immanent vulnerability to imitation, falsification, and illegitimacy. This is not to say that Balzac's signature is without conflict, but to suggest only that his struggle with pseudonymity was effectively deflected by his return to a significantly reinvented surname.

By 1831 Balzac had discovered that his mother had had adulterous affairs. We should note at the outset that anything we say in regard to Balzac's relation to his mother is an exercise in speculative biography, since there is no indisputable evidence to confirm precisely *when* Balzac made this discovery; all that is certain is that he definitely knew of her infidelities by 1831. While we cannot absolutely confirm that this discovery triggered Balzac's decision to abandon his pseudonymous authorship, it is surely significant that in 1831 he made his mother's infidelities the subject of one of his major early works. Did he suspect a maternal fault early on and then confirm his suspicions around 1831, or did he make the discovery after 1829 and use it to justify and consolidate the patriarchal position he had come to independently? The crucial point here is that we recognize the necessary, though always problematic, link between the relation to the mother and the question of pseudonymous authorship. In Balzac's case, the period from 1829 to 1831 was marked by a number of cross-purposes and conflicting identifications, all of which were presumably resolved by his self-assertive assumption of his father's name. Honoré's return to the legitimacy of his name entailed an irreducible judgment upon his mother's conduct, and the struggle to sign and re-sign his proper signature would be unending. We might regard the particle "de" as a defensive countermeasure intended to anticipate the disruptive intrusions of the maternal fault.

Balzac's art, his language, and the form of his narratives are themselves forged within the crucible of the signature. In order to set the scene, let us begin with the fact that one of Madame Balzac's adulterous affairs resulted in the birth of Honoré's half-brother, Henri. Pierre Citron presents the relevant facts concerning Madame Balzac's affairs: "Let us recall that Madame de Balzac [sic] was married to a man thirty years older than herself and that she most probably had a lover, M. de Margonne, and was courted by a Spanish refugee, Ferdinand Heredia, Count de Prado Castellane. Whether or not she became his mistress is irrelevant since, against all appearances, her son believed she was."[1] Citron goes on to say that Balzac certainly knew of his mother's fault by 1831. There is, however, no reason why the discovery could not have occurred earlier. Furthermore, we might assume that a discovery of such magnitude would have been something Honoré struggled with over a period of months or years. Even though the gravity of the maternal fault remains indecipherable, Honoré chose to believe the worst, perhaps because he had long resented the preferential treatment his mother had always shown to Henri.

On the basis of the evidence provided by Balzac's short story "La Grande Bretèche," written in 1831 and published a year later, Citron concludes that Balzac discovered the adultery with de Margonne during this period. Since de Margonne was indisputably the father of Balzac's half-brother, and since "La Grande Bretèche" presents us with the story of a woman's adultery with a Spanish nobleman, we can conclude with Citron that Balzac became convinced around this time that his mother was also guilty of adultery with Heredia. "La Grande Bretèche" would thus offer the narrative form that underlies and authorizes Balzac's turn from the tragically flawed mother to the idealized father. What is encrypted in "La Grande Bretèche" is at once the maternal fault and the author's reliance on pseudonyms. Balzac scapegoats the mother in order to ensure his own legitimacy.

"La Grande Bretèche" is nothing less than an allegory of the mother's adultery and of the consequences of her concealment of the crime. The story registers the psychological and narrative complexities that were at work in Balzac's own emerging will to power as an artist. In his depiction of the woman's cruel suppression of all traces of her adultery, Balzac reveals the maternal crime and even acts as his mother's accomplice. In order to legitimate his assumption of the name of the father, Balzac must silence the mother. This is one of the most conventional and time-honored gestures of patriarchal culture. My focus in *Maternal Fictions* is on the link between the author's pseudonymous identity and his or her relation to the mother, which is precisely what Balzac tries to erase in "La Grande Bretèche," where adultery becomes a crime that must be suppressed at all costs, including murder.

"La Grande Bretèche" is part of *Autre étude de femme,* in which three men, de Marsay, Montriveau, and Bianchon, relate stories of unfaithful women and their tragic demise and punishment. In "La Grande Bretèche" Bianchon tells the story of Madame de Merret and her Spanish lover, Count de Feredia, whom she allows to be walled in by her irate husband when he discovers his wife's adultery. The horror of the tale resides with the character of Madame de Merret herself, who swears on the cross to her husband that nobody is in her closet when she, of course, knows the consequences of her lie. Monsieur de Merret also knows perfectly well that the lover is hiding within, and his wife's assent enables him to proceed with his cruel vengeance by having his mason enclose the ill-fated Spaniard behind brick and mortar.

Madame de Merret's unfortunate lover, Monsieur de Feredia, was first called de Heredia, which was the name of the man whom Honoré believed was Madame Balzac's lover: "In 1832, in 'La Grande Bretèche,' Heredia . . . was his name in the manuscript before it became Feredia."[2] Only at the last minute, just before publication, did Balzac change Heredia to Feredia. Madame de Merret's sacrilegious oath and criminal silence thus become unmistakable traces of the adultery of Madame de Balzac.

The trace of the maternal fault is literally inscribed as a fissure, a *brèche* (breach). *Brèche* also refers to the cement that has set once one has sealed up a wall. "La Grande Bretèche" is Balzac's name for the trace of the division within the proper name; it names an irreducible instability, a break, against which the proper name must constitute and define itself. The *brèche* is at once the gap and that which seals the gap up and covers it over. It is on and in the *brèche* that the disruptive fault of the mother is inscribed within the name of the father; the guilt of Madame de Merret and her lover is concealed behind the *brèche.* The homonymic slippage from *brèche* to *Bretèche,* from the common to the proper name, becomes the cipher for the movement from the mother to the father, from the pseudonym to the paternal name.

Mothers, *mères*, are everywhere in this story; in the surname de Merret most obviously, but also in Balzac's repetition of the words *maire* (mayor) and *mairie* (city hall; de Merret tells his wife he is going there to see the mayor). The text literally resonates with homonyms of *mère*. Madame de Merret is *la mère* par excellence, not simply *une mère*, but *Mère* herself. This wordplay is strategic on Balzac's part and on the part of his characters as well. When de Merret tells his wife that he is going to see the *maire*, his intention is to mislead her into thinking she has time enough to make a breach (*brèche*) in the wall that now encloses her lover.[3] Her attempted rescue is thwarted, however, for her husband has not sought out the *maire* but has stayed behind precisely in order to confirm his suspicions of the (allegorical Balzacian) *mère* and to prevent her effort to dislodge what we might call *la grande brèche*, the great seal that walls up the maternal fault and keeps it silent.

Balzac thus stands as a counterexample to the writers with whom I am principally concerned. Stendhal, Sand, Rachilde, and Bataille write pseudonymously because they neither wish to suppress the maternal secret nor are capable of doing so; rather than try to contain it, they quite obsessively seek to rehearse it and explore it in a variety of ways. Balzac's narratives seek to establish patriarchal legitimacy by repeatedly silencing the figure of the erring mother. I say repeatedly because Balzac is by no means finished with the maternal fault in "La Grande Bretèche"; for Balzac, writing is synonymous with the perennial effort to (re)bury the maternal fault, to seal up the *brèche*, and endlessly to reexamine the workmanship.

We might indicate here some significant stages in Balzac's effort to isolate the destabilizing force of the maternal relation and thus the always present threat of an insurgent pseudonymous identity. For example, the mother is killed by her favorite son at the end of *La Rabouilleuse* (1842); she reappears, however, in an even more threatening incarnation as the titular spinster of *La Cousine Bette* (1845). "I am going to begin *La Cousine Bette*," wrote

Balzac, "a horrible novel since the main character will be a composite of my mother, Madame Valmore, and Aunt Rosalie. It will be the story of many families" (Je vais me mettre sur *La Cousine Bette*, roman terrible, car le caractère principal sera un composé de ma mère, de Mme Valmore et de la tante Rosalie. Ce sera l'histoire de bien des familles).[4]

The shift from the bad mother to the illegitimate brother defines a generalized shift within Balzac's fiction. Fraternal rivalry provides a very effective cover for the mother's fault even while it replays and elaborates its most unhappy consequences. The mother remains at once inside and outside the text: contained, held at bay, in an encrypted vault, an outside that is walled up inside the text. Balzac's return to the father's name in 1829 must be continually sustained by walling up or otherwise excluding or containing the mother's desire. The father's name functions for Balzac like the *brèche* in "La Grande Bretèche": it is what keeps the fault from showing, and it eliminates what could call his legitimacy into question.

For Balzac, the proper name serves to speak from a place of authority while hiding sordid family secrets. The pseudonym is for him a replacement, a temporary falsehood, a counterfeit signature.[5] For the four writers whom I study in detail in *Maternal Fictions*, a pseudonymous identity is part of an ongoing struggle against the authority of the name of the father. At its most extreme, in certain texts of Bataille, for example, we come very close to the structures of psychotic foreclosure that are familiar through Lacanian psychoanalysis and through the writings of such famous psychotics as Freud's Daniel Paul Schreber or Antonin Artaud. For our four main writers, the maternal secret can be revealed only from behind the protective cover of a pseudonym. While Stendhal, Sand, and Rachilde use pseudonyms throughout their careers, Bataille uses a pseudonym on and off throughout his work—whenever he signs a pornographic text. The pseudonymous signing of these four writers facilitates the maternal return throughout their writing, whereas Balzac's signing of the paternal name keeps the mother at bay, holds her at a distance, and blocks her return. This does not, however, mean that the return of the maternal figure is any less haunting, disruptive, or potentially negative for them than it was for Balzac, but only that their pseudonymous identities were explicitly constituted in relation to the maternal.

In each of these four instances, the pseudonym is an attempt to resist the father's law, to put his name under erasure, to invent a self free of paternal oppression. Is pseudonymity a questioning of the possibility of escaping from a father-centered discourse? In each of the following chapters, we will see that pseudonymity describes the site of a continuing unresolved conflict and transformation.

In *This Sex Which Is Not One*, Luce Irigaray attacks psychoanalysis for the reductive model it offers to women: "Psychoanalytic discourse on female sexuality is the discourse of truth. A discourse which tells the truth about the logic of truth: namely, that *the feminine occurs only within models and laws devised by male subjects.* Which implies that there are not really two sexes but only one."[6] Under the cover of pseudonyms, Stendhal, Sand, and Rachilde reevaluate this phallic model. It is precisely because they do not share the values of patriarchal society that they reject the father's name. For Freud, writes Irigaray, woman "remains forever fixated on the desire for the father, remains subject to the father and to his law, for fear of losing his love, which is the only thing capable of giving her any value at all."[7] Irigaray's revision of the Freudian paradigm repeats analytically what Stendhal, Sand, Rachilde, and Bataille enact through fictional narrative.

The proper name only suggests the submission to patriarchy, ownership, propriety, and inheritance. It does not enforce or enact such submission. We do not want to suggest that resistance to patriarchal authority can only take place through pseudonymous signing. What is at stake here is the broader implication that pseudonymity is at work even through the father's name. The Balzacian counterexample demonstrates a certain survival of the pseudonym beneath the paternal name. The pseudonym simply concretizes a suppressed or marginalized relation to the maternal that is there whether or not one uses a pseudonym.

The novelist's pseudonym is more an occasion for the reinvention of the self than it is an occasion for an escape from conventional norms. As an artist, the pseudonymous novelist simply makes explicit the act of self-creation that many novelists are engaged in. As Julia Kristeva remarks, "Social protocol views multiplication of names as a series of repudiations, all of them inauthentic. Nonetheless, the creation of novelistic characters becomes the most faithful expression of that masquerade, in fact unveiling the aim of pseudonymity: to impose the infinite power of a writing that kills the author and, out of that sacrifice, to generate masks henceforth caught in the dialectics of an unending negation and reformulation."[8] In other words, the creation of fictional narrative, character, the entire effort of imaginative work, is an exercise in pseudonymity. For our purposes, this immense field of reinventing the world comes into focus through the much more specific focus of the pseudonymous identity that speaks of a suppressed maternal relation—indeed, of pseudonyms that sign what are essentially maternal fictions.

For Stendhal, the suppression of the paternal name, Beyle, and the invention of a pseudonym belie an unconscious desire to discover the figure of the lost mother. While Balzac's fiction encrypts its secrets, Stendhal strives to become his own creator by opening up a path toward his childhood and his mother's name. After his mother's early death, Stendhal's entire childhood appeared to him as a confinement from which he sought to escape. The father image thus becomes the very symbol of pettiness, oppression, and illegitimacy (he goes so far as to call his father "the bastard" in letters to his sister Pauline). The most significant patterns of identification emerge within the family myth of *Vie de Henry Brulard* (1836). In Victor Brombert's words, "Henry Brulard's hatred of his father is not a fortuitous factor to be dismissed as a regrettable antipathy and the original cause of the young boy's rebellious nature. Its deeper significance is that it justifies and almost requires the notion of a double paternity. Stendhal repeatedly explains that 'his true father' was his grandfather, Dr. Gagnon."[9] In substituting the fiction of a maternal grandfather for the reality of his father's paternity, Stendhal insists on being different from Henri Beyle. When he refers to himself as "Mr. Gagnon's son," he indulges in a fiction wherein he is his mother's brother. His recasting of his genealogy can no longer be contained by the opposition between the maternal and the paternal but seeks a symbolical self-engendering.

In *Vie de Henry Brulard*, Stendhal asks: What is a mother *without* her son? Stendhal substitutes his own death for his mother's and thus tries to cancel the unbearable loss he suffered. His reconstruction of the oedipal scene entails a new significance for the maternal function. By ignoring Jocasta's death, Freud also ignores her desire and her guilt. Has his silence provided cover for a certain idealization of the mother, and has it prompted us to believe in the innocence of mothers? Are mothers any better able to escape the destiny that their children must face? Stendhal's answer is a resounding no. *Armance* (1827), *Le Rouge et le noir* (1830), and *Les Cenci* (1837) force us to confront the recurring figure of the mother. Stendhal's self-invention takes place through his reinvention of the mother as beloved sacrificial victim.

Yet another maternal scenario awaits us in the case of George Sand. In the aftermath of the death of Aurore Dupin's father, her mother and grandmother continued to struggle for influence over her. In the absence of any paternal figure, Aurore (George Sand) was forced to live with her grandmother at Nohant while longing to be reunited with her mother in Paris. At her grandmother's death, Sand finally joined her mother, only to experience maternal abuse and disappointment. The traditional oedipal scenario states the law of the nonreturn of the daughter to the mother and her exile in the masculine, paternal world. Sand's delayed return to her mother defines her experience of the division within the maternal, and her fiction reopens this fissure again and again.

In her autobiography, *Story of My Life* (1847–54), and her novels *Indiana* (1832), *Mauprat* (1837), and *Le Péché de M. Antoine*

(1845), Sand elaborates upon the double structure of the mother-grandmother figure and upon the gender anxiety it produces. The idea of "two mothers" gives a new twist to the Freudian theories of castration anxiety and the uncanny. Because her relationship to her mother was never complete or satisfying, Sand repeats with her daughter Solange the bad relationship she had with her mother, Sophie Dupin. The impossibility of either foreclosing or internalizing the identity of the mother can also be linked to Sophie Dupin's pleasure in dressing Aurore as a boy and introducing her as "my son."

The split between masculine and feminine identifications calls out for the suture of a brèche; and this is where the pseudonym Sand comes in. (Her son Maurice would take his mother's famous name as his legal name.) Sand's pseudonym announces her triumph over the crisis of gender identification. Her solution to the problem of the proper name also marks her turn away from Sophie Dupin. Although her artistic theories can be seen as the feminization of the male canon, Sand refused to restrict herself to a single-gendered vision. Her language of resistance and her independence as a female writer constitute a rigorously antithetical code. In 1848, in a letter addressed to the "Comité Central de la Gauche," Sand stated her opposition to women's political emancipation, that is, the right to vote.[10] I believe that Sand's political views of women's rights are the result of her low opinion of her mother. The lack of trust she expressed in this letter is the most distressing evidence of Sand's resistance to the feminist perspective.

George Sand's political distrust of women is taken several steps further by Rachilde (Marguerite Eymery), who carries Sand's views to the extreme in her famous Pourquoi je ne suis pas féministe in 1928.[11] This pamphlet is an autobiographical account of the reasons why she is not a feminist. In this text the domineering and mad figure of the mother makes impossible any normal relationship between mother and daughter. Rachilde describes her mother, Gabrielle Eymery, as a forbidding presence from whom she distanced herself very early. Belittled by her mother on several occasions, Rachilde explored the mother-daughter relation in a very negative way. The power of the mother is always seen as abusive and tyrannical, but also as utterly indestructible. For her, the mother is the crucial accomplice of patriarchal domination. Rachilde is thus at once aware of women's victimization and certain that there can be no emancipation. She repeats her distrust of the maternal relation throughout her fiction. Rachilde's narratives stage the daughter's revolt against maternal, social, and religious authority. The subsequent defeat of the young rebel assumes various forms in *Monsieur Vénus* (1884), *La Marquise de Sade* (1887), and *Le Meneur de louves* (1905). The half-hearted battle that daughters fight against powerful mothers results only in uncovering an incontrovertible social malaise.

Maurice Barrès referred to Rachilde as "Mademoiselle Baudelaire," which speaks directly to the gender ambivalence within her pseudonymous identity. My reading of Rachilde elaborates the decadent and anarchist motifs that Barrès suggested through his witty renaming of Rachilde. Jennifer Birkett remarks that "in Rachilde's work, decadence makes the clearest confession of its own impotence. We do not live or make history; our symbols do it for us."[12] Rachilde's description of political impotence and sexual perversions provide important insights into the role of women during the fin de siècle. While she glamorizes female submission to male authority, she is also very ironical about gender relations and remains aware of the inequality of relations between the sexes. She recognizes the destructive nature of the old patriarchal order even while her hatred of her mother compels her to endorse it.

In *Face à la peur* (1941), written while France was occupied by the Germans, Rachilde is particularly candid and outrageous. Abandoning her human lineage entirely, Rachilde claims that she is a werewolf (*loup-garou*) that traces its lineage to her great-grandfather. Her numerous accounts of the family curse (her great-grandfather was a defrocked priest who got married during the French Revolution in 1789) reveal that she would rather belong to an accursed line than be the daughter of Joseph and

Gabrielle Eymery. Her parents wanted a boy, and Rachilde was an unwelcome child. Her solution is to be neither male nor female—to become an animal. Her numerous expressions of disgust at women's reproductive function belie a deep bitterness. The fissure in the maternal relation is so profound that it can never be plastered over or sealed up. Rachilde's extreme solution, her version of the *brèche*, is the desperate effort to free women of their biological destiny and to transform them into forces of unencumbered animal ferocity.

Like Rachilde's *Face à la peur,* part of Georges Bataille's *L'Expérience intérieure* was written in 1941 during the Occupation. The writing of memoirs during the war triggered in both Rachilde and Bataille a flood of memories and revelations. In a universe stripped of all means of transcendence, whether religious or scientific, the historical limits of the subject's destiny can no longer be ignored. Bataille's *L'Expérience intérieure* (1943) and *Le Coupable* (1944) are texts of intense anguish which replay Bataille's experience of the loss of his father in 1915 and the loss of his lover Laure in 1938. The resemblance that Bataille sees between the faces of his dead lover and his dead father is at the origin of the guilt he felt at abandoning his crippled father in Rheims to the invading Germans in 1915. While Rachilde's *Face à la peur* reinterprets the meaning of her pseudonym during the Occupation, Bataille's *L'Expérience intérieure* investigates the Hegelian theory of history in terms of his own personal guilt. Furthermore, Bataille's confession must take place in connection with the pseudonym, for he insists on reading *Madame Edwarda* (1941) along with *L'Expérience intérieure,* as though to stress the link between pseudonymous pornography and the theoretical writing of the father's name.

Madame Edwarda was published under the pseudonym Pierre Angélique, while *L'Expérience intérieure* was signed by Georges Bataille. The same division can be seen in the pairing of *Ma Mère,* which was written in 1962 under the name Pierre Angélique, and *Le Coupable,* which was signed by Bataille. Although *Ma Mère* was published posthumously in 1966, it is clearly linked to this division within the signature. My thesis is that the theoretical texts attempt to wall up the mother's fault, while the pornographic texts speak her guilt. The figure of the saintly whore in *Madame Edwarda* and *Sainte* and that of the sex-crazed mother in *Ma Mère* are projections of idiosyncratic oedipal desires on the part of Bataille/Angélique. For Bataille, the maternal relation conceals a psychotic element that threatens the very basis of society. It is only from behind the cover of a pseudonym that Bataille can risk prying away the suture that marks and conceals the unsettling maternal function. The figure of the mother lies at the origin of Bataille's thinking about the nature of transgression.

Ma Mère and *Madame Edwarda* also constitute the dual enigma of maternity and femininity in Bataille's work. In *Le Bleu du ciel* (1935), Bataille wrote, "but a couple arrived—a mother and son" (mais un couple arriva que formaient la mère et le fils),[13] as if to stress the incongruity of the couple. Here the mother has already been encrypted within a discursive space. The Bataillean incestuous couple is ineluctably confronted with the paradox according to which "mother" has become the site of the law. *La mère,* in other words, is *l'expérience intérieure* of guilt and truth. Because she remains unnameable, unspeakable, and unknowable, she arouses in Bataille "the anticipation of the impossible."

As we move from Stendhalian nostalgia for the maternal figure to the brutality of Bataillean maternal necrophilia, the modes of experience that are registered by the pseudonym change radically. Though it is difficult to generalize concerning the overarching form of the narrative that unfolds between Stendhal and Bataille, it is perhaps a question of a certain gradual, irresistible demonization of the maternal figure, a darkening of the promise that she appeared to offer, and perhaps a certain betrayal of the hope for an escape from conventions, norms, and authority. The ambivalence of the maternal figure that begins in Sand becomes menacing in Rachilde and Bataille.

The pseudonym is not, of course, the only means of access to the maternal, but, as I have said, it makes explicit what is everywhere implicit in modern French literature. The pseudonym appears as a metaphor for a number of narrative strategies by which modern French writing inscribes its fictions of the maternal. It liberates the proper name from its constraints and opens up all that has been foreclosed and occluded by patriarchal law and institutions. But this is not a story of liberation. The maternal fictions that I decipher from *Armance* (1827) to *Ma Mère* (1966) describe a shift within paternal law toward maternal law and back to paternal law once again. Resuscitating the mother is at once the subversion of patriarchy and its reinscription. While in Stendhal the return to the mother is marked by the work of incessant mourning, the work of the other three writers reveals that the liberating promise of the maternal fiction soon becomes as tyrannical and oppressive as the patriarchal regime it had tried to subvert.

Chapter One

STENDHAL:
THE OEDIPAL PALIMPSEST

I often feel it to be so; who can see himself? It's less than three
years since I discovered the reason why.
                    STENDHAL, *The Life of Henry Brulard*

The Name of the Mother in *The Life of Henry Brulard*

Stendhal's oedipal struggle might be seen as the novelist's most
typical representation of the double postulation of authority and
subversion. For Stendhal, to use a pseudonym was to engage in an
act of protest. In *The Living Eye*, Jean Starobinski showed that the
young Henri Beyle concocted the most extraordinary reasons for
denying any connection with the Beyle family:

> A common illusion is to believe that our destinies and truths
> are inscribed in our names. To some extent Stendhal suc-
> cumbed to this illusion. If he refused the name Beyle, it was
> because it signified a predestined fate of which he wanted no
> part. His name bound him to France, to Grenoble, to the
> bourgeois class, and to his father's world of hoarding and
> sordid calculation. By choosing a new name he gave himself
> not only a new face, a new rank in society with the noble
> particule *de*, new nationalities. Only in Italy, moreover, was

happiness free to flourish, and in his young imagination young Henri Beyle established a whole genealogy for himself on his mother's side.[1]

If the name is truly an identity, then repudiation of the patronymic is a substitute for parricide. It is the most discreet form of murder in effigy. To kill the father means also to supplant him; the filial challenge occurs with the paternal relationship and is sustained only by upholding the authority that its values come to threaten. The rejection of the name transmitted by his father is also a strategy aimed at retrieving the memory of his dead mother. Stendhal's love for his mother offers countless scenarios of the great oedipal passion tearing apart and yet resuscitating the maternal figure. Henri still contains the mother's name Henriette and systematically displaces the name of the father to the name of the mother: "for I considered myself a Gagnon and I never thought of the Beyles except with a distaste which I still feel in 1835" (car je me regardais comme Gagnon et je ne pensais jamais aux Beyle qu'avec une répugnance qui dure encore en 1835).[2] The strong identification with the mother subverts the patronymic while bringing Stendhal's forbidden passion back through the names of his heroines. Stendhal's oedipal confession looms high in *Vie de Henry Brulard* (1836) and constitutes the horizon against which I want to examine the pattern Stendhal follows to retrieve the figure of the mother. *Armance* (1827), *Le Rouge et le noir* (1830), and *Les Cenci* (1837) describe the return to the maternal and its tragic ending. But at the start of the oedipal complex, the death of the mother is immediately recalled in Stendhal's memoirs. In *Armance*, *Le Rouge et le noir*, and *Les Cenci*, Stendhal performs his restorative work by giving tragic variants of his oedipal complex. I will examine how, in each of these three texts, Stendhal's maternal fictions originate from his oedipal confession in *Vie de Henry Brulard* and the ontological questioning it inspired.

Writing one's autobiography is, according to Stendhal, not only difficult but unavoidably incomplete, since one cannot say:

STENDHAL

"I was born/I died." Brulard's questions—"What sort of man have I been? Have I been a wit? Have I had any sort of talent?" (Qu'ai-je donc été? Ai-je été un homme d'esprit? Ai-je eu du talent pour quelque chose?) (*Henry Brulard*, 2–3/7)—are necessarily unanswerable. Failing a reply, he can only try to destroy the spell, to elude "the dazzling" character of such questions: "This is the only way I can hope to reach the truth about a subject which I cannot discuss with anyone" (C'est ma seule ressource pour arriver au vrai dans un sujet sur lequel je ne puis converser avec personne) (*Henry Brulard*, 12/19). Stendhal's story of his life becomes, of course, enmeshed with immortality and the pleasure of writing:

> So my confessions will have ceased to exist thirty years after being printed if the I's and me's prove too boring for their readers; nevertheless I shall have the pleasure of writing them and of searching my conscience thoroughly.

> Mes confessions n'existeront donc plus trente ans après avoir été imprimées, si les Je et les Moi assomment trop les lecteurs; et toutefois j'aurais eu le plaisir de les écrire, et de faire à fond mon examen de conscience. (*Henry Brulard*, 5/10)

One wonders why Brulard, an unsuccessful lover, "an utter ignoramus," as Mr. Daru used to call Stendhal, is restlessly in quest of himself. The structure of Stendhal's desire for literary immortality, which Louis Marin describes as "auto(biothanato)graphy," from the Greek *bios* (life) and *thanatos* (death), also describes the fascination experienced by Stendhal in saying: "I was told that I died at . . . in. . . ." The Stendhalian "I died" is the "original 'gaze' of auto*biothanato*graphy when the subject appropriates and identifies himself from the unspeakable double border of his birth and death."[3] But what exactly happened in this merging of birth and death? In which unnameable passion is Stendhal locked?

The lack of differentiation between life and death recalls the death of Stendhal's mother, Henriette Gagnon, in childbirth: "Please be kind enough to remember that I lost her in childbed when I was barely seven" (Qu'on daigne se rappeler que je la perdis par une couche quand à peine j'avais sept ans) (*Henry*

Brulard, 22/29). The loss of the mother is irrevocably linked to Stendhal's oedipal desire. Stendhal's memoirs would then simply express the passion of a man who seeks in writing the power which might shelter him from the anguish he felt at his mother's death. The creation of Henry Brulard then becomes the strongest expression of his dread, for it is precisely the avowal of Brulard's oedipal desire which puts his memoirs at risk: "But I have too long deferred telling something which must be told, one of the two or three things perhaps which will make me throw these memoirs in the fire. My mother, Mme Henriette Gagnon, was a charming woman and I was in love with my mother" (Mais je diffère depuis longtemps un récit nécessaire, un des deux ou trois peut-être qui me feront jeter ces mémoires au feu. Ma mère, madame Henriette Gagnon, était une femme charmante et j'étais amoureux de ma mère) (*Henry Brulard*, 21/28). *Brulard* (from *brûler*, to burn) indicates that something within the name is "burning" (*brûlant*), that something unspeakable risks destroying the speaker's proper identity. By distancing himself from Brulard, Stendhal can thus undertake the task of analyzing his oedipal complex based on his recollections: "I wanted to cover my mother with kisses, and without any clothes on. She loved me passionately and often kissed me. I abhorred my father when he came to interrupt our kisses" (Je voulais couvrir ma mère de baisers et qu'il n'y eût pas de vêtements. Elle m'aimait à la passion et m'embrassait souvent. J'abhorais mon père quand il venait interrompre nos baisers) (*Henry Brulard*, 22/29). If incest was never committed, Stendhal's imaginary scenarios still consisted of elaborating his oedipal fantasms and acting them out in all his novels. Previous to his mother's death, Stendhal recalls another memory which is not without Freudian implications: "One evening, when for some reason I had been put to bed on the floor of her room on a mattress, she leaped over my mattress, lively and light-footed as a doe, to reach her own bed more quickly" (Un soir, comme par quelque hasard on m'avait mis coucher dans sa chambre par terre, sur un matelas, cette femme vive et légère comme une biche sauta pardessus mon matelas pour atteindre plus vite son lit) (*Henry*

Brulard, 23/31). What Stendhal as a child actually saw is silenced by the next sentence: "Her room remained closed for ten years after her death" (Sa chambre est restée fermée dix ans après sa mort) (*Henry Brulard*, 23/31). This dramatic interruption, which marks a gap in the narrative, signals the link between Stendhal's oedipal complex and death.

Is it in fact, as Freud argues in his essay "Medusa's Head" (1922), the sight of the mother's genitals which provokes "the horror of castration"? Freud's interpretation suggests that to decapitate is to castrate: "The terror of Medusa is thus a terror of castration that is linked to the sight of something. It occurs when a boy, who has hitherto been unwilling to believe the threat of castration, catches sight of the female genitals, probably those of an adult, surrounded by hair, and essentially those of his mother."[4] Although we do not actually know what Stendhal saw when Henriette leaped over his mattress, we can argue that the child's first sight of a woman's genitals took place then. The lack of details, which might be due to the considerable period which separates Henriette Gagnon's death in 1790 from the time Stendhal begins his memoirs in 1835, might also indicate that something is occulted in Stendhal's silence. In linking the myth of the Medusa's head to the castration complex, Freud establishes the equivalence between the fear of losing one's sight (being turned to stone) and that of losing one's sex. For Stendhal, the castration complex, and more specifically man's impotence, constitute his first attempt at understanding sexuality in the pathological manifestations of its absence.

If the Medusa's head takes the place of a representation of the female genitals in mythological themes, Stendhal's representation of the castration scene will take place in the aftermath of the mother's demise. The sight of Henriette leaping above his head is instantly followed by her disappearance. Stendhal's creativity seems to repeat this primary scenario. The desire for the mother is cut short by her death. This unresolved oedipal complex is accompanied by incredible separation anxiety. I have called this particular Stendhalian structure the "oedipal palimpsest." The privileged, if short-lived, relation between Stendhal and his mother makes him also dependent on a primary event or text. The precursor text thus becomes the primary source of inspiration for Stendhal. It textually replays the oedipal drama Stendhal wants to protect himself against. Stendhal's fiction is based on repetition within difference; *Armance* (1827) repeats *Olivier* (1825), by Henri de Latouche, while creating its own fictive space. The return to "the mother text" is the condition of Stendhal's writing and repeats itself throughout his work: *Le Rouge et le noir* (1830) was first suggested to Stendhal by the criminal case of Antoine Berthet in *La Chronique des tribunaux*. Later on, Stendhal claimed that he translated *Chroniques italiennes* (1837–39) from old Italian manuscripts. These few examples show Stendhal's need for an originary text which he then appropriates. In short, the precursor text is used as the reading that allows Stendhal to replay fictively in his writing his separation anxiety. The oedipal desire is thus the trope which at its best defines Stendhal's creative work.

I propose to read Stendhal's first novel, *Armance, ou quelques scènes d'un salon de Paris en 1827*, in parallel with *The Life of Henry Brulard*. In *Armance*, Stendhal problematized the hero's impotence, while Brulard confessed that he was not honored with most women's favours. When Brulard declared that "the usual condition of my life has been that of an unhappy lover" (l'état habituel de ma vie a été celui d'amant malheureux) (*Henry Brulard*, 10/16), the statement could also be applied to Octave, the hero of *Armance*. In *Stendhal: Fiction and the Theme of Freedom*, Victor Brombert gives us the literary origin of *Armance*: Latouche's *Olivier* is *babilan* (impotent) and must annul his marriage; his story is repeated in the character of Octave in Stendhal's *Armance*.[5] The passage from the masculine name Olivier to the feminine Armance shows that the title has been surreptitiously changed and indicates that the shift from Olivier to Armance is a ruse destined to occult Octave. In *Armance*, the Stendhalian discursive space refers immediately to another discourse already said and known, which saves Stendhal the embarrassing task of "explaining" Octave's impotence.[6] Superimposing Octave upon Olivier is like a textual reduplication which illuminates what is not said in *Armance*. Can we then go so far as to say that Stendhal's oedipal structure and Henry Brulard's oedipal desire constitute the figure of the forbidden in the guise of impotence?

When Brulard declares, "I have too delicate a skin, a woman's skin (later on I always had blisters after holding my sword for an hour), the least thing takes the skin off my fingers, which are very well shaped; in a word the surface of my body is like a woman's" (J'ai la peau beaucoup trop fine, une peau de femme [plus tard j'avais toujours des ampoules après avoir tenu mon sabre pendant une heure], je m'écorche les doigts, que j'ai fort bien, pour un rien, en un mot la superficie de mon corps est de femme) (*Henry Brulard*, 122–23/147–48), one wonders if this is not Stendhal's way of identifying himself with the maternal body. In *Armance*, Octave is described as having features as delicate as a woman's; his physical ambiguities discreetly imply that Octave is not completely a man. One might also recall that in *Le Rouge et le noir*, Madame de Rênal's first glance at Julien mistook him for a girl. The enigma of the feminized Stendhalian hero triggered Julia Kristeva's amazing statement: "The Stendhalian lover is secretly a lesbian."[7] Although Kristeva does not explicitly develop what she means in saying that Stendhal is "secretly a lesbian," she implies that the social code, in Stendhal's world, is based on female homosexuality. I think that Stendhal's total identification with the dead mother caused him to undergo a complete breakdown of gender identity. Stendhal's "secret lesbianism" is still another scenario taking Stendhal one step further away from the paternal model of identification. Besides, it allows Stendhal to create a kind of sexuality ideally cerebral and aesthetic. The Stendhalian *babilan* who is necessarily heading for sexual fiascos is the trope around which Stendhal organized *Armance*, his first novel. Thus, *Armance* is constructed around several maternal identifications which allow Octave momentarily to escape his impotence while denying sexuality. In Stendhal's life, the mother's loss is always experienced as incomprehensible; her death must be repeated throughout his fiction because it has never been fully accepted: "But it seemed to me that I was going to see her the next day; I did not understand death" is followed by "Thus, forty-five years ago, I lost the being I loved best in the whole world" (Mais il me semblait que je la reverrais le lendemain, je ne comprenais pas la mort. Ainsi il y a quarante-cinq ans que j'ai perdu ce que j'aimais le plus au monde) (*Henry Brulard*, 22/29). The death of the mother is so powerfully inscribed in the Stendhalian imagination that autobiography and fiction are like a palimpsest endlessly rewriting and erasing her demise: the deaths of Lucrecia and Beatrice Cenci, Madame de Rênal, la Sanseverina, and Clélia are all miming the tragic loss of the mother while fictitiously resurrecting her at the same time. In the wake of Kristeva's work on Stendhal, we might wonder who is put to death: "With those dead women, there may be above all a specifically Stendhalian manner of idealizing the loved one as she loses her characteristic of being an other—an other sex—and unites with the lover's desired power."[8] In *Henry Brulard*, the dead mother is celebrated by Stendhal as Beatrice was celebrated by Dante; the juxtaposition between the mother's death and her reading Dante's *Divine Comedy* brings back the memory of the dead mother:

> Her features expressed nobility and utter serenity; she was very lively, preferring to run about and do things for herself rather than give orders to her three maids, and she was fond of reading Dante's *Divine Comedy* in the original. Long afterwards I found five or six copies in different editions in her room, which has remained shut up since her death.

> Elle avait une noblesse et une sérénité parfaite dans les traits; très vive, aimant mieux courir et faire elle-même que de commander à ses trois servantes et enfin lisant souvent dans l'original la *Divine Comédie* de Dante dont j'ai trouvé bien plus tard cinq à six exemplaires d'éditions différentes dans son appartement resté fermé depuis sa mort. (*Henry Brulard*, 22/29)

The mother's liveliness and her love for *The Divine Comedy* seem to be enclosed in her room, immortalizing her absence in the presencing of her favorite reading. Furthermore, Starobinski argues that Stendhal established an Italian genealogy for himself on his mother's side: "He settles his memory of her in the warm and sensuous Lombard countryside."[9] Beatrice is therefore the Italian model to which Henriette is compared. One should notice here that Stendhal chose to describe Henriette as a young woman rather than as his mother. One should note also that this feminine figure, too, is that of a dead woman. The memory of the mother is called into being and at the same time withheld, kept out of reach.

Stendhal's mourning for the mother assumes in *Brulard* the Freudian structure of the *fort/da*. In *Armance,* Madame de Malivert designates Armance de Zohiloff as the right woman to marry her son Octave. The rigor of their mutual exclusions (Octave must leave his mother in order to marry Armance) ensures their resemblance, folds what is apparently outside inside, and turns distance into proximity. It is precisely this proximity which "kills" Octave and makes his suicide inevitable. By marrying Emilie and Armance, Olivier and Octave are respectively excluded from their marriages in both Latouche's *Olivier* and Stendhal's *Armance.* Although it appears that their respective impotence is the reason the marriage cannot be consummated, Octave's suicide subverts the alleged justification of the text. If we consider Olivier's and Octave's decision to leave their wives after their marriages, we notice that the name is in both texts privileged:

> In a month she can be free. She will be a young, rich, very beautiful and courted widow; and the name of Malivert will suit her better to find an *amusing husband* than the name of Zohiloff still unknown.

> Mais je puis la laisser libre dans un mois. Elle sera une veuve jeune, riche, fort belle, sans doute fort recherchée; et le nom de Malivert lui vaudra mieux pour trouver un *mari amusant* que le nom encore peu connu de Zohiloff.[10]

In Olivier's farewell letter, he leaves his wife Emilie free to take either her married or her maiden name:

Thus, you will be able to have my name or take back the one you had till now. Only in choosing to take your husband's name will you be free to silence the pressing curiosity of society.

Vous pourrez donc ainsi porter mon nom, ou reprendre celui que vous avez eu jusqu'ici. Il me semble que ce n'est qu'en prenant le nom de mon épouse, que vous pourrez répondre à l'empressement curieux de la société.[11]

In Stendhal's and Latouche's texts, the husband's name ironically erases the name of the father while stressing the social pressures of marriage. Although in Octave's fantasies the name Malivert should facilitate Armance's remarriage, there is one moment in the text when he is locked in the constant presencing of the name Zohiloff. It seems to me, however, that Stendhal is less concerned with the meaning of Armance's name, Zohiloff, than with using the initials of her first and last names:

The commonest objects reminded him of Armance. His madness was so great that he could not see the letter A or Z on top of a billboard or on a shopsign, without being violently forced to think of this Armance de Zohiloff whom he had sworn to forget. All the surrounding objects manifested Armance's presence. The shortening of this beloved name followed by some interesting date was everywhere written.

Les objets les plus indifférents lui rappelaient Armance. Sa folie allait au point de ne pouvoir apercevoir à la tête d'une affiche ou sur une enseigne d'une boutique un A ou un Z, sans être violemment entraîné à penser à cette Armance de Zohiloff qu'il s'était juré d'oublier. Tous les objets qui l'environnaient portaient les marques du souvenir d'Armance. L'abrégé de ce nom chéri, suivi de quelque date intéressante, était écrit partout. (*Armance*, 127)

Octave's obsession with Armance is here summarized by reading her name in every object around him. A–Z also represents the alphabet, as well as being the two letters which would constitute Stendhal's memory of Madame Azur (Alberthe de Rubempré, with whom he had an affair in 1829). Nine years after the publication of *Armance,* Stendhal returned to the meaning of A–Z when he began writing *The Life of Henry Brulard,* first tracing in the dust the names of women he loved:

> I discovered that my life could be summed up by the following names, the initials of which I wrote in the dust, like Zadig, with my walking-stick, sitting on the little bench behind the Stations of the Cross of the *Minori Osservanti* built by the brother of Urban VIII: Virginie (Kubly), Angela (Pietragrua), Adèle (Rebuffel), Mélanie (Guilbert), Mina (de Griesheim), Alexandrine (Petit), Angeline, whom I never loved (Bereyter), Métilde (Dembowski), Clémentine, Giula. And finally, for a month at most, Mme Azur whose Christian name I have forgotten. Most of these charming creatures never honoured me with their favours; but they literally took up my whole life.

> Je trouvai que ma vie pouvait se résumer par les noms que voici, et dont j'écrivais les initiales sur la poussière, comme Zadig, avec ma canne, assis sur le petit banc derrière les stations du Calvaire des *Minori Osservanti* bâti par le frère d'Urbain VIII: Virginie (Kubly), Angela (Pietragrua), Adèle (Rebuffel), Mélanie (Guilbert), Mina (de Griesheim), Alexandrine (Petit), Angeline, que je n'ai jamais aimée (Bereyter), Métilde (Dembowski), Clémentine, Giula. Et enfin, pendant un mois au plus, Mme Azur dont j'ai oublié le nom de baptême. La plupart de ces êtres charmants ne m'ont point honoré de leurs bontés; mais elles ont à la lettre occupé toute ma vie.
> (*Henry Brulard,* 9–10/15–16)

Then follows the drawing of the convent, of the road leading to Albano, and two names, Zadig-Astarté, are written under the first picture of *Brulard.* Beyle rewrites these names later in his memoirs and compares his gesture to Zadig's. Stendhal's life is inscribed within these names which he gives us to read. According to Louis Marin, the "Zadig-Astarté" inscription is the key to understanding the pause marked by the forgetting of Mme Azur's real name: "A list of names, more precisely twelve letters already inscribe—since the beginning—his life, sealing his tomb, another's tomb whose others would read the epitaph, Zadig. Above the Lake of Albano, *Albe, aube* [dawn], white, A, B, the alphabet, Beyle-Brulard, his whole life contained in twelve letters, it's Zadig, Z, the last letter, the ultimate one."[12] It is clear when reading Voltaire's *Zadig* that it was Astarté and not Zadig who wrote Zadig's name in the sand: "Zadig was curious to see what she was writing. He saw the letter Z, then an A; he was surprised: then a D; he started. Never was astonishment greater than his when he saw the last two letters of his own name."[13] In replacing Astarté's name with Zadig's, Brulard commits an error which allows him to identify momentarily with Zadig. For Stendhal, writing one's own life had already been performed by another writer, Voltaire. This is precisely what Marin called "the excommunicated voice." In *La Voix excommuniée*, subtitled *Essais de mémoire*, Marin transformed the Stendhalian excommunication into his autocommunication.[14] Stendhal used the same textual strategy when incorporating Voltaire's voice in his own story. Here, I am "excommunicating" neither Stendhal nor Marin from his autocommunication. More specifically, my intention is to discover Stendhal's gender identification while he was secretly naming the mother in his writing. In order to discover himself, Stendhal/ Brulard must inscribe his story in the list of the lovers' names while retrieving the past in another's voice: "My entire life summed up by the initials of twelve women's names over there, above Lake Albano, written on a page this November night. Here it has already been written by Zadig, Voltaire's character: a fiction."[15] It is Zadig's reading Astarté's writing his name in the sand which surprises him, not writing his own name. In *Armance*, the name Armance de Zohiloff must be erased and replaced by Armance de Malivert, blurring mother and wife together in the same name. The marriage with Armance reveals a doubling of the maternal figure that anticipates Brulard's astonishing oedipal desire: "When I loved her [Henriette Gagnon] at about the age of six, in 1789, I showed exactly the same characteristics as in 1828 when I was madly in love with Alberthe de Rubempré" (En l'aimant à six ans peut-être, 1789, j'avais absolument le même caractère qu'en 1828 en aimant à la fureur Alberthe de Rubempré) (*Henry Brulard*, 21/28). Falling in love with women is for Stendhal exactly like loving his mother, and it is precisely in retrieving his mother's love that Octave will end his life, by breaking away from the social bondage of marriage. The recurrence of Stendhal's oedipal passion in his affair with Alberthe de Rubempré signals the return of the repressed. Earlier in *Henry Brulard*, Stendhal could only remember her under her pseudonym, Madame Azur. Here, the figure of the maternal seems to be hidden in the forgetting of the lover's name. The nondifferentiation between Henriette Gagnon and Madame Azur takes place in the efface- ment of the name. After all, *azur* means a solid blue sky. The sublime memory of the mother remains occulted in the AZ of *azur*, which also encompasses the alphabet.

Marin's reading of Stendhal's *Life of Henry Brulard* consists of unfolding the fort/da structure of Brulard's oedipal confession and linking the presence/absence of the mother to the recollec- tion of his lovers' names. When Henriette leaps over her six-year- old son Henri, then, she constitutes what Marin calls "a reading event": "a leap between readable and visible, a figural letter, a matrix, two gazes of reading and vision which are reading, at once active and receptive—the one who is reading and who starts writing is read because already written, the one who looks at what is forbidden sees an eye which bedazzles him: *dazzling*."[16] The Stendhalian eye/I echoes phonetically the questions trou- bling Brulard: "I often feel it to be so; who can see himself?" (Je sens cela souvent, quel oeil peut se voir soi-même?) (*Henry Brulard*, 4/9). "Which eye can see itself?" asks Stendhal while questioning the relevance of writing one's confessions. The link between *Brulard* and *Armance* establishes the "dazzling" as the condition of writing; or, as Starobinski noted, "Desire for erotic potency, desire for metamorphosis, and desire for command of a new language are oddly juxtaposed."[17] By normal standards of coherence such conflicting desires should not be mentioned side by side. The wish for erotic power and the dream of meta- morphosis express two aspects of a single will to power; Stendhal cannot abolish the gap that separates him from his dead mother any more than Octave can abolish the insurmountable obstacle which keeps him away from Armance. The Stendhalian "dazzling" acknowledges the profound connection between the "pleasure principle" and the desire for writing: "To tell the truth, I'm quite uncertain whether I have enough talent to get myself read. I sometimes very much enjoy writing, that's all" (A vrai dire, je ne suis rien moins que sûr d'avoir quelque talent pour me faire lire. Je trouve quelquefois beaucoup de plaisir à écrire, voilà tout) (*Henry Brulard*, 4/8). If Stendhal's dazzling is the stratagem aimed at thwarting the gaze in amorous rapture and depriving him of the ability of seeing things clearly, then writing restores his authorial lucidity. The Stendhalian dazzling is always under the threat of sexual fiascos and blindness, carrying the metaphor of castration to its extreme.

In the third chapter of *Memoirs of Egotism* (1832), Stendhal recalls his amorous fiasco with the beautiful Alexandrine, kept in a brothel "in the rue du Cadran": "I failed her completely; it was a perfect *fiasco*. I then tried to make amends in another way, and she seemed to countenance it. Not knowing exactly what to do next, I tried to go on with my sleight of hand, but she put a stop to it. She seemed astonished at my behavior"[18] (Je la manquai parfaitement, *fiasco* complet. J'eus recours à un dédommagement, elle s'y prêta. Ne sachant trop que faire, je voulus revenir à ce jeu de main qu'elle refusa. Elle parut étonnée).[19] Stendhal's momentary impotence in 1821, which is reinscribed in the *Memoirs* of 1832, marks that sexual lack which constituted *Armance*. It is that gesture of replacing one's sex by one's hand that Marin describes in these terms: "To substitute the writing pen to the failing sex, that is to say 'I,' 'my' glorious sex, the quill, the tip. To substitute the writing hand, this compensation, the sleight of the hand already used in the *fiasco* scene and which already traces Beyle's desire in Alexandrine's body, outside his pleasure."[20] Acknowledgment of the profound connection between sexual pleasures and the desire for metamorphosis, as has already been mentioned, can be found in a curious text written by Stendhal near the end of his life, *Les*

Privilèges du 10 avril 1840. Here Stendhal formulates vividly his concern. The text begins with the notation: "God grants me the following privileges" (God me donne le brevet suivant):

> Article 3: The *mentula* [penis], like the index finger for rigidity and movement, the latter at will. Size, two inches longer than the big toe, same thickness. But pleasure through the *mentula*, only twice a week. Twenty times a year, the grantee may become whomever he wishes to be, provided that individual exists.

> Article 3. La *mentula,* comme le doigt indicateur pour la dureté et pour le mouvement, cela à volonté. La forme, deux pouces de plus que l'article, même grosseur. Mais plaisir par la *mentula,* seulement deux fois par semaine. Vingt fois par an le privilégié pourra se changer en l'être qu'il voudra, pourvu que cet être existe.[21]

Sexual potency, painless death, and metamorphosis are among the privileges Stendhal lists first. In the first article of *Les Privilèges,* Stendhal wishes to die painlessly of a stroke in his sleep, a wish which will be realized in 1842. The "miracles" repeat, two years before his death, Stendhal's lifelong concerns for these three privileges.[22] In *Les Privilèges,* Stendhal ironically transforms the dread of impotence and death into superhuman achievements. In the list of miracles, he also mentions speaking new languages. While sexual potency and a polyglot's talents are combined together facetiously in *Les Privilèges,* there is no miracle at work in *Armance,* and impotence and mutism afflict Octave tragically. Would *Armance* then be the "privileged" place from which young Stendhal staged impotence while warding off its threat? Could we perhaps enlarge the meaning of impotence in *Armance* and examine how it dramatizes the *impuissance* of the Restoration generation?

    Armance, subtitled *Or Some Scenes of a Parisian Salon in 1827,* and *Le Rouge et le noir* (1830), subtitled *Chronicle of 1830,* take into account the part played by the salon culture of the Restoration. Particularly in *Armance,* the salon is the paralyzing force which affects society. The individual cannot survive the suffocating effects of the salon's empty discourse unless he accepts its rules. For both Henri de Latouche and Stendhal, impotence and salon culture have a stifling effect on the individual. Something of what remains unsaid in Octave's discourse might be illuminated by a remark of Lacan's: "Even if it communicates nothing, the discourse represents the existence of communication; even if it denies the evidence, it affirms that speech constitutes truth; even if it is intended to deceive, the discourse speculates on faith in testimony."[23] Octave's censored discursive space denounces the lies of a society incapable of telling the truth. The "truth" of the discourse is doubly occulted by the social masquerade and by Octave's "fatal word," which he never can speak. In both *Olivier* and *Armance*, the confession cannot take place because it is silenced by the salon discourse. As Julien ironically remarks about Marquis de La Mole's salon in *Red and Black*:

> Provided one didn't joke about God, or the priests, or the king, or the men in power, or the artists protected by the court, or about any part of the establishment, provided one said nothing good about Béranger, or the opposition newspapers, or Voltaire, or Rousseau or of anything which involves the use of free speech; provided, above all, that one never talks politics, one could talk freely about anything whatever.

> Pourvu qu'on ne plaisantât ni de Dieu, ni du roi, ni des gens en place, ni des artistes protégés par la cour, ni de tout ce qui est établi; pourvu qu'on ne dît du bien ni de Béranger, ni des journaux de l'opposition, ni de Voltaire, ni de Rousseau, ni de tout ce qui permet un peu de franc-parler; pourvu surtout qu'on ne parlât jamais politique, on pouvait librement raisonner de tout.[24]

Octave is powerless in Restoration culture, particularly when Louis XVIII's Indemnity Law places him in the position of a rich and attractive heir. As Brombert stated, "Impotence, in this instance, is not merely an individual's physiological deficiency, but the hidden symbol of the shameful deterioration of an entire social class."[25] Octave's social and physical positions are doubly crippling for him. The two million in allowance restores the Marquis de Malivert's credit and thus strengthens the father's name: "Thus I am no longer a beggar and neither are you, your fortune will again match your rank, and I can now look for a spouse for you and not beg for one" (Ainsi je ne suis plus un gueux, c'est-à-dire tu n'es plus un gueux, ta fortune va se trouver de nouveau en rapport avec ta naissance, et je puis maintenant te chercher et non plus te mendier une épouse).[26] Octave's *parole vide* is constantly censured by silences and escapes; he is a by-product of the Restoration. Impotence is pathologically linked to language, and throughout his life Stendhal was unable to separate one from the other. Octave constantly invents new names and social functions that place him out of reach of his father, the Marquis de Malivert. Here Octave replays Stendhal's gesture of severing the paternal bond by abandoning the proper name; Octave's imaginary pseudonyms introduce a radical disjunction between his world and his father's. This is precisely the moment when the impotent Octave coincides with the pseudonymous Stendhal:

> The first [project] is to be called Mr. Lenoir; under this beautiful name, I would go to the province to tutor in arithmetics and applied geometry. I hesitate telling you the best of my projects; I would take up Pierre Gerlat's name, I would begin in Geneva or Lyon and I would become the servant of some young man destined to play the same part than me in the world. Pierre Gerlat would bear the Viscount of Malivert's excellent certificates.

> Le premier est de me faire appeler M. Lenoir; sous ce beau nom, j'irais en province donner des leçons d'arithmétique, de géométrie appliquée aux arts. J'hésite à vous avouer le plus beau de mes projets; je prendrais le nom de Pierre Gerlat, j'irais débuter à Genève ou à Lyon et je me ferais valet de chambre de quelque jeune homme destiné à jouer à peu près le même rôle que moi dans le monde. Pierre Gerlat serait porteur d'excellents certificats du vicomte de Malivert. (*Armance*, 106–7)

THE OEDIPAL PALIMPSEST

Octave's self takes up new identities, allowing him to give birth to a new self by rejecting both the name of the father and his nobility. M. Lenoir and Pierre Gerlat are substituted for Octave de Malivert so that the Stendhalian fantasm of being one's own creator can be fulfilled. In rewriting *Olivier*, Stendhal radicalizes the fiction in Octave's suicide, which is the final avowal of his impotence. It is precisely in his name, (*babil*)*an* (babble, also impotent), that the return to the babble precipitates the end of the fiction. Octave's suicide definitively occults the avowal of his impotence and sends both his mother and wife to take the veil in the same convent.

According to Luce Irigaray, "speaking is never neuter," that is to say, speaking is always gendered. Speaking his impotence, his "neutrality," is for Octave the crucial debate of his life. Octave's dilemma can be summed up in Irigaray's remarks: "The rule of saying everything calls into question the forbidden, the *unnamed* articulation of the word, this *in-between* which goes from the inside to the outside of the discourse."[27] Interdiction is connected with the paternal law; incest with the mother is denied the son by the father's interdiction. The son's impotence suggests that there is a total abrogation of being in the face of the father's interdiction. Impotence, as a calculated evasion, is Octave's master trope. It is the bodily mark that makes the relationship to the mother unreadable:

> "I stay where I am the happiest man," said Octave. "There are times when I believe you," used to answer his happy mother; "but if for two days I only saw you in the world, reason gets the upper hand." "Alas! Dear mother, the sight of all the men saddens me equally; you are the only one I love in the world."

> "Je reste où je suis le plus heureux," disait Octave. "Il y a des moments où je te crois" répondait son heureuse mère; "mais si pendant deux jours je ne t'ai vu que dans le monde, la raison reprend le dessus." "Hélas! Chère maman, la vue de tous les hommes m'attriste également; je n'aime que toi au monde." (*Armance*, 35)

The feminine duos constituted by Octave's mother and Armance and by Madame de Bonnivet and Armance make Octave the object of exchange. For Kristeva, the lover positioned between two women is Stendhal's most typical gesture: "Julien Sorel between Madame de Rênal and Mathilde; Fabrice del Dongo between Sanseverina and Clélia, between Sanseverina and Marietta, between Sanseverina and Fausta, and, to begin with, between Sanseverina and his own mother."[28] This strategy of being "between two women" also suggests a "safeguarding strategy," a stratagem of masculine sexuality obsessed with castration anxiety. Stendhal's impotent hero is for Kristeva the paradoxical defense against sexual fiascoes. Similarly, the classification of Stendhal's lovers is nothing more than the warding off of the fear of castration. The alphabetization of women becomes the culminating Stendhalian passion, an impotent passion that reduces women to letters.

Perhaps it should not be forgotten that what is at issue as potentially lacking in castration is not so much the penis as the phallus, or the signifier of desire. And it is in the mother that castration must be located by the child if he is to exit from the imaginary orbit of maternal desire and be returned to the father, to the possessor of the phallic emblem that makes the mother desire him and prefer him to the child. But because Stendhal never could exit from the imaginary orbit of maternal desire, he is caught in the real threat of castration, the absence of the penis, that is, impotence. The alphabetization of women thus becomes the ruse which allows Stendhal/Octave to return to the imaginary bliss of mother's love.

For Irigaray, logocentrism can be understood as a consequence of the castration of gaze and voice: "The letter is a finite, single, unique, distinct and distant shape, separable. It is indifferent, except by phonetic relation to the other letters: nonserial, numeral, associable, groupable, operable. . . . An individual of a species and gender with no link to any family, it remains without possible genealogy or affiliation, except by proxy, delegation, artifice."[29] The letter is cut off from the rest of the alphabet and still part of it; it is separated and yet can be reunited; it has no generation. Irigaray argues that the letter represents nothing, that it merely arouses the presence of its *prescripteur,* a word which designates a precursor script. It is in the presencing of that other scene that the Stendhalian alphabet takes its full meaning.

Stendhal blinds himself (*s'aveugle*) looking at what should not have been seen, should not have been described. If the fear of blinding oneself like Oedipus is connected with the fear of castration, it is generally linked to the father's death. In his essay "The Uncanny" (1919), Freud shows how in Hoffmann's "The Sandman," Nathaniel's childhood is constructed around the split father imago: whereas the one threatens to blind him, that is, to castrate him, the other, "good" father intercedes for his sight. It is remarkable that in this essay Freud attributed the child's castration anxiety to the split father figure, whereas it would be attributed in "Medusa's Head" (1922) to the sight of the mother's genitals. In *Henry Brulard,* the different figures of blindness are all linked to the mother's death. The first case Brulard reports is related to Zadig, who almost lost his eye in the first chapter of *Zadig:* "Zadig's hurt was more dangerous. An arrow had hit him near the eye and made a deep wound. The great doctor Hermes was sent from Memphis. He visited the sick man and said he would lose his eye."[30] If Brulard's "pre-scriptor" is Zadig in his memoirs, the fear of being a one-eyed man is again activated by a personal anecdote: Stendhal is recollecting the evening when he was taken by his uncle to see *Le Cid.* This was in 1790, a few months after his mother had died, and he remembers the accident which occurred at the theater: "As he recited the Stanzas, or at some other point, wielding his sword with too much fervour, the Cid hurt himself near the right eye. 'He very nearly put out his eye,' people were saying round me" (En disant les Stances, ou ailleurs, en maniant son épée avec trop de feu, le Cid se blessa à l'oeil droit. Un peu plus, dit-on autour de moi, il se crevait l'oeil) (*Henry Brulard,* 31/40).

Brulard's linguistic slippage from *deuil* to *duel* (mourning to dueling) combines, in the same metaphor of blindness, mourning for the mother and the Cid's near loss of sight in a duel. Zadig's blindness and that of the Cid provide a symbolical reading for Brulard's fear of never seeing his mother again: "Shall I never see her again?" "How can you see her again if they're going to take her away to the churchyard?" ("Je ne la reverrai jamais?" "Comment veux-tu la revoir, si on l'emportera au cimetière?") (*Henry Brulard*, 26/33). Death is for young Stendhal equivalent to blindness—the impossibility of seeing the loved mother ever again. The figural opacity that Marin stresses when interpreting the list of women's names in *Brulard* becomes the sign of another reading: "Vaammaaamacga or VAa MmAaaMAcga: to mummy, ancient voice, obscure voice which is reinscribing this former reading, today, in the other one, I am seeing in the V which has become the first letter of this strange, unspeakable name, a proffering mouth or a listening ear."[31]

The specificity of the alphabet is to be assembled or disassembled and to constitute partitions, topographical divisions, and frameworks. In the scene where Stendhal's mother leaped over him, there is indeed an opening, a V figure which he will repeat in his fiction. The V of the mother's legs is a motif Freud adduces in his account of the Wolf-Man's dread of butterfly wings. For both Stendhal and the Wolf-Man, the mother's genitals and the primitive scene constitute the fear of castration. It is rather troubling to see the child's echolalia reconstituted in Stendhal's list of women's names, as if "Vaammaaamacga" were still calling for the mother. Because the call, sadly, is never answered, Stendhal is thinking of new scenarios protecting him from the mother's death. As the staging of castration is never ended, mourning for the mother is never performed, since Stendhal reverses it into the mother's mourning for the dead son.

In *Armance*, *Le Rouge et le noir*, and *La Chartreuse de Parme*, the son's death precipitates the end of the fiction. It is therefore at the very moment when the Stendhalian "I" (Octave, Julien, Fabrice) dies that his fiction stops in the mother's demise. The textual vampirization in Stendhal's works marks the passage from the originary text to his own fiction that unveils the entire oedipal structure. It is his dependence on the dead mother that is repeated in the act of being "penetrated" by, pulled into the sway of, the precursor text. Stendhal's appropriation and transformation of other writers' discourse rehearse his need for pseudonymous identities. In the guise of the other text, Stendhal is reinventing his own discursive space. In *Henry Brulard*, Stendhal addressed the problem of authorship: "One could, of course, write using the third person: he said, he did. But then how could one describe one's own hidden emotions?" (On pourrait écrire, il est vrai, en se servant de la troisième personne, il fit, il dit. Oui, mais comment rendre compte des mouvements intérieurs de l'âme?) (*Henry Brulard*, 3–4/8). Although no literary text is ever created ex nihilo, in the case of Stendhal it is his insistence on the rewriting of an anterior text which suggests an unusual parasitic need.

I will now specifically consider the palimpsestic slippage from *Olivier* to *Armance*. In both *Olivier* and *Armance*, Olivier and Octave are respectively in love with the marchioness of Nanteuil and Armance. In the two narratives, Olivier and Octave dread marriage for reasons which are never openly acknowledged. In both cases, Latouche and Stendhal describe the tragic effect of social pressures on the individual: "Nothing can be hidden for long in society when the main occupation, I was going to say the main concern, is conversation" (Il n'est rien de longtemps caché dans une société où la conversation est le principal emploi du temps, j'allais dire la principale affaire).[32] It is precisely because Olivier's visits to the marchioness of Nanteuil are known that the jealous Baroness of B. forces them into marriage: "Well then! we will be united. We must be married since your honor as much as mine demands it" (Eh bien! oui . . . nous serons unis. Il le faut maintenant, votre honneur l'exige autant que le mien) (*Olivier*, 91). Once the marriage is publicly announced, Olivier leaves his wife Emilie, and the end of the narrative is told in a letter sent to his wife by Olivier. She receives Olivier's letter after he has entered the monastery under the name of Brother Emilien. The absorption of the feminine name Emilie into Brother Emilien marks the symbolic disappearance of Olivier. In Stendhal's *Ar-*

mance, Octave's suicide is followed by Madame de Malivert's and Armance's taking the veil in the same convent. Here, Stendhal cannot resist rewriting the story. We already noted the passage from *Olivier* to *Armance* in the effacement of the masculine name. The title indicates that something we are not exactly certain of occurred outside the fiction, even though *Armance*'s ending is typical of nineteenth-century French fiction in having both women withdraw into the same convent. However, the rewriting of *Olivier* is unsettling in *Armance* because it draws a parallel between impotence and the feminine. Why is Octave effaced in the title *Armance*? In the renaming of *Olivier* as *Armance*, Stendhal inverts the role in having Armance take the veil, not Olivier (Octave). The substitution is clearly intentional.

But what does the title mean? In *Parages*, Jacques Derrida questions the problem posed by Maurice Blanchot's title, *La Folie du jour* (1973). In arguing that "*La folie du jour* est une folie du titre,"[33] Derrida insists on the transgressions operated by the narrative. Derrida is retrieving here another "story of the eye," in which the narrator becomes insane as he recovers from an eye injury. The specificity of Blanchot's narrative is relevant to our study as long as we keep in mind that in both narratives blindness (madness) and impotence constitute the enigma of the text. The quotable (*citationnel*) relation between *Olivier* and *Armance* reveals the duplicity of the narrative, since it replays the precursor text under the feminine guise of the title. In questioning the countless meanings of *La Folie du jour*, Derrida insists on one in particular: "It is the most obvious meaning of a text which tells or fails to tell the impossible attempt of a *narrative*, of a traumatic event which nearly cost the *sight*—thus the life—of somebody supposed to say 'I.'"[34]

If the symbolical equivalence between the French *coûter la vue/coûter le jour* (to cost one's sight/to cost one's life) brings us back to the moment in *Henry Brulard* when Stendhal loses his mother and dreads never seeing her again, we must also bear in mind that she died when giving birth (*donner le jour*). *Coûter le jour/donner le jour* becomes the tragic paradigm of the Stendhalian texts. In *Armance*, textual appropriation goes back to an earlier text of Madame de Duras's *Olivier, ou le secret* (1822), in which Olivier stabs himself to death to avoid telling Madame de Nanteuil his secret. Olivier's impotence, which is never revealed in either text, constitutes "the secret" of the narrative and is kept as such in *Armance*: "Except for the way he killed himself, he enjoyed telling everything to his Armance" (Excepté le genre de sa mort, il s'accorda le bonheur de tout dire à son Armance) (*Armance*, 189). Readers are left to guess Octave's reason for committing suicide. Like *La Folie du jour*, *Armance* fails to come to terms with the traumatic event it is supposed to tell. In saying that "this is precisely what is madness, that logos is mad, that the discourse of reason cannot take on one meaning," Derrida comes to the conclusion that "in a way, the title will not have taken place" (le titre d'une certaine manière n'aura pas eu lieu).[35] The decentering of the logos turns *La Folie du jour* into pure madness. The avatars of the title deprive the narrative of its logic. In *La Folie du jour* as well as in *Armance*, the title is deceitful and enigmatic, since it does not correspond to what it is supposed to describe. Under the cover of a woman's name, Stendhal is effectively telling the story of a man.

The next question to ask is then the following: in the guise of Armance de Zohiloff, is Stendhal surreptitiously adding his own story? Would he already write from a female point of view although Armance has not yet become Lamiel? In *L'Hermaphrodite*, Michel Serres analyzes Balzac's *Sarrasine* and remarks that Zambinella, once the letter Z has been removed (*ambinella*), means "the two in her" in Italian.[36] In reconstructing *Sarrasine* around the meaning contained in the name Zambinella, Serres argues that the sculptor's death is necessary if Zambinella's statue is to live: "La mort engendre les arts."[37] In *Armance*, we could argue that *Octave*, from the Latin *octavus*, meaning "eighth," designates the period of eight days which follows each of the main celebrations in the year. In music it also means the interval of eight scale degrees. Octave already contains his own end: "The wedding took place. Octave himself could not help seeing Armance's happiness. He had the weakness to delay his departure for eight days" (Le mariage se fit. Octave lui-même ne pouvant se dissimuler le bonheur d'Armance, eut la faiblesse, de retarder son départ de huit jours) (*Armance*, 187–88). In delaying his departure for Greece, where he intends to kill himself, Octave gives himself eight days of "survival," which later in the text will be the exact length of his pretended agony: "Octave saw after eight days that they [the sailors] despaired of his return to life" (Octave vit au bout de huit jours qu'on désespérait de son retour à la vie) (*Armance*, 188). Stendhal is in effect asking the same question as Derrida: "If one could go write-on-living-on, would one write on the condition of being dead already or of living on? Is it an alternative?"[38] The alternative chosen by Octave/Stendhal is to survive through his writing, here in the posthumous letter Octave sends to Armance. The eight days which Octave grants himself to survive nonetheless mark the limit of his survival. The narrative of impotence is here the narrative of effacement of one text by another. *Armance* constitutes finally the Stendhalian supplement to the other *Oliviers* by reaffirming the maternal survival.

It is Octave's passion for his mother which makes him different from the other Oliviers: "Except during the time when I enjoyed being alone with you, my unique pleasure consists of living isolated, and without anyone in the world to speak to me" (Excepté dans les moments où je jouis du bonheur d'être seul avec toi, mon unique plaisir consiste à vivre isolé, et sans personne au monde qui ait le droit de m'adresser la parole) (*Armance*, 34). *Armance* manifests the painful severance from the mother and replays it in different registers, different "octaves." The reappropriation of the mother into language marks Stendhal's attempt at recentering Octave in the very lacuna of his impotence. The shift from Madame de Malivert to Armance is catastrophic because it forces Octave to face his "monstrous nature." The mother is the site of infantile bliss, whereas Armance becomes the ominous promised wife: " 'Yes, my dear,' said he, looking finally at her, 'I adore you, but which man is he who loves you? He is a monster' " ("Oui, chère amie," lui dit-il en la regardant enfin, "je t'adore, mais quel est l'homme qui t'adore? C'est un monstre") (*Armance*, 175).

The speech act does not produce here anything besides its own enigma. What is censored in Octave's speech is the risk of dissolution, dismemberment. Severance from the mother cannot be assumed; impotence is the metaphor which protects Octave from being separated. The Freudian *fort/da* oscillates on the side of the *da*; there is no *fort*, no coming back. This is precisely the moment that Gilbert Lascault describes: "The monstrous shape is figuring one moment of this flickering oscillation: *fort*, the moment of absence, death, zero, *impouvoir*. It is the aberration which suggests shapelessness, the dissolution of body, speech, and social organization. It is the rejected, excluded shape."[39] To speak is then to risk naming one's physical aberration: "Octave stopped right in front of her [Armance] as if struck by horror and not daring to continue. His frightened eyes looked straight ahead as if he had the vision of a monster" (Octave était arrêté droit devant elle comme frappé d'horreur et n'osant continuer. Ses yeux effrayés regardaient fixement devant lui comme s'il eût la vision d'un monstre) (*Armance*, 175). Speech is constantly silenced by visions; it has lost its function of communication. Stendhal's separation anxiety is here replayed by Octave's loss of communicative skills and his suicide.

Monsieur de Malivert and Octave's uncle, Monsieur de Soubirane (also called the commander), both represent patriarchal authority: "The commander, my father himself! they do not love me; they like the name I bear, they cherish in me an ambitious pretext" (Le commandeur, mon père lui-même! ils ne m'aiment pas; ils aiment le nom que je porte, ils chérissent en moi un prétexte d'ambition) (*Armance*, 43). It is Monsieur de Soubirane who devises a plot destined to break up the marriage between Octave and Armance. Unsuccessful in doing so, he will nonetheless succeed in having Octave kill himself. Finding that the marriage is not advantageous to the family and to him in particular, Monsieur de Soubirane has a letter addressed to Méry de Tersan, Armance's best friend: "Once the model of the letter was chosen, it was presented to his autograph writer who imitated Mademoiselle de Zohiloff's writing to perfection. Armance was supposed to write a long letter to her friend Méry de Tersan regarding her future marriage with Octave" (Le modèle de lettre arrêté fut présenté à son calqueur d'autographes qui imita à s'y tromper l'écriture de mademoiselle de Zohiloff. Armance était supposée écrire à son amie Méry de Tersan une longue lettre sur son prochain mariage avec Octave) (*Armance*, 181). The letters are exchanged when Octave finds Monsieur de Soubirane's letter while placing one of his own in the orange tree box. His letter is the one which reveals his impotence to Armance: "He kept his word. He wrote a ten-line letter and addressed it to Mademoiselle de Zohiloff" (Il tint parole. Il écrivit une lettre de dix lignes et y mit l'adresse de mademoiselle de Zohiloff) (*Armance*, 179). However, the "fatal letter" will be torn up and its pieces kept when the counterfeit letter is discovered: "Octave was struck with horror. To deserve such an exception, I should have been pleasant and joyful, and that is what I lack. I was wrong; all I have to do is to die" (Octave resta frappé d'horreur. Pour mériter une telle exception, il eût fallu être aimable et gai, et c'est ce qui me manque. Je me suis trompé; il ne me reste qu'à mourir) (*Armance*, 183). If it takes only an apocryphal letter for Octave to kill himself, it shows that the original letter does not have a very authentic existence.[40] The forged letter nullifies Octave's confession.

Octave's "survival" is left to his posthumous letter, in which "he enjoyed telling the truth to his Armance" (il s'accorda le bonheur de tout dire à son Armance) (*Armance*, 189). The secret is thus revealed outside the fiction itself—Octave's suicide hides Brulard's dread of impotence/castration and repeats that other scene of desire: "In any case, on another scene since nothing can take place on this scene—without gaze, or voice, or erection—a *scene* created entirely by the alphabetic economy."[41] It is precisely this alphabetic economy which constitutes the return of the repressed in Brulard's confessions. The truncated names of Stendhal's lovers which form the "Vaammaaamacga" call for the mother appear as the total sum of a life already contained in its origin. It is in the presencing of the mother's ghostly voice that Stendhal writes: "She died in the flower of her youth and beauty in 1790; she must have been twenty-eight or thirty. That was when the life of my mind began" (Elle périt à la fleur de la jeunesse et de la beauté en 1790, elle pouvait avoir vingt-huit ou trente ans. Là commence ma vie morale) (*Henry Brulard*, 22/29). In *Armance*, Stendhal was testing the limits of retelling the dread of impotence; in *Le Rouge et le noir*, he will adapt several affairs from the *Gazette des tribunaux* to describe castration anxiety.

The Horror of the Name: Julien Sorel

> Being is tested by being split up into offspring, copies and fakes. These disperse and miniaturize the potency of the gaze. Of mirrors.
>
> LUCE IRIGARAY, *Speculum of the Other Woman*

In *Le Rouge et le noir* (1830), Stendhal's concern shifts from the dread of impotence and castration to the horror of decapitation. Early in *Le Rouge et le noir*, when Julien Sorel enters the church at Verrières before going to the Rênals', he discovers a scrap of printer paper which attracts his attention: "He glanced at it and saw: *Details of the execution and last moments of Louis Jenrel, executed at Besançon, on the ——.* The paper was torn. Who could have left this paper here? thought Julien. Poor fellow, he added with a sigh, his name has the same ending as mine" (Il y porta les yeux et vit: *Détails de l'exécution et des derniers moments de Louis Jenrel, exécuté à Besançon, le. . . .* Le papier était déchiré. Qui a pu mettre ce papier là, dit Julien? Pauvre malheureux, ajouta-t-il avec un soupir, son nom finit comme le mien) (*Red and Black*, 20/48). The irony is that Julien recognizes a resemblance between the names as both ending in *rel*, but fails to notice that Louis Jenrel is the anagram of Julien Sorel. Louis Jenrel's trial and execution are in effect the perfect *récit en abyme*. There is an irony in Sorel's "son nom finit comme le mien" insofar as it anticipates Julien's uncanny "ending," which is just like that of Jenrel.

Pursuing the anagram of Louis Jenrel, Peggy Kamuf writes:

The name(s) of the author—Stendhal/Henri Beyle—does not simply point to someone behind the scenes, pulling the strings. It too is displayed in the scene like a fragment of text set out in order to be read. The assonance or near rhyme of those two names—Louis Jenrel/Henri Beyle—signals that the proper name of the signatory has not simply been left out of the loop to be replaced or protected by the device of encrypting. What is more, the name Rênal, which is also circulating in the scene, ends like Stendhal.[42]

Here the name functions as the subject of a death sentence; like Julien Sorel, the name of Louis Jenrel is pseudonymous, veiling the actual name of Antoine Berthet. In providing the general outlines of Stendhal's plot, Antoine Berthet's criminal proceedings and execution are repeated in Julien's trial and decapitation.[43] The pseudonym Jenrel is another of Stendhal's calculations deliberately to remove the name from its origin. Kamuf calls this removal or detachment "the signature piece": "The process by which Henri Beyle can take Stendhal, the proper name of a place, as signature is the same process that has to allow 'Stendhal' to become detached again from the signatory. It is already detached and the signatory is already outlived by the signature even when, at the moments he signs, his death is only announced or prefigured as a still further event."[44] Brulard's "auto-biothanatography" is here replayed by Stendhal in *Le Rouge et le noir*, unknown to Julien. The problem of the name is also connected with the naming of a place.

In his preface to Stendhal's *Ecrits intimes*, Ernest Abravanel establishes the historical circumstances which seem to have given Beyle the idea of taking the name of the town Stendal: "Part of Germany is still occupied by the French army. As an officer Henri Beyle is appointed to govern Sagan. His duty calls him to repress a small riot in the neighboring town of Stendal. Why, among so many names, does this one stay in his memory? Why, among all his pseudonyms, does this one live on?"[45] Perhaps Stendhal wants to mark strongly the separation from the father's name in establishing his military victory as the origin of his name. However, the addition of the letter H (pronounced *hache* in French; the word *hache* means axe in English) to the name Stendal remains unexplained. The H/*hache* marks also the semantic connection between Stendhal and Beyle/*Beyl* (axe), which is now spelled *Beil* in German. Arguing that Stendhal thus wanted to keep a trace of his paternal name Beyle, Nicholas Rand points to the relation between Verrières, the town of *Le Rouge et le noir*, Stendhal, and the guillotine.[46] Pseudonymous Stendhal offers for Rand a cryptonymic link between Stendhal, Beyle, and Verrières. From the outset, the idea of decapitation is contained in both names, Stendhal and Verrières, and reinscribed in Louis Jenrel's execution. From the *Gazette des tribunaux* to *Le Rouge et le noir*, we see that Stendhal cannot write from a safe distance: his name/pseudonym is always inevitably caught up with ideas of severance, which bring us back to his mother's death and the loss of his own life. How can we read Verrières in the context of Julien's decapitation and Stendhal's name?

In his introduction of the *Wolf-Man's Magic Word*, Rand shows how the description of Verrières, which occupies the first chapter of *Le Rouge et le noir*, hides the author himself. Verrières contains the word *verre* (glass) and also designates a *verrière* (glass house), a transparency which opens to that other town of Stend(h)al. Rand establishes that, hidden behind Verrières, the guillotine is the key to deciphering the novel. The idea of cutting, severing, contained in the axe (*hache*) is also contained in the word *verrière*. From the very beginning, *Le Rouge et le noir* is detached from Antoine Berthet's criminal proceedings and given as a fragment of missing pieces: "The paper was torn. On the other side were the first words of a line: *The first step* . . ." (Le papier était déchiré. Au revers on lisait les deux premiers mots d'une ligne, c'étaient: Le premier pas . . .) (*Red and Black*, 20/48). The incompleteness of Julien's reading can here be juxtaposed with Brulard's dread of being unable to write his finished autobiography. What is missing in Stendhal's writing? For Rand, the guillotine has become symbolically the metaphor of language: "[In this passage] the action of the guillotine may be further interpreted as a clue suggesting that certain words in the novel are uncompleted."[47] The effects of this textual dissimulation are not gratuitous; if some words are incomplete, for instance *to guillotine*, they can evoke another narrative, such as Antoine Berthet's murder case, or another scene, such as Henriette Gagnon's death, in which past/present are undifferentiated in a perfect crypt. Creation for Stendhal will thus repeat the mother's death in childbirth; creation is the impossible reconciliation between life and death. In this condition, Brulard's musings on writing his incomplete autobiography are similar to Julien's musings on dying: "It's a funny thing, the verb guillotine can't be conjugated in all its tenses. One can very well say, I will be guillotined, you will be guillotined, but it's impossible to say: I have been guillotined" (C'est singulier, le verbe guillotiner ne peut pas se conjuguer dans tous ses temps; on peut bien dire: je serai guillotiné, tu seras guillotiné, mais on ne dit pas: J'ai été guillotiné) (*Red and Black*, 389/551).

Julien's impossible utterance "I have been guillotined" anticipates Brulard's impossible "I died at. . . ." In such impossible locutions Stendhal betrays his impossible love for his dead mother: "She cannot be offended because I am taking the liberty of revealing the love I had for her; if ever I meet her again, I shall tell her about it once more" (Elle ne peut pas s'offenser de la liberté que je prends avec elle en révélant que je l'aimais; si je la retrouve jamais je le lui dirais encore) (*Henry Brulard*, 22/31). Brulard's guilt—"As for me, I was as criminal as possible, I was passionately in love with her charms" (Quant à moi j'étais aussi criminel que possible, j'aimais ses charmes avec fureur) (*Henry Brulard*, 22/31)—is blocked forever in the impasse of oedipal desire. In *Le Rouge et le noir*, Stendhal kills both son and "mother" as if to resuscitate his own mother in the same "criminal" passion. This is what Julia Kristeva describes as the dialectics of an unending negation and reformulation: "The madness made up of Stendhalian women's unreasonable courage is perhaps the moment when the dead mother comes to life as death drive—as passion."[48] In claiming that "the figure of the Patriarch casts the longest shadow in *Le Rouge et le noir*,"[49] Carol Mossman places the emphasis elsewhere. But as I have shown, the castrating role of language and the paternal shadow are always articulated on an irreducibly maternal scene. Indeed, while the first part of the novel accounts for Julien's search for a father in lieu of his own, Sorel *père*, *Le Rouge et le noir* ends with the fulfillment of Madame de Rênal's tragic premonition: "I shall die soon. But you will be a monster" (Je mourrai bientôt. Mais tu seras un monstre) (*Red and Black*, 95/151). The "matricide" will be finally the cause of Julien's death.

Accused of adultery in an anonymous letter sent to her husband, Madame de Rênal asks Julien to counterfeit another letter in order to discredit the sender, who she thinks is Monsieur de Valenod:

> The whole point of my acting is to make my husband think the letter comes from M. Valenod, as I don't doubt it does. Now you must furnish me with my anonymous letter; you'll need patience and a pair of scissors. Cut out of a book the words with which I'll furnish you; then glue them on the sheet of blue notepaper enclosed here; it was sent by M. Valenod. If you don't find the exact words, take time to form them letter by letter.

> Tout le but de ma conduite, c'est de faire penser à mon mari que la lettre vient de M. Valenod; je ne doute pas qu'il en soit l'auteur. C'est toi qui vas me fournir la lettre anonyme; arme-toi de patience et d'une paire de ciseaux. Coupe dans un livre les mots que tu vas voir; colle-les ensuite avec de la colle à bouche, sur la feuille de papier bleuâtre que je t'envoie; elle me vient de M. Valenod. Si tu ne trouves pas les mots tout faits, aie la patience de les former lettre à lettre. (*Red and Black*, 96/152)

The letter that Julien must reconstruct is made of fragments, of cut-out letters severed from their origin. The counterfeit letter here accedes to the same status of authenticity as the original letter. The falsification of truth plays the same role as in Monsieur de Soubirane's letter: it subverts the original. Both Octave and Monsieur de Rênal are deceived by "another" text which imitates the primary text: Armance's handwriting, M. Valenod's style. Stendhal's process of creation proceeds through the deconstruction of another text. The enterprise of creating a text out of another describes Stendhal's appropriation and disfiguration of his sources. As Mossman argues, "Origins begin to lose their referential anchors, authenticity proves unfathomable, and the Word plays a subversive role in this comedy of falsification."[50] Counterfeit and anonymous letters simulate reality while falsifying it in *Armance* and *Le Rouge et le noir*. Besides reproducing creation itself in Stendhal's writing, the scene reveals Madame de Rênal's strange judgment of herself.

In this passage, Madame de Rênal steps out of the path of traditional maternal devotion. Stendhal radically transforms the role of Madame de Rênal in having her say to Julien: "Whatever happens, you may be sure of one thing: I shall never survive our final separation, not for a day. Ah, what a wicked mother! Two empty words I have written there, dear Julien. They have no meaning for me; at this moment I can think only of you, and I wrote them only to forestall your blame" (Quoi qu'il puisse arriver, sois sûr d'une chose: je ne survivrais pas d'un jour à notre séparation définitive. Ah! mauvaise mère! Ce sont deux mots vains que je viens d'écrire là, cher Julien. Je ne les sens pas; je ne puis songer qu'à toi en ce moment, je ne les ai écrits que pour ne pas être blâmée de toi) (*Red and Black*, 97/153–54). In momentarily abandoning her children for Julien's sake, Madame de Rênal points to the difference between the "good mother" and the "bad mother."[51] She registers the difference between herself and women whose unique concern is motherhood. In "Stabat Mater," Kristeva argues that "we live in a civilization where the *consecrated* (religious or secular) representation of femininity is absorbed by motherhood."[52] The irresistible death drive represented by Madame de Rênal's passion for Julien contains the end of the novel: "Mme de Rênal was true to her word. She never tried in any way to take her own life; but three days after Julien, she died in the act of embracing her children" (Madame de Rênal fut fidèle à sa promesse. Elle ne chercha en aucune manière à attenter à sa vie; mais trois jours après Julien, elle mourut en embrassant ses enfants) (*Red and Black*, 408/576). Stendhal's filial and incestuous fantasm is created by the foreclosure of the primal scene. The scene where young Beyle saw his mother leap over his bed is followed by her death. Stendhal's guilty secret has become this *coupure de l'écriture*, which is repeated by Octave's impotence and Julien's decapitation. The sign of the letter H/*hache* cryptically repeats the severance from the mother while announcing the son's death.

In Kristeva's words, Stendhalian women "have the strength of destiny, the power of ancient divinities."[53] Stendhal's women seem to have the power to change the course of history. One thinks of course of Madame de Rênal's disastrous letter sent to M. de La Mole, which still remains the true generator of the novel's conclusion. In fact, the letter has been inspired to her by her confessor: "The letter written to M. de La Mole had been the work of the young priest who was Mme de Rênal's confessor, and she had copied it out" (La lettre écrite à M. de La Mole avait été faite par le jeune prêtre qui dirigeait la conscience de Mme de Rênal, et ensuite copiée par elle) (*Red and Black*, 394/558). It is curious to note how Stendhal brings about Julien's downfall by having Mme de Rênal become the instrument of his fate. Death by the guillotine finally shortcircuits Julien's "novel" by leaving paternity dangling. Julien's unborn "son" problematizes what is good motherhood: "He found himself once more face to face with that idea which so distressed Mathilde: in fifteen years, Mme de Rênal will adore my son, and you will have forgotten him" (Il se trouvait de nouveau vis à vis de cette idée si choquante pour Mathilde: dans quinze ans Mme de Rênal adorera mon fils, et vous l'aurez oublié) (*Red and Black*, 380/538). As a father who will never know his son—if son it be—Julien also fails in having Madame de Rênal take care of his son, since she dies three days after he does. In bequeathing his father his estate, Julien/Stendhal is upsetting the order of succession and mocking paternal law. Here Stendhal is giving the decisive stroke to bad fatherhood: "'I will give a thousand francs to each of my brothers, and that remainder to you.' 'All right,' said the old man, 'that remainder is my due.' That's paternal affection for you! thought Julien, with desolation in his heart" ("Je donnerai mille francs à chacun de mes frères et le reste à vous." "Fort bien," dit le vieillard, "ce reste m'est dû." Voilà donc l'amour de père! se répétait Julien, l'âme navrée) (*Red and Black*, 399/564–65). Since Julien achieves no final relationship to any of his figures of paternity, it is, as Peter Brooks demonstrates, "Sorel the carpenter who re-emerges in the place of the father at the end, and Julien attributes to him the jolly thought that the expectation of a legacy of three or four hundred louis from his son will make him, like any father, happy to have that son guillotined."[54] The problem of "bad motherhood" unmistakably unveils what is "bad fatherhood."

The mother's victimization is finally what Stendhal is aiming at. In systematically trying to subvert the father's law, Stendhal is showing how he fails in doing so: "And the victory of Sorel *père* over his son is perhaps an ironic representation of the novelist's ultimate and absolute paternal power to put his creatures to death."[55] It is after all M. Valenod who condemns Julien to death:

> M. le baron de Valenod marched in, solemn and theatrical, followed by the other jurors. He coughed, then declared that Julien Sorel was guilty of murder, and murder with premeditation: this finding carried with it the death penalty, and it was pronounced a moment later.
>
> M. le baron de Valenod s'avança d'un pas grave et théâtral, il était suivi de tous les jurés. Il toussa, puis déclara qu'en son âme et conscience la déclaration unanime du jury était que Julien Sorel était coupable de meurtre avec préméditation: cette déclaration entraînait la peine de mort; elle fut prononcée un instant après. (*Red and Black*, 388/549)

Julien's execution is shortly followed by Mme de Rênal's death, repeating in effect two of Brulard's assertions: "I am in despair because of Métilde; she dies; I'd rather she were dead than unfaithful" (Je suis au désespoir à cause de Métilde, elle meurt, je l'aimais mieux morte qu'infidèle) (*Henry Brulard*, 9/15), and of course the well-known "the whole joy of childhood ended for me when my mother died" (il se trouva qu'avec ma mère finit toute la joie de mon enfance) (*Henry Brulard*, 29/38). Strangely enough, death resembles an execution in Stendhal's writing. True, the son's and mother's deaths give the father his final victory. However, Sorel *père* and the baron of Valenod are both ludicrous representations of fatherhood and legality respectively; if *Le Rouge et le noir* is the failed attempt at subverting the father's law, Julien's decapitation still reveals the inanity of such a vengeful law.

One has to wait for the rewriting of *Les Cenci* (1837), which Stendhal claimed to have translated from *Chroniques italiennes*, to get the incredible staging of the father's death. The story of Cenci's parricide offers a definitive example of the "oedipal palimpsest" in Stendhal's works. In *Les Cenci*, Stendhal establishes a literal equivalence between killing the father and blinding him. Here Stendhal seems to take the figure of the blind Oedipus and displace it onto the father's so that his punishment fits the monstrosity of his crimes.

Specular Analysis: *Les Cenci*

> Laius/Jocasta . . . Jocasta/Oedipus . . . Oedipus/Antigone and Ismene—there we have the Greek tragedy that spans the origins and end of the unhappy hero whom Freud chose as the model for every human destiny.
>
> CHRISTIANE OLIVIER, *Jocasta's Children*

The graceful picture of a young girl, her bust swathed in a white mantle and a white turban around her head, has for years been pointed out to visitors at the Barberini Gallery as the portrait of Beatrice Cenci. Corrado Ricci claims that "passion and bad faith, in fact, began their work of deforming truth on the very day the fate of the Cenci was decided."[56] For different reasons, Beatrice Cenci's fate inspired many authors: Shelley's *The Cenci* (1819), Stendhal's *Les Cenci* (1837) in *Chroniques italiennes*, Corrado Ricci's

Beatrice Cenci (1923), and Antonin Artaud's *Les Cenci* (1935), to name but a few writers interested in retelling Beatrice Cenci's tragic fate. One can first question why so many male writers devoted so much time to telling the same story. Does incest between father and daughter constitute such a powerful drama that men cannot recount it enough?

Let us juxtapose here Freud's theory of the father's seduction: "In the period in which the main interest was directed to discovering infantile sexual traumas, almost all my women patients told me that they had been seduced by their father. I was driven to recognize in the end that these reports were untrue and so came to understand that hysterical symptoms are derived from phantasies and not from real occurrences."[57] The seduction is, of course, covered up both in theory and practice by a normative statement, a law which denies it. As Irigaray argues, "It is neither simply true, nor indeed false, to claim that the little girl fantasizes being seduced by her father, since it is equally valid to assume that the father *seduces his daughter*."[58] That being said, it is nevertheless the father's desire which prescribes the modes of the law he lays down, a law that reduces to the state of "fantasy" the little girl's seduction. Stendhal's dramatization of the Cencis' case poses unequivocally the tragic effects of the father's power in the absence of law.

In arguing that "when it suspends the realization of a seduced desire, law organizes and arranges the world of fantasy at least as much as it forbids, interprets, and symbolizes it,"[59] Irigaray seems to address urgently the question of the seductive function of law itself. In having both mother and daughter subjected to the mad, tyrannical power of the father, Stendhal's text comes close to personal experience. The mother is here forced to see and witness the father's crime:

> He tried with threats and by using force to rape his own daughter Beatrice; he was not ashamed to be in bed with her. Then he used to take her to his wife's bed, so that poor Lucrecia could see what he was doing with Beatrice by the candlelight. He made this poor girl believe the horrible heresy

that I hardly dare to repeat, namely, that when a father knows his own daughter, the children who are born are necessarily saints.

Il tenta avec des menaces, et en employant la force, de violer sa propre fille Béatrix; il n'eut pas honte d'aller se placer dans son lit. Puis il la conduisait dans le lit de sa femme, afin qu'à la lueur des lampes la pauvre Lucrece pût voir ce qu'il faisait avec Béatrix. Il donnait à entendre à cette pauvre fille une hérésie effroyable, que j'ose à peine rapporter, à savoir que, lorqu'un père connaît sa propre fille, les enfants qui naissent sont nécessairement des saints.[60]

The staging of the daughter's rape unveils the father's pathological desire to have the mother see them committing incest and plays out the reversal of the primal scene. Why does Stendhal's rewriting of the incest scene contradict Ricci's account of the historical facts? In Ricci's *Beatrice Cenci*, two serving women report: "It seems that he [the father] installed himself for some days in the chamber where Lucrezia and Beatrice slept. It seems also that he paid not the slightest consideration to the presence of Beatrice" (*Beatrice Cenci*, 1:123). In dramatizing the incest scene Stendhal clearly superimposes another: he focuses on the singular horror of the mother at the spectacle of Beatrice in Cenci's bed. Whereas the child interprets the "primal scene" on the basis of what s/he sees in the Freudian scenario, Stendhal places the mother in the role of the witness. Stendhal's characteristic compulsion to repeat and rewrite his own primal scene is clearly at work in this refashioning of the father's crime. Against all evidence, he centers the scene around the mother's gaze. Stendhal appears more concerned with replaying his own obsessions surrounding the mother than with chronicling the historical incident.

Here the act of blinding the incestuous father is the equivalent of Brulard's *vie morale*, which began at his mother's death. The mother's death puts an end to her son's incestuous desires; Brulard then undergoes a complete transformation under the father's tutelage. In *Les Cenci*, the failure of the incest prohibition recalls Stendhal's tormented and insatiable oedipal desire. The task is that of imagining a symbolic order which might lead the child out of the oedipal dilemma. But the problem of *Les Cenci* is precisely that one discovers that the site of the presumed paternal symbolic order is in fact the site of unprecedented lawlessness and violence. In being forced to witness the father's crime, Lucrecia, the mother, is transformed into a "speculum" mirroring the father's fault and the collapse of paternal law. In emphasizing that the chronicle of the Cenci was written when Stendhal was also engaged in writing his autobiography, Marin again stresses the link between fiction and the autobiographical *Vie de Henry Brulard*: "The unspeakable, forgotten wager is to write about a single gaze fixed, a long time ago, onto what should not have been seen, what could not be seen."[61] The son's inability to understand what he has just seen in the place of the presumed origin is followed by a *coupure* in the text, a stop or *arrêt* followed by his mother's death. In depicting the mother's vision of what should remain unseen in *Les Cenci*, indeed in occupying the place of the mother as witness, is not Stendhal reversing the Medusa's-head scenario? The Medusa's mortal look becomes here an apotropaic act; and by forcing Lucrecia to look at the incest scene, Cenci brings upon himself the revenge of his wife and daughter. The parricide is indeed the incredible staging of Cenci's blinding by the paid murderers: "One of them had a big nail which he put vertically on the sleeping old man's eye; the other one had a hammer with which he drove the nail into his head" (L'un d'eux avait un grand clou qu'il posa verticalement sur l'oeil du vieillard endormi; l'autre, qui avait un marteau, lui fit entrer ce clou dans la tête) (*Les Cenci*, 2:695). The elaboration of the parricide in the Stendhalian text repeats another scene in which castration, blinding, and death are undifferentiated.

Stendhal manipulates the historical truth in several ways. While, as we have seen, he transforms incidents to suit his imaginative predilections, in other instances he adduces facts that are elided in other versions of the story. In stressing, for example, the horrible details of Francesco Cenci's death, Stendhal uses details that Shelley eliminates in his play: "We strangled him that there might be no blood."[62] Shelley's fiction of strangling conceals the gory details of the father's murder. In Stendhal's *Les Cenci*, the parricidal blood is almost immediately afterwards identified with Beatrice's menstrual blood: "Early in the morning, she gave a blood-stained bed sheet to a washing woman in the fortress, telling her not to be surprised by such loss of blood since she bled a lot all night long" (Dès le grand matin, elle avait donné à une femme qui blanchissait le linge dans la forteresse un drap tâché de sang, lui disant de ne pas s'étonner d'une telle quantité de sang, parce que, toute la nuit, elle avait souffert d'une grande perte) (*Les Cenci*, 695). Although the scene corresponds to Ricci's own description, one can wonder if the parricide does not stand for the scene when his mother died in childbirth: "I could write a whole volume on the circumstances of the death of so beloved a person. That is to say: I am wholly ignorant of the details; she died in childbed apparently owing to the clumsiness of a surgeon named Hérault" (J'écrirais un volume sur les circonstances de la mort d'une personne si chère. C'est-à-dire: j'ignore absolument les détails, elle était morte en couches apparemment par la maladresse d'un chirurgien nommé Hérault) (*Henry Brulard*, 24/32). The mother's blood in *Brulard* would thus seem to spill over into the account of the father's murder in *Les Cenci*. The mother's death is more than simply a literary scenario for Stendhal; it is *the* traumatic experience of his childhood: "That age, which everybody says is the happiest in one's life, was for me, thanks to my father, one long sequence of cruelly painful and disgusting experiences" (Cet âge, que la voix de tous dit être celle des vrais plaisirs de la vie, grâce à mon père n'a été pour moi qu'une suite de douleurs amères et de dégoûts) (*Henry Brulard*, 53/66).

In rewriting *Les Cenci*, Stendhal repeats Henriette's deadly leap; both Henriette and Lucrecia die in the same symbolic act of opening their legs (*enjambement*): "Ignorant of what she [Lucrecia] should do, she asked Alexander, the first executioner, how she must behave. He answered that she had to ride the prisoner's seat.

But this seemed to offend her modesty, and she took a long time to do it" (Ne sachant ce qu'elle avait à faire, elle demanda à Alexandre, premier bourreau, comment elle devrait se comporter. Il lui dit de se placer à cheval sur la planche du cep. Mais ce mouvement lui parut offensant pour la pudeur, et elle mit beaucoup de temps à le faire) (*Les Cenci*, 705–6). The limit of the forbidden is here bypassed by the mother's leap, which is always followed by Stendhal's silence, which in turn leads (in *Les Cenci*) to the next scene: "The executioner showed the head to the people and then wrapped it up in the black taffeta veil" (Le bourreau montra la tête au peuple et ensuite l'enveloppa dans le voile de taffetas noir) (*Les Cenci*, 706). Lucrecia's step painfully echoes the scene that haunts Stendhal's unconscious in *Henry Brulard*: "[When] I went into the drawing-room and saw the coffin, under its black pall, *in which my mother lay,* I was seized with the most violent despair; I realized at last what death was" (En entrant au salon et voyant la bière couverte de drap noir où *était ma mère* je fus saisi du plus violent désespoir, je comprenais enfin ce que c'était que la mort) (*Henry Brulard*, 29/37).

The mother's execution and death allow the return of paternal law, or rather, the father's violent imposition of the will that passes for law. For Stendhal, as for Ricci, the Pope's sentence reestablishes paternal law at any cost: "The sentence contains not a word of commiseration for the condemned, not even a word of reprobation for Francesco Cenci. Their [Lucrecia's and Beatrice's] punishment was necessary that they might not boast of the monstrous crime they had committed" (*Beatrice Cenci*, 2:192). In unconditionally reestablishing paternal law, Pope Clement VIII conceals the father's fault.

Since the gaze is always at work in Stendhal's texts, we might return to Irigaray's analysis of the gaze in the Freudian construction of the castration complex:

By rights, though, the question should still be raised of the respective relationships between the gaze and sexual difference, since, [Freud] tells us, you have to see it to believe it. And therefore, one must lose sight of something to see it anew? Which leads to envy of the omnipotence of gazing, knowing? About sex/about the penis? To envy and jealousy of the eye-penis, of the phallic gaze? Displaced castration? *The gaze is at stake from the outset.* Don't forget, in fact, what "castration," or the knowledge of castration, owes to the gaze, at least for Freud.[63]

Irigaray stresses ironically the omnipotence of gazing/knowing which in the Freudian scenario leads to penis envy for the little girl. As I mentioned earlier, the relationship Freud establishes between castration anxiety, the fear of losing one's sight, and the fear of one's father's death in "The Uncanny" is disrupted by the "Medusa's Head" essay. In *Les Cenci,* Stendhal condensed both interpretations of castration anxiety in rewriting the incest scene. Beatrice Cenci's rape is immediately followed by the parricide, which links castration anxiety to the father's death. However, the parricide is then superseded by the mother's and daughter's death. The woman-mother is "uncanny" (*unheimlich*) not only by reason of a repression of a primitive relationship to the maternal but because her sex and sexual organ are different; while *heimlich* as a mother, woman would remain "un" as a woman. Freud describes the passage from *heimlich* to *unheimlich*: "This *unheimlich* place, however, is the entrance to the former *heim* (home) of all human beings, to the place where everyone dwelt once upon a time and in the beginning. . . . 'This place' is familiar to me, we may interpret the place as being his mother's genitals or her body."[64] While writing *Les Cenci,* Stendhal was also writing *Henry Brulard.* In a letter to Levavasseur, he could not hide the fact that he was effectively writing his confession: "I am writing a book now which is perhaps a big mistake; it is *My Confessions,* except for the style, like Jean-Jacques Rousseau, with more honesty" (J'écris maintenant un livre qui peut-être une grande sottise; c'est *Mes Confessions* au style près, comme Jean-Jacques Rousseau, avec plus de franchise).[65] Stendhal's *Les Cenci* replays *The Life of Henry Brulard* in the guise of the Cencis' story.

The spectral image of the castrated mother who dies in childbirth is finally the dominant thematic around which Stendhalian autobiography and fiction are written. They are all narratives of dissimulation and repetition leading invariably to the kernel of thanatos within the shell of the maternal. As Irigaray remarks, is not the mother "torn to pieces by Oedipus' hatred when she is cut into stages, each part of her body having been invested then disinvested so that she can grow up. And when Freud speaks of the father's dismemberment by the sons of the primitive horde, doesn't he forget the woman who was torn between son and father, between sons."[66] Stendhal's love for his mother offers countless scenarios of the oedipal passion destroying and yet resuscitating the maternal figure. In Beatrice Cenci, Stendhal doubtless hears an echo of Dante's Beatrice, who was so loved by his mother.

What is most essential to understanding the Stendhalian gaze of/on the beloved and the gaze of/on the mother is precisely its blinding, "dazzling" character. In *Les Privilèges*, he writes of a radically nonvisual, indeed tactile, rapture: "Miracle. The grantee having a ring on his finger and clasping this ring while looking at a woman, she falls madly in love with him like we think Heloïse fell in love with Abelard" (Le privilégié, ayant une bague au doigt et serrant cette bague en regardant une femme, elle devient amoureuse de lui à la passion, comme nous voyons qu'Héloïse le fut d'Abélard) (*Les Privilèges*, 1525). This wish which could never be fulfilled is the repetition, fifty years later, of Stendhal's impossible love for his dead mother and his persistent hatred for his father: "I remember that she [his aunt Elisabeth] opposed my hatred for my father and scolded me roundly because once, talking to her about him, I spoke of him as *that man*" (Elle combattait, je m'en souviens, ma haine pour mon père, et me gronda vertement parce qu'une fois en lui parlant de lui je l'appelai *cet homme*) (*Henry Brulard*, 95/114). Here we might return to Marin's question: "What would be a gaze which writes itself or writes the story of its eye, the life of its subject?"[67] Stendhal's repositioning of himself, of his narrative I/eye, in and around the place of the mother leads finally to something blinding, something that can only be felt, not seen, to a phenomenology beyond the visual field but nevertheless sustaining it. This is the truly blinding element of the oedipal scenario. The recurring figure of the blind Oedipus haunts Stendhal's writing in search of the truth about himself. This form of vision which is unsatisfied with its effort to imagine itself as a consciousness turned back upon itself, always failing to grasp itself, at once destroying and realizing itself in the "dazzling" moment that constitutes its apogee: this would be a general description of the sort of dilemma the impotent Octave intends when he is horrified at his own monstrosity.

Stendhal's mother makes her last posthumous appearance in 1840 in *The Last Romance: Earline*.[68] In his edition of the story, Henri Martineau remarks that the name Earline is a pseudonym of the Countess Cini, whose name derives from *cinis*, ashes in Latin. In calling her Countess Sandre (*cendre*, ashes), Stendhal is in effect returning once again to the ashes of the dead. The cryptonym functions here to assure the mother's "survival." Stendhal's obsession with the problems of paternity and authority is always the cipher for something else, the retrieval of the dead, the love of women he never possessed: "Most of these charming creatures never honoured me with their favours; but they literally took up my whole life. After them came my writings" (La plupart de ces êtres charmants ne m'ont point honoré de leurs bontés; mais elles ont à la lettre occupé toute ma vie. A elles ont succédé mes ouvrages) (*Henry Brulard*, 10/16). It is as if Stendhal had decided to enclose within the pseudonym Sandre the "dazzling" essence of his oedipal love. Stendhal's "tales of love" create a pattern of sublimation motivated by his passion for his mother. As we will see in the last chapter, Georges Bataille's obsessive theme of blindness in *L'Expérience intérieure* (1954), which culminates in the posthumous autobiographical fiction *Ma Mère* (1966), continues and radicalizes Stendhal's search for the sublime abjection of oedipal desire which surpasses the very limits of vision and experience.

Chapter Two

SAND: DOUBLE IDENTITY

Which paternal eye was then opened on mankind the day it
decided to divide itself by placing one sex under the domination of the other sex?

GEORGE SAND, *Lélia*

What is a name in our revolutionized and revolutionary society? A cipher for those who do nothing; a sign or an emblem
for those who work or fight. The one I was given, I earned
myself, after the event, by my own toil.

GEORGE SAND, *Story of My Life*

Inventing a Name and a Self

Like Stendhal's *Vie de Henry Brulard*, Sand's *Histoire de ma vie* (1855)
was profoundly influenced by Rousseau's *Confessions* (1781).
Though she admired Rousseau's autobiography, Sand nevertheless criticized his lack of integrity:

Forgive me, Jean-Jacques, for blaming you when I finished
your admirable *Confessions!* In blaming you, I pay you greater
tribute, because this blame does not obviate my respect and
enthusiasm for the whole of your oeuvre.

> Pardonne-moi, Jean-Jacques, de te blâmer en fermant ton ad-
> mirable livre des *Confessions!* Je te blâme, et c'est te rendre
> hommage encore, puisque ce blâme ne détruit pas mon respect
> et mon enthousiasme pour l'ensemble de ton oeuvre.[1]

Sand's point is to tell "the story of her life," not, like Rousseau, by
giving herself the freedom to invent and to lie, but by chronicling
the most important events as precisely as possible. She begins by
establishing her genealogy:

> I was born the year Napoléon was crowned, Year Twelve of the
> French Republic (1804). My name is not Marie-Aurore de
> Saxe, Marquise de Dudevant, as several of my biographers
> have "discovered," but Amantine-Lucile-Aurore Dupin, and
> my husband, M. François Dudevant, claims no title.

> Je suis née l'année du couronnement de Napoléon, l'an XII de
> la République française (1804). Mon nom n'est pas Marie-
> Aurore de Saxe, marquise de Dudevant, comme plusieurs de
> mes biographes l'ont découvert, mais Amantine-Lucile-Aurore
> Dupin, et mon mari, M. François Dudevant, ne s'attribue aucun
> titre. (*Story of My Life*, 76/OA, 1:13)

Sand's dual origin makes her Maréchal de Saxe's great-granddaughter on her father's side and a plebeian woman on her
mother's side. This dual origin will have endless repercussions in
her life and will provide the dramatic structure for her early
novels. The family discrepancy between aristocrat and com-
moner will be replayed at her father's death by, respectively, her
grandmother Madame Dupin (born Marie-Aurore de Saxe) and
her mother Sophie Dupin (born Delaborde). Sand herself thinks
that the confusion surrounding her name might be attributable to
the confusion, on the part of her biographers, between two
generations: "Marie-Aurore de Saxe was my grandmother; my
husband's father was a colonel in the cavalry during the Empire"
(Marie-Aurore de Saxe était ma grand-mère, le père de mon mari
était colonel de cavalerie sous l'Empire) (*Story of My Life*, 76/OA,
1:14). In fact, this confusion is not accidental or a mere error on
the part of her biographers; it is instead fundamental to under-

standing her identity. Aurore was always caught between two generations, her mother's and her grandmother's. Her life and her writing are constituted by that division, and, no less than for Rousseau, a certain fictionality is thus essential to Sand's self-understanding as well, since it was never a question of an authentic or irreducible self versus some fictive counterpart. For Sand the "story of her life" was always already a fiction.

My intention in this chapter is to show how Sand's dual maternal identification will be replayed in her first novels. I will examine how the choice between mother and grandmother is acted out in the recurrent feminine double who appears throughout Sand's early writing.

The question I will pose throughout my reading of Sand concerns the difficulties that confront any attempt to limit or restrict the nature of the conflict emerging around Sand's name, which, rather than being simply organized along a male-female axis, disrupts gender difference even as it constitutes it. Furthermore, Sand's conflicted identity spills beyond the question of gender and comes to determine her understanding of the relation between the isolated communities she depicts in her novels and civil society at large. Divided between two proper names, it was ultimately, of course, a third, masculine name, George Sand, that Aurore bequeathed to the world. Let us begin to reconstruct the paleography of this complex field of Sandean names and identities.

In *Story of My Life*, Sand explains that, first, her mother-in-law forbade her to use the family name Dudevant on "printed covers." Second, her literary collaboration with Jules Sandeau did not last. Abandoning her claim to authorial credit for their first effort, *Rose et Blanche* (1831), Aurore appears to have allowed Sandeau to take the credit and to sign under his pseudonym, Jules Sand, which, interestingly enough, he never used again. In a sense, then, she signs precisely by *not* signing, or rather, she signs within the very aberration of Sandeau's signature. She describes the emergence of her pseudonym in the following passage from *Story of My Life*:

I sketched out a first work that Jules Sandeau then entirely revised, and Delatouche put the name "Jules Sand" on it. This work attracted another publisher, who asked for another novel under the same pseudonym. I had written *Indiana* while at Nohant. I wanted to give it to the publisher under the pseudonym requested, but Jules Sandeau, out of modesty, did not wish to take credit for fathering a book which he knew nothing about. A name is a selling point, and as the little pseudonym had created a good demand, he really wanted to keep it. Delatouche was consulted and settled the question by a compromise: Sand would remain intact, and I would find another first name which would be uniquely mine. Without looking further, I quickly chose George, which seemed to me appropriate for someone from rural Berry.

Un premier ouvrage fut ébauché par moi, refait en entier ensuite par Jules Sandeau, à qui Delatouche fit le nom de Jules Sand. Cet ouvrage amena un autre éditeur qui demanda un autre roman sous le même pseudonyme. J'avais écrit *Indiana* à Nohant, je voulus le donner sous le pseudonyme demandé; mais Jules Sandeau, par modestie, ne voulut pas accepter la paternité d'un livre auquel il était complètement étranger. Le nom est tout pour la vente, et le petit pseudonyme s'étant bien *écoulé*, on tenait essentiellement à le conserver. Delatouche, consulté, trancha la question par un compromis: Sand resterait intact et je prendrai un autre prénom qui ne servirait qu'à moi. Je pris vite et sans chercher celui de George qui me paraissait synonyme de Berrichon. (*Story of My Life*, 907/OA, 2:139)

Sand was evidently aware of acquiring, as she said, "half of the name of another writer," but she accepted it with good humor: "It was a whim of Delatouche which gave it to me" (*Story of My Life*, 908). Is this not Sand in a Rousseaustic moment of fictive reinvention, as she implies that the pseudonym is mere serendipity and not the leitmotif of her entire experience as a woman and as an artist?

The irreducible conflict within Aurore's experience of her name and identity was first forced upon her when her mother dressed her in a military uniform like that of her father and even introduced her as "my son" to the great Napoleonic general, Murat. While this disguise was meant to please Murat, Sand recalls it with horror: "But I felt hot under the fur, I felt smothered under the gold braiding, and I was very happy when we arrived at home and my mother again put on my Spanish costume of the time—the black silk dress, edged in white-mesh silk net starting at the knees and falling in fringes to the ankle" (Mais j'avais chaud sous cette fourrure, j'étais écrasée sous ces galons, et je me trouvai bien heureuse lorqu'en rentrant chez nous, ma mère me remettait le costume espagnol du temps, la robe de soie noire, bordée d'un grand réseau de soie, qui prenait au genou et tombait en franges sur la cheville) (*Story of My Life*, 444/*OA*, 1:569). Though the instability of her gender identification was apparently difficult for the young Aurore (at least according to Sand's autobiography), we must also recall that Aurore (as George) would, as a young woman, come to adopt exactly such masculine attire:

> I had already observed and experienced these things before I dreamed of settling in Paris, and had brought up the problem with my mother; how to make do with the cheapest mode of dress in this frightful climate, short of living confined to one's room seven days a week. She had replied to me, "At my age and with my habits, it's not hard; but when I was young and your father was short of money, he got the idea to dress me like a boy." At first this idea seemed amusing to me, and then very ingenious. Having been dressed like a boy during my childhood, then having hunted in smock and gaiters with Descartes, I did not find it at all shocking again to put on a costume which was not new to me.

> J'avais fait déjà ces remarques et ces expériences avant de songer à m'établir à Paris, et j'avais posé ce problème à ma mère: comment suffire à la plus modeste toilette dans cet affreux climat, à moins de vivre enfermée dans sa chambre sept jours sur huit? Elle m'avait répondu: "C'est très possible à mon âge et avec mes habitudes; mais quand j'étais jeune et que ton père manquait d'argent, il avait imaginé de m'habiller en garçon." Cette idée me parut d'abord divertissante et puis très

ingénieuse. Ayant été habillée en garçon durant mon enfance, ayant ensuite chassée en blouse et en guêtres avec Deschartres, je ne me trouvai pas étonnée du tout de reprendre un costume qui n'était pas nouveau pour moi. (*Story of My Life*, 892–93/*OA*, 2:117)

Sand's masculine identification was further encouraged by financial difficulties, since masculine attire cost considerably less than the more complicated feminine wardrobe. "Idée divertissante," "ingénieuse"—such words indicate that for Sand the reinvention of gender, and more specifically cross-dressing, was from the beginning her privileged access to the experience of self-creation, not really of adopting or replicating an available identity but of fashioning a new one.

Sand's "Two Mothers"

In a letter dated 15 January, 1867, to Gustave Flaubert, George Sand makes the rather novel proposal that we should abolish the very notion whereby sexual difference is conventionally regarded in terms of anatomical difference. Sand is suggesting that, when considered more closely, apparent anatomical differences begin to dissolve and what appears is not two distinct sexes but one, though this *one* sex is still, we must remember, based on anatomical knowledge:

> And still further, there is this for those strong in anatomy: *there is only one sex*. A man and a woman are so entirely the same thing, that one hardly understands the mass of distinctions and subtle reasons with which society is nourished concerning this subject.

> Et puis encore, il y a ceci pour les gens forts en anatomie: *il n'y a qu'un sexe*. Un homme et une femme c'est si bien la même chose que l'on ne comprend guère les tas de distinctions et de raisonnements subtils dont se sont nourries les sociétés sur ce chapitre-là.[2]

What is the relation between what are in effect Sand's "two mothers" and her notion here of "one sex"? Might it be that Sand's creative and highly idiosyncratic experience of self-fashioning revealed to her at a relatively early age that within and between the apparent anatomical distinctions between the sexes there was another element, another component that traversed these differences even as it marked them out? And is not this late notion of "one sex" finally a metaphor for the act of self-creation that Sand has always been heir to? In what follows, we shall try to find some indications, some preliminary outlines, of an answer.

Sand's father's premature death (Aurore was then four years old) confused her greatly, and like Stendhal, she was too young to understand death. She recalled asking her grandmother this cruel question: "But when my daddy is through being dead, he'll come back to see you, won't he?" (Mais quand mon papa aura fini d'être mort, il reviendra bien te voir?) (Story of My Life, 464/OA, 1:598). The death of the father also marked the end of normal family life, hence the impossible choice between her grandmother, who lived at Nohant, and her mother, who went to Paris. Sand's fiction is organized around family scenarios which try to find a remedy for the family impasse. Young Aurore's "novels" were fundamentally linked to the mother and were composed in order to please her: "I was composing aloud interminable stories which my mother referred to as my novels. I have no recollection whatever of those droll compositions which my mother spoke of to me a thousand times, long before I had any thought of writing" (Je composais à haute voix d'interminables contes que ma mère appelait mes romans. Je n'ai aucun souvenir de ces plaisantes compositions, ma mère m'en a parlé mille fois, et longtemps avant que j'eusse la pensée d'écrire) (Story of My Life, 426/OA, 1:542). The relation between Sand's mother and her writing warrants extensive development.

In this early literary context, let us now consider the divine and androgynous Corambé, Sand's desperate attempt at reconciling the masculine with the feminine. Even retrospectively, Sand is incapable of giving a meaning to Corambé: "I shall limit myself to recalling that I had started—at so early an age, I could not say exactly when—an unwritten novel made up of thousands of stories linked together through a main fantastic character called Corambé (a name without any significance, whose syllables put themselves together by chance in a dream)" (Je me bornerai à rappeler que j'avais commencé, dans un âge si enfantin que je ne pourrai le préciser, un roman composé de milliers de romans qui s'enchaînaient les uns aux autres par l'intervention d'un principal personnage fantastique appelé *Corambé* [nom sans signification aucune, dont les syllabes s'étaient rassemblées dans le hasard de quelque rêve]) (*Story of My Life*, 925/OA, 2:165). The function of the imaginary Corambé is to resituate the family drama. Since, according to Freud, dreams have childhood material at their command and since we know that material is for the most part blotted out in our consciousness, it is not surprising that Sand does not remember the meaning of the dream in which Corambé first appears. Nor is it surprising that many critics have sought to impose a meaning upon this mysterious name. My intention is to demonstrate why Sand's writings actually made it impossible for Corambé to survive.

Sand herself insists on the absence of sexual specificity of Corambé, and Corambé's presexual anticipation of the idea of "one sex" appears to undermine in advance any notion of sexual difference organized around normative anatomical notions:

> And then, I also had to complement it at times with a woman's garb, because what I had loved best and understood best until then was a woman—my mother. Hence it often appeared to me with female features. In sum, it had no sex and put on many different guises.

> Et puis, il me fallait le compléter en le vêtant en femme à l'occasion, car ce que j'avais le mieux aimé, le mieux compris jusqu'alors, c'était une femme, c'était ma mère. En somme, il n'avait pas de sexe et revêtait toutes sortes d'aspects différents. (*Story of My Life*, 605/OA, 1:813)

Helene Deutsch's Freudian analysis of Corambé is relevant here, for even though it is clearly mistaken, Deutsch's remarks will help us to clarify the relation between Sand's notion of sexual difference and her experience of the dilemma of the proper name.

For Deutsch, Sand's "split personality" is "a clear example of a conflict between femininity and masculinity."[3] She links Sand's experience of "bisexuality" to what she calls the "masculinity complex," and she argues that Sand takes this essentially defensive measure because of her father's early death and her abandonment by her mother to the care of her grandmother. By way of background here, we should recall that Sand's grandmother, in order to ensure that all links between Aurore and her mother were severed once and for all, told Aurore that her mother had been a prostitute, which was in fact the truth. Among the highly disruptive effects this had on Aurore was the shock it presented to her notion of her own legitimacy. Whose daughter might she actually be? This is an issue that, as we will see later, looms large in Sand's narrative imagination. But to return to the question of Corambé, which, as Deutsch interestingly remarks, disappeared during an interval following the revelations of Aurore's grandmother, Corambé is precisely a figure of the relation between writing and the maternal, a relation which, for Sand, is always unstable, threatened, vulnerable: "If my mother was detestable and hateful, then I, the fruit of her womb, was, too. Terrible harm had been done to me that could have been irreparable" (Si ma mère était méprisable et haïssable, moi, le fruit de ses entrailles, je l'étais aussi. On m'avait fait un mal affreux qui pouvait être irréparable) (*Story of My Life*, 634/OA, 1:858). For Sand, the major difficulty is to differentiate between two opposed maternal models which have been sublimated in Corambé's dreamlike parental union. Thinking back on her childhood following the revelations, Sand says that she herself became machinelike and that Corambé fell silent. The temporary death of Corambé might indicate that s/he was linked with the mother's fault and could not endure the damage done to the maternal representation, but also that, for the mature Sand, writing itself became in effect the sublation of Corambé, the dialectical negation, uplifting, and preservation of Corambé at a higher level of complexity. Deutsch, somewhat more narrowly, sees Corambé as marking the dominance of the masculine disposition which pursues Sand throughout her life and proves, in Deutsch's estimation, to be a limiting factor and ultimately the cause of Sand's repeated sexual failures: "This attachment to Corambé seems to have been a great obstacle to her feminine love life."[4]

Deutsch divides the name *Corambé* into *coram*, the Latin word for "in the presence of," and *bé*, "b," the second letter of the alphabet. When Aurore was still very young and her father was away, her mother tried to teach her the alphabet. Sand showed talent and application but had one curious difficulty: the letter "b" did not exist for her, and she obstinately omitted it from her list. Deutsch's argument is to demonstrate that the "b" repressed in her childhood is identical with the *bé* that later turned up as the suffix to *coram*: "The whole word could then mean, 'in the presence of b.' If the b repressed in childhood referred to the absent father whom she hardly knew at the time, then its turning up in Corambé would be quite understandable."[5] If the massive repression resulted from her father's death, then the complete meaning of Corambé becomes "in the father's presence." When Sand transformed her father's demise into the comforting presence of an androgynous Corambé, she was also exposed to the gravest obstacle to her feminine nature. This explanation is, however, inadequate, since Corambé neither followed Sand, nor did Sand ever really abandon the name. It was, rather, as we have suggested, transformed, sublated, into something else, and as such remained the silent link conjoining Sand's life of writing to the constitutive division of the two mothers; Corambé names the very principle that traverses anatomical difference and makes "one sex" possible—a utopian possibility, to be sure, and one that is crucial to understanding her future notion of the utopian community, as we shall see later in this chapter. By Sand's own account, the disappearance of Corambé coincided with her sexual maturation.

The transformative disappearance of Corambé led Sand to,

among other things, the writing of *Indiana* (1832). Writing will itself at once replace the androgynous Corambé and make his/her return (im)possible:

> Meanwhile, my poor Corambé vanished as soon as I started to feel in a mood to persevere with a certain subject. He was of too tenuous an essence to bend to the demands of form. I had hardly finished my book when I wanted to regenerate my usual flow of reveries. Impossible! The characters of my manuscript, shut in a drawer, were happy to remain quiet. I hoped in vain to see Corambé reappear, and with him those thousands of beings who lulled me every day as pleasant day dreams.

> Mais mon pauvre Corambé s'envola pour toujours, dès que j'eus commencé à me sentir dans cette veine de persévérance sur un sujet donné. Il était d'une essence trop subtile pour se plier aux exigences de la forme. A peine eus-je fini mon livre, que je voulus retrouver le vague ordinaire de mes rêveries. Impossible! Les personnages de mon manuscrit, enfermés dans un tiroir, voulurent bien y rester tranquilles; mais j'espérai en vain voir reparaître Corambé et avec lui ces millers d'êtres qui me berçaient tous les jours de leurs agréables divagations. (*Story of My Life*, 925/*OA*, 2:165)

The sublation of Corambé is an essential stage in Sand's reinvention of her identity and her art. Philippe Berthier has spoken of the frustration and the difficulties of this transition. He divides Corambé into *cor* (the heart) and *ambo* ("two," "the two of us"): "The name of Corambé would emblematize its function in the child's inner life: it would inscribe in her the sensibility perturbed by the family disequilibrium, the promise and already the presence of a pacified reunion in a euphoric shared love."[6] In the idealized figure of Corambé, Aurore could project her need to love and be loved in the legitimacy of a true couple. Corambé is at the same time the fantasm of conjugal unity (her father is already dead) and the reconciliation dreamed of between her forbidding grandmother and her too-permissive mother.

The Coming to Writing: *Indiana*

Indiana describes the tragic effects of Colonel Delmare's tyranny upon his wife, Indiana, and Raymon's seduction of Noun. The novel reveals Sand's family tensions even while it transforms them. The female double Indiana/Noun, in conjunction with Noun's suicide, amounts to another symbolic killing of Corambé. As Berthier remarks: "This is a kind of hierogamy which is here celebrated: Aurore stages the imaginary wedding of her parents, including herself in it in a retro-projective way shaping both past and future according to her desire."[7] While repeating this oscillation between her conflicted childhood and her sexual difficulties in adult life, *Indiana* also registers, in the guise of the Delmare couple, her bitter criticism of her failed marriage and of marriage in general.

As George Sand remarks in her 1842 preface to the novel, *Indiana* describes the catastrophic consequences of a bad marriage:

> When I wrote *Indiana*, I was young; I acted in obedience to feelings of great strength and sincerity which overflowed thereafter in a series of novels, almost all of which were based on the same idea: the ill-defined relations between the sexes, attributable to the constitution of our society. These novels were all more or less inveighed against by the critics, as making unwise assaults upon the institution of marriage.

> Lorsque j'écrivis le roman d'*Indiana*, j'étais jeune, j'obéissais à des sentiments pleins de force et de sincérité, qui débordèrent de là dans une série de romans basés à peu près tous sur la même donnée: le rapport mal établi entre les sexes, par le fait de la société. Ces romans furent tous plus ou moins incriminés par la critique, comme portant d'imprudentes atteintes à l'institution du mariage.[8]

It will be helpful here to summarize the plot of *Indiana*. It revolves around Indiana Delmare; she is married to old Colonel Delmare, who mistreats her. She falls in love with Raymon de Ramière, who tries in vain to seduce her. Leaving her husband in

Bernica at the Ile Bourbon, Indiana returns to France and finds that de Ramière has married the rich Laure de Nangy. Destitute and dying, Indiana is saved by her cousin, Ralph Brown, who has spent his life with the Delmares. Ralph and Indiana decide to return to Bernica since M. Delmare is dead. Both Ralph and Indiana are unknown in the island:

> In the year that had passed since the *Nahandove* brought Sir Ralph and his companion back to the colony, he had not been seen in the town three times; and, as for Madame Delmare, her seclusion had been so absolute that her existence was still a problematical matter to many of the people.

> Depuis près d'un an que le navire *la Nahandove* avait ramené M. Brown et sa compagne à la colonie, on n'avait pas vu trois fois sir Ralph à la ville; et, quant à madame Delmare, sa retraite avait été si absolue, que son existence était encore une chose problématique pour beaucoup d'habitants. (*Indiana*, 4:317/343)

Sand never identified herself with Indiana. It was Deutsch, among other critics, who forced Sand's identification with her heroines. In *Indiana*, autobiography and fiction are two separate but inextricable elements. Sand's identification with her own text produces in *Indiana* a new development in her social criticism which revolves around the strangely haunting figure of the female double. Sand gives a strong indication of this in her astonishing confession in *Story of My Life*:

> I have created many female characters and I think that when people have read the present account of the impressions and reflections of my life, they will clearly see that I never portrayed myself in feminine guise. If I had wanted to show myself in serious depth, I would have told a life story which, up to that point, bore more resemblance to that of the monk Alexis (in the not very entertaining novel *Spiridion* [1839]) than to the passionate young Creole, Indiana.

> J'ai présenté beaucoup de types de femmes, et je crois que quand on aura lu cet exposé des impressions et des réflexions de ma vie, on verra bien que je ne me suis jamais mise en scène

sous des traits féminins. Si j'avais voulu montrer le fond sé-
rieux, j'aurais raconté une vie qui jusqu'alors aurait plus ressem-
blé à celle du moine Alexis (dans le roman peu récréatif de
Spiridon) qu'à celle d'Indiana la créole passionnée (*Story of My
Life*, 921–22/OA, 2:160)

The difficulty that Sand experiences in portraying herself "in
feminine guise" reveals her dread of being identified with other
women insofar as this also entails her exclusion from society.
Sand's strong identification with male writers echoes Nancy
Miller's remark that "through literature, and more specifically
through the use of the male pseudonym and male personae,
women writers have been able to liberate themselves and attain a
whole human experience."[9] Writing "as a man" reveals at once
Sand's response to the exclusion of women from literature while
at the same time marking her ambivalence toward identifying
with women, and thus a certain ambiguity toward feminism.

The subtleties of role playing are, as a result, very complex in
Sand's writing. In discussing three novels written between 1832
and 1845—*Indiana, Mauprat* (1837), and *Le Péché de Monsieur Antoine*
(1845)—I want to examine these issues in the context of Sand's
artistic and intellectual shift of focus from the representation of
"maternal fictions" to the future of utopian communities.

In spite of Sand's mask of masculinity and Deutsch's diagnosis
of a "masculinity complex," we will repeatedly rediscover the
more powerful mediating figure of the recurrent female double
and the phenomenon of female cross-dressing in Sand's major
fiction; this includes not simply women dressing as men but
women dressing as *other* women. Whereas for Deutsch "bisexuality" is uniquely linked to Sand's "masculinity complex," Naomi
Schor's notion of "bisextuality" (at once bisexual and bitextual, an
irreducible doubling that cuts across writing and gender) enables
us to mark the oscillation between masculine and feminine on
either side of the symbolic axis of castration. In other words, as
Schor demonstrates, these undecidable identifications and per-
mutations are characteristic of Sand: "In Sand's texts, this perverse oscillation takes the form of a breakdown of characteriza-

tion which is quite possibly Sand's most radical gesture as a writer."[10] Ultimately, the occasional adoption of male costume does not constitute an act of subversion but rather belongs to a long tradition of cross-dressing in fiction, drama, and opera. What Schor finds most interesting is the phenomenon of women dressing as other women, which I, in turn, will link to Sand's experience of the feminine double: "*Female travesty* in the sense of women dressing up as or impersonating other women constitutes by far the most disruptive form of bisextuality."[11]

Sand's feminine doubles, for instance, Indiana/Noun, Lélia/Pulchérie, and Valentine/Louise (each of which results from Sand's interminable impasse between her grandmother and her mother), are exemplary "bisextual" phenomena. Noun's suicide provides a fictional solution to the crisis that Sand herself experienced as insoluble. The feminine double is the figure at the intersection of two opposing maternal powers, and to choose either one is to end in tragedy. Perhaps Sand's writing enabled her to avert the tragedy for which she herself seemed destined.

Addressing issues raised in *Story of My Life*, which offers unparalleled insights into the deep-seated conflicts in Sand's nature, Thelma Jurgrau characterizes Sand's sexual "double bind": "The experiences of womanhood to which Sand herself directs us in *Story of My Life* are a primary source of evidence of gender anxiety, for they give readers a sense of the unusual origins and development that explain her inability to adapt to the typically constrained life of a woman of her time."[12]

The fluctuation between masculine and feminine identifications took a disturbing turn in a dream that Sand recounts in *Story of My Life*. In this passage, Aurore is fascinated by the green wallpaper of her bedroom and particularly by two figures shown in medallions over each doorway:

> The one I saw on waking in the morning was a nymph, or a dancing Flora. This one gave enormous pleasure. The one facing her . . . had a totally different expression. She was a serious bacchante. I held the bacchante in awe, having read the story of Orpheus torn apart by similarly cruel ones; in the

evening, when the shimmering light illuminated her extended arm and the thyrsus, I thought I saw the head of the divine poet on the end of a javelin.

Celle que je voyais le matin en m'éveillant était une nymphe ou une Flore dansante. Celle-là me plaisait énormément. Celle qui lui faisait vis à vis . . . était d'une expression toute différente. C'était une bacchante grave. Je regardais la bacchante avec étonnement, j'avais lu l'histoire d'Orphée déchiré par ces cruelles et le soir, quand la lumière vacillante éclairait le bras tendu et le thyrse, je croyais voir la tête du divin chantre au bout d'un javelot. (*Story of My Life*, 477–78/OA, 1:619)

Aurore's dream fulfills her foreboding sense that something terrible was about to happen. Emerging from her medallion, the bacchante becomes a furious maenad who chases both Sand and the nymph and pierces both of their bodies with her sharp lance. The feminine double, bacchante/nymph, which again recalls Sand's hatred/love for the mother/grandmother figure, becomes another figure for Sand's tormented experience of gender identification.

This early scenario in Sand's life is replayed in *Indiana*. Instead of having two distinct and opposed figures (the bacchante and the nymph), Indiana and Noun represent the blurring of identities between the two Creoles. For Sand, the dream evokes Orpheus' death and the horror of his dismemberment. The dread she feels while looking at the wallpaper figures is expressed by the doubling of the female bacchante/nymph. In *Indiana*, Raymon de Ramière feels a similar dread when he is unable to differentiate between Indiana and Noun. The terror he experiences is closely related to Sand's horror at imagining the bacchante emerge from the wallpaper, with "the head of the divine poet on the end of a javelin." Raymon imagines that his mistress, Noun, is really the disguised Indiana, and thus that in making love to his mistress he is in fact making love to the chaste Indiana:

If she [Noun] had not been as drunk as he, she would have understood that in his wildest flights Raymon was thinking of another woman. But Noun appropriated all these transports to herself, when Raymon saw naught of her but Indiana's dress. If he kissed her black hair, he fancied that he was kissing Indiana's black hair. It was Indiana whom he saw in the fumes of the punch which Noun's hand had lighted; it was she who smiled upon him and beckoned him from behind those white muslin curtains.

Si elle n'eût pas été ivre comme lui, elle eût compris qu'au plus fort de son délire Raymon songeait à une autre. Mais Noun prenait tous ces transports pour elle-même, lorsque Raymon ne voyait d'elle que la robe d'Indiana. S'il baisait ses cheveux noirs, il croyait baiser les cheveux noirs d'Indiana. C'était Indiana qu'il voyait dans le nuage du punch que la main de Noun venait d'allumer; c'était elle qui l'appelait et qui lui souriait derrière ces blancs rideaux de mousseline. (*Indiana*, 4:63/86)

The ghostlike shape of Indiana behind the "white muslin curtains" stresses the instability of Raymon's desire. In loving a "ghost," Raymon replays the Sandean scenario in which the absent woman is always the one most cherished.

In "The Uncanny" (1919), Freud describes the psychological phenomenon that arouses horror and dread. The uncanny registers the fact that something familiar has become "uncanny" (*unheimlich*), unfamiliar, through repression.[13] *Indiana* offers an exemplary incident of such a transformation in its account of Raymon's disorientation when, after Noun's suicide, he experiences an uncanny return of the repressed when he discovers that he has mistaken the hair of the dead Noun for that of Indiana: after Noun's suicide, Indiana offers Raymon a mass of cut hair, which he assumes to be that of Indiana, only to be overwhelmed when he realizes that it is that of his dead mistress. Raymon becomes a figure for Sand herself before the impasse of the double feminine identification. The familiar hair of the mysterious Indiana becomes unfamiliar once Raymon realizes it belongs to his late intimate companion. The familiarity/unfamiliarity of the hair and the women to whom it belongs crosses and recrosses. The central issue here is the instability that characterizes all these identifications.

Freud in effect describes the structure of Sandean "bisextuality" when he remarks that "among its different shades of meaning, the word *heimlich* [familiar] exhibits one which is identical with its opposite *unheimlich*. What is *heimlich* thus comes to be *unheimlich*."[14] In other words, *heimlich* contains the meanings of both "canny" and "uncanny," "familiar" and "unfamiliar." So too does feminine identity in Sand. It contains within itself both the selfsame and the other. The experience of this doubleness causes Raymon to faint:

> He looked more closely and saw a mass of black hair, of varying lengths, which seemed to have been cut in haste, and which Indiana was smoothing with her hands.
>
> "Do you recognize it?" she asked.
>
> Raymon hesitated, looked again at the handkerchief about her head and thought that he understood.
>
> "This is not yours," he said, untying the kerchief which concealed Madame Delmare's hair.
>
> "Don't you recognize this?"
>
> Raymon sank upon a chair; Noun's locks fell from his trembling hand. He shivered from head to foot and fell in a swoon on the floor.

> Il se pencha, et vit une masse de cheveux noirs irrégulièrement longs qui semblaient avoir été coupés à la hâte et qu'Indiana rassemblait et lissait dans ses mains.
>
> "Les reconnaissez-vous?" lui dit-elle.
>
> Raymon hésita, reporta son regard sur le foulard dont elle était coiffée, et crut comprendre.
>
> "Ce ne sont pas les vôtres!" dit-il en détachant le mouchoir des Indes qui lui cachait ceux de madame Delmare.
>
> "Ne reconnaissez-vous donc pas ceux-là?"
>
> Raymon se laissa tomber sur une chaise; les cheveux de Noun échappèrent à sa main tremblante. Il frissonna de la tête aux pieds, et roula évanoui sur le parquet. (*Indiana*, 4:163–64/183–84)

As he recognizes that he is holding the hair of the dead Noun, Raymon experiences the return of the repressed. Raymon's uncanny confusion between the dead and the living causes his desire to misfire and puts an end to his love for Indiana:

> When he came to himself, Madame Delmare was on her knees beside him, weeping copiously; but Raymon no longer loved her.
> "You have inflicted a horrible wound on me," he said; "a wound which it is not in your power to cure."
>
> Quand il revint à lui, madame Delmare, à genoux près de lui, l'arrosait de larmes et lui demandait grâce; mais Raymon ne l'aimait plus.
> "Vous m'avez fait un mal horrible," lui dit-il; "un mal qu'il n'est pas en votre pouvoir de réparer." (*Indiana,* 4:164/184)

The uncanniness of the feminine double creates yet another form of psychological disturbance. The sexual instability of Raymon's love for Indiana is transformed into hatred: "He swore that he would be her master, were it but for a single day, and that then he would abandon her, to have the satisfaction of seeing her at his feet" (Il jura qu'il serait son maître, ne fût-ce qu'un jour, et qu'ensuite il l'abandonnerait pour avoir le plaisir de la voir à ses pieds) (*Indiana,* 4:172/191). Raymon's loss of consciousness emerges at the very moment the characteristic Sandean dilemma arises. That the crisis of the impossible but necessary need to choose between the two maternal models of identification emerges here within a male character and is envisioned from a male perspective simply reduplicates the process of doubling and division that has been at work from the outset. By virtue of the fetishistic remainder/reminder of the hair, the dead woman *is* the living one. Raymon's paralyzing inability to differentiate between them replays Sand's guilt. The unsettling effect that the scene has upon Raymon poses the question of the division within the Sandean ego.

We have, then, two pairs of doubles here: Indiana/Noun and Sand/Raymon. An important piece of evidence regarding this latter identification is surely the fact that the last words spoken by Raymon's dying mother exactly repeat the dying words of Sand's grandmother. Madame de Ramière says to her son, " 'You are about to lose your best friend' " ("Vous perdez, lui dit-elle, votre meilleure amie" (*Indiana,* 4:244/264); while Sand's grandmother, on her deathbed, tells Aurore, " 'You are losing your best friend.' Those were her last words" (Tu perds ta meilleure amie. Ce furent ces dernières paroles) (*Story of My Life,* 799/OA, 1:1106). The male who faints in *Indiana* is yet another figuration for the invariable Sandean experience of what lies at the limits of consciousness. The anguished choice between two modes of feminine identification, one the severe superego, the other the libidinally free ego ideal, is thus linked to the crisis of gender identification itself: am I a man or a woman? These are asymmetrical but inextricably linked dilemmas, and they lie at the heart of the structure and language of *Indiana.* They are asymmetrical because the other who calls on the ego to inhibit its desires, who prohibits the realization of desire, may or may not be female; and, conversely, the other who induces the ego to more pleasure, to more libidinal freedom, may or may not be male. The superego identification of the "thou shalt" variety and the ego-ideal identification with a positive rather than a negative model of desire form the constitutive parts of the unconscious dilemma of the Sandean ego, both in life and in art. The ego who responds to the call for more pleasure has no feminine models at its disposal, and hence it responds to the inducement to enjoy by taking on a masculine persona, cross-dressing, and all the other familiar Sandean motifs. On the other hand, the prohibition of desire by that other unconscious component in the Sandean ego forces it into its dialectically necessary conventionality; thus Sand must always be at once the archetypal Victorian matron and the archetypal Victorian artist-rebel. The crossings of these inescapable modes of identification lead us to a definitive typology of both Sand's life and her writing.

I would like to return to this process of doubling and division in one of Sand's dreams, which stages her gender anxiety at an early age. In this dream, she describes in detail a Pulcinella dressed in red and gold which she received as a gift when she was very young. The clown could not be kept in the same box with her favorite doll because she felt that the Pulcinella was a danger to it. Aurore had a foreboding that something terrible would happen to the feminine doll if she remained too near the Pulcinella. Having hung him from the stove, opposite her bed, Aurore fell asleep: "At night I had a terrible dream: Pulcinella, now dressed in a red spangled vest, his hump in front, had gotten up, caught fire on the stove, and was running all around, after me, after my doll who fled in a panic, while he reached us with long jets of flame" (La nuit, je fis un rêve épouvantable: polichinelle s'était levé, sa bosse de devant, revêtue d'un gilet de paillon rouge, avait pris feu sur le poêle, et il courait partout, poursuivant tantôt moi, tantôt ma poupée qui fuyait éperdue, tandis qu'il nous atteignait par de longs jets de flamme) (*Story of My Life*, 424/*OA*, 1:539). For Sand, the Pulcinella's violence, like Raymon's loss of consciousness, constitutes a moment of intense anxiety. While Pulcinella gave Sand a great *souffrance morale*, Raymon complains that a horrible wound (*un mal horrible*) has been inflicted on him. Aurore's passion for the fire is henceforth transformed into dread: "And instead of playing with the fire, as had been my passion until then, just one look at the fire left me in great terror" (Et, au lieu de jouer avec le feu comme jusque-là j'en avais eu la passion, la seule vue du feu me laissa une grande terreur) (*Story of My Life*, 424/*OA*, 1:539). As for Raymon, he swears that "he would triumph over her [Indiana]. It was no longer a matter of snatching a new pleasure, but of punishing an insult; not of possessing a woman, but of subduing her" (qu'il triompherait d'elle. Il ne s'agissait plus pour lui de conquérir un bonheur, mais de punir un affront; de posséder une femme, mais de la réduire) (*Indiana*, 4:172/191). The difference between and within the sexes is always an enigma for Sand. The Pulcinella dream, like Raymon's loss of consciousness, reveals her anxiety about both gender difference and the nature of feminine identity itself. Sand's writing is a defense against having to choose her gender, having to choose between the alternative maternal fictions she is presented with. Noun's suicide and Indiana's failures are figures of Sand's effort to evade the demands of reality.

Sand's writing is thus also an evasion, a foreclosure, a disavowal of the reality of death. Her refusal to choose between the fictions of her mothers is also a refusal to choose between life and death.

For Freud, death cannot be represented in our unconscious: "The psycho-analytic school could venture on the assertion that at bottom no one believes in his own death, or, to put the same thing in another way, that in the unconscious every one of us is convinced of his own immortality" (SE, 14:289). It is part of Freud's clinical experience to discover that although the unconscious is ruled by the pleasure principle, it can be threatened by the death drive, thanatos. In *Beyond the Pleasure Principle* (1919), Freud argues that the life instincts have more contact with our internal perceptions, while the death instincts seem to do their work unobtrusively: "The pleasure principle seems actually to serve the death instincts." Life is finally in the service of death. In Sand's scenarios, the doll, Noun, and Indiana are symbolic figures of the death drive. The different registers of thanatos are probed in Sand's dreams and writing.

Sand's work unveils that the death drive is secretly at work in most of our life practices. Following Freud's theses in *Beyond the Pleasure Principle*, Julia Kristeva poses the question of how the death drive functions within a divided ego: "Thus, if the death instinct is not represented in the unconscious, must one invent another level in the psychic apparatus where—simultaneously with *jouissance*—the being of its nonbeing would be recorded? It is indeed a production of the split ego, made up of fantasy and fiction—in short, the level of the imagination, the level of writing which bears witness to the hiatus, blank or spacing that constitutes death for the unconscious."[15] The abandoned Indiana is, for Sand, like the dismembered Orpheus, a figure of the destructive forces at work in the act of artistic creation. In *Indiana*, Noun's suicide and Indiana's failed suicide explicitly raise these questions.

Abandoned a first time by Raymon de Ramière, Indiana tries to drown herself in the Seine. She is saved by her cousin Ralph, who asks her to promise to join him in committing suicide together sometime in the future. This strange bond suggests that the union between man and woman is possible only in death:

> "Well then," rejoined Ralph, "swear to me that you will not resort to suicide without notifying me. I swear to you on my honor that I will not oppose your design in any way. I simply insist on being notified: as for life, I care about it as little as you do, and you know that I have often had the same idea."

> "Eh bien, jurez-moi," reprit Ralph, "de ne plus avoir recours au suicide sans m'en prévenir. Je vous jure sur l'honneur de ne m'y opposer en aucune manière. Je ne tiens qu'à être averti; quant au reste, je m'en soucie aussi peu que vous, et vous savez que j'ai souvent eu la même idée." (*Indiana*, 4:203/222)

The joint suicide occupies a privileged place in the narrative since it stands as a substitute for the marriage between Indiana and Ralph. It is thus also a kind of regressive reverie, a symbolic return to the womb: the Ile Bourbon, which is the place of origin, also becomes the site chosen for the suicide pact. Kristeva describes the death drive in similar terms when she speaks of "a total oceanic death."

Sand describes a fantasm of absolute plenitude in *Story of My Life* when she recalls the aesthetic sensations that overwhelmed her in the midst of a drowning experience: "But right in the middle of the ford, a dizziness seized me, my heart leaped, my vision blurred, I heard the fatal Yes roaring in my ears. I reined my horse abruptly to the right and found myself in deep water, wracked by hysterical laughter and joy" (Mais au beau milieu du gué, le vertige de la mort s'empare de moi, mon coeur bondit, ma vue se trouble, j'entends le *oui* fatal gronder dans mes oreilles, je pousse brusquement mon cheval à droite, et me voilà dans l'eau profonde, saisie d'un rire nerveux et d'une joie délirante) (*Story of My Life*, 793/OA, 1:1096). Suicide is indeed for Sand "oceanic" and jubilant, and it coincides with this other voice, this voice of the other that cries *oui* as it reaches beyond the pleasure principle.

In *Indiana,* Sand again runs the risk of complete dissolution. Though the suicide pact of Indiana and Ralph never transpires, it succeeds in inscribing Sand's narrative within a familiar male narrative paradigm. Bernardin de Saint-Pierre's *Paul et Virginie* (1788) "legitimates" *Indiana* insofar as Ralph and Indiana reiterate the terms of this earlier text. As Ralph says to Indiana: "When I read you the story of Paul and Virginie, you only half understood it. You wept, however; you saw only the story of a brother and sister where I had quivered with sympathy, realizing the torments of two lovers. The book made me miserable, whereas it was your joy" (Quand je vous lisais l'histoire de Paul et Virginie, vous ne la compreniez qu'à demi. Vous pleuriez, cependant; vous aviez vu l'histoire d'une frère et d'une soeur là où j'avais frissonné de sympathie en apercevant les angoisses de deux amants) (*Indiana,* 4:301/324). The resemblance between *Paul et Virginie* and *Indiana* stops at the last chapter, as if Sand deliberately wanted to mark the difference by "adding" another ending, an ending that averts suicide. Nancy Miller says of the different endings: "At stake here is what I think amounts to *a mise en abyme,* as it were (the pun is not only terrible and irresistible but important), of a female signature, the internal delineation of a writer's territory."[16] Sand's distancing from the legitimacy of the precursor text also asserts the triumph of life over death. In their evasion of suicide, Indiana and Ralph transform *Paul et Virginie*'s tragic end into a Sandean utopia, which nevertheless lies beyond the pleasure principle. In brief, the utopia is another kind of death.

For Isabelle Naginski, the novel's double ending finds its true significance in the creation of an authentic language system: "There is a legitimate reason for the false suicide to be transmuted into a happy ending, a logic behind the two heroes' flight to a paradise lost, as they engulf themselves in a circular mythological time."[17] As Naginski argues, Ralph and Indiana achieve a new system of communication. Moreover, the novel's double ending prepares the birth of the future socialist commune which will liberate Sand from the anguish-ridden family scenarios.

Sand's early ambivalent feeling for her mother and grand-mother is resolved in this way. At first, hatred was the grand-mother's portion and love the mother's. Later a reversal took place: the grandmother was loved and the mother was hated, because she disappointed her daughter. In returning with Ralph to Bernica, Indiana recalls all she owes to both her cousin and the island: "Do you know that his mother was my mother's sister? that we were born in the same valley; that in our early years he was my protector; that he was my mainstay, my only teacher, my only companion at Ile Bourbon; that he has followed me everywhere" (Vous ne savez donc pas que sa mère était la soeur de la mienne; que nous sommes nés dans la même vallée; que son adolescence a protégé mes premiers pas; qu'il a été mon seul appui, mon seul instituteur, mon seul compagnon à l'île Bourbon; qu'il m'a suivie partout) (Indiana, 4:121/144). The maternal link is underlined here, and this is what justifies the utopian departure of the lovers to the island, which in turn marks its supplementary difference from Paul et Virginie.

In founding their "Indian cottage" outside wedlock, Ralph and Indiana subvert the traditional endings of the nineteenth-century French novel. Union libre offers here an alternative that remained unacceptable in the nineteenth century. Nevertheless, it defines the concept of a "happy" ending that she will elaborate in her later fiction. Georges Bataille has spoken of "the commu-nity of those who do not have a community," which is an apt description for the utopian exclusion Ralph and Indiana experi-ence at Ile Bourbon. The return to the place of origin again points to the question of the maternal and indicates as well Sand's need to legitimate her origin and identity. However, this maternal link must be broken in order for Ralph to tell the story of his life to Indiana: "I was hardly born when I was cast out of the heart which I most needed. My mother put me away from her breast with disgust" (A peine né, je fus repoussé du coeur dont j'avais le plus besoin. Ma mère m'éloigna de son sein avec dégoût) (*Indiana*, 4:298/321). Sand's ambiguity toward her mother is reiterated by Ralph's words. And there is something more; the desire to differentiate herself from Bernardin de Saint-Pierre is only part of the story. As Nancy Miller observes, although *Indiana* also marks the end of the collaboration between Sand and Jules Sandeau, "the traces of a certain doubling seem to remain."[18] There is no end to the doublings at work in *Indiana*, for Sand is always invariably expressing both her attachment to and her separation from the past.

After her grandmother's death, Aurore was forced to go and live with her mother in Paris. The long-dreamt-of maternal proximity was quickly transformed into a painful "absence of community." In her memoirs Sand indicates the difficulties of their relation: "[Aurore's mother] said that she had thus been informed by one of the closest friends of the family. I did not say anything in response; I could not say anything. I felt sick and disgusted. She went to bed, victorious over having crushed me" (Elle se disait renseignée ainsi par un des plus intimes amis de notre maison. Je ne répondis rien, je ne pouvais rien répondre. Le coeur me levait de dégoût. Elle se mit au lit, triomphante de m'avoir écrasée) (*Story of My Life*, 815/*OA*, 1:1129). Sand's disgust transforms the once-desired maternal relation into what Kristeva calls an "impregnable and thus malevolent, detestable exteriority."[19] Separation from the mother, which was once dreaded, now becomes desirable; it is symbolically acted out by the double's suicide. One after the other, mother and grandmother are symbolically eliminated in Sand's fiction. Instead of reading Sand's ambiguous gender identification within the traditional opposition of masculine/feminine, we might understand it as an effort to regulate the dreaded maternal double and the gender trouble it produces by eliminating it.

In *Indiana*, for example, Ralph's mother is expressive of the bad mother, while Raymon's mother offers a positive vision: "That evening Madame de Ramière died in her son's arms. Raymon's grief was deep and bitter. His mother was really necessary to him; with her he lost all the moral comfort of his life" (Le soir, madame de Ramière mourut dans les bras de son fils. La douleur de Raymon fut amère et profonde. Sa mère lui était réellement nécessaire; avec elle il perdait tout le bien-être moral de sa vie) (*Indiana*, 4:244–45/265). There is no end to the doubling of the maternal figure in Sand's fiction.

Toward the New Community

If "Sand," as we discussed earlier, was the name that Delatouche gave her, "Piffoël" was the name that she gave herself. In *Entretiens journaliers avec le très docte et très habile docteur Piffoël* (1837–1841), Piffoël is at once Sand and the voice of the other within. In the entry of 3, 4, 5 July 1837, Sand notes her mother's illness (she would die the following month): "Misery, despair, bitter tears, I did not know I loved her so much this poor woman!" (Misère, désespoir, larmes amères, je ne savais pas que je l'aimais ainsi cette pauvre femme!), which is followed by a deep depression: "Your heart is troubled. Piffoël, which worry is eating you up? Which fear of living makes you wish illness and death?" (Ton coeur est troublé. Piffoël quel ennui te ronge? Quelle peur de vivre te fait donc souhaiter la maladie et la mort?).[20] Sand's melancholia is transferred to Piffoël, whom she calls "melancholy and abominable beast" (bête mélancolique et abominable), and who represents her psychic split. Sand's immediate specular identification with the mother is here inverted into a death-bearing maternal image. Piffoël takes the place of the analyst who allows the transference to occur. Thus the feminine as an image of death is constantly transformed into a masculine representation that keeps at bay the threat of confusional love. Piffoël becomes the pseudonym which plays a role similar to that of Brulard. Both *Vie de Henry Brulard* and *Entretiens journaliers* enable their authors to distance themselves by creating another voice. Both Brulard and Piffoël are pseudonymous identities which symbolically allow Stendhal and Sand to cope with their traumatic memories. In both cases, autobiography is a return to the maternal archive with a view toward reinventing it.

The suicide pact of Ralph and Indiana is a version of the threatened fatality of maternal fusion: " 'Be my husband in heaven and on earth,' she said, 'and let this kiss bind me to you for all eternity!' " ("Sois mon époux dans le ciel et sur la terre," lui dit-elle, "et que ce baiser me fiance à toi pour l'éternité!") (*Indiana*, 4:314/338). The suicide pact expresses at once the impossibility of community and the basis for a new type of community. In this connection there is a particular pertinence to Jean-Luc Nancy's remark that "the true community of mortals, or death as the community, is their impossible communion."[21] Recall Sand's experience of the other, nonsubjective voice she hears on the verge of drowning: "I could not tear myself away from the river bank at will and began to question myself, Yes or No, often enough and for a long enough time to risk being thrown by a Yes to the bottom of the clear water which attracted me" (Je ne pouvais plus m'arracher de la rive aussitôt que j'en formais le dessein, et je commençais à me dire: Oui ou Non? assez souvent et assez longtemps pour risquer d'être lancée par le Oui au fond de cette eau transparente qui me magnétisait) (*Story of My Life*, 793/OA, 1:1096). The basis of Sand's thinking about the nature of community entails a link to this voice, this "yes" that cries out from the other side of subjectivity. The temptation of suicide is also the solicitation of this other voice and of the new community that it portends.

The yes/no alternative of suicide is definitively abandoned in the conclusion of *Indiana*. In her supplementary ending to *Paul et Virginie*, Sand breaks away from traditional nineteenth-century institutions while accepting the assumption that culture is fully subsumed under patriarchal laws. In Sir Ralph's words: "Society should demand nothing of the man who expects nothing from it. As for the contagion of example, I do not believe in it; too much energy is required to break with the world, and too much suffering to acquire that energy" (La société ne doit rien exiger de celui qui n'attend rien d'elle. Quant à la contagion de l'exemple, je n'y crois pas; il faut trop d'énergie pour rompre avec le monde, trop de douleurs pour acquérir cette énergie) (*Indiana*, 4:327/353). The end of the novel moves from France to its colonies and points to the limits of the dominant culture. *Indiana* does not, however, issue in a strong protest against that culture, since the social implications of the decision of Indiana and Ralph to live for love in a world beyond convention relegate them to a marginal role. Sand's abandonment of the romantic suicide pact gives way to Sir Ralph's criticism of society. In this gesture, we can see a movement that will develop in Sand's subsequent novels. In *Mauprat* (1837), she succeeds in integrating her personal myths with the utopian notion of a better society to come.

Sand's "Wild Horde": *Mauprat*

The totem may be inherited either through the female or the male line. It is possible that originally the former method of descent prevailed everywhere and was only subsequently replaced by the latter.

SIGMUND FREUD, *Totem and Taboo*

For Sand, the question of the community is linked to her socialist commitments. The historical novel *Mauprat* reexamines the eighteenth century from the perspective of Bernard Mauprat's privileged vision. Bernard's enlightenment elaborates Sand's belief in the perfectibility of the human race. In telling the story of his life to his two guests, Bernard Mauprat reconstitutes the mythical scene of storytelling: "A man so unfortunate as I have been deserves to find a faithful biographer, who will clear his memory of all reproach. So listen to me and drink some coffee" (Un homme aussi infortuné que je l'ai été mérite de trouver un historiographe fidèle, qui lave sa mémoire de tout reproche. Ecoutez-moi donc et buvez du café).[22] Here Sand is interested in setting forth a myth of origin and telling us about its transmission. Bernard Mauprat's story is located between the pure oral tradition of Corambé and the form of the novel. The scene of the narrative gathers three people around the same fire: "Come close to the fire and keep quiet. You cannot please me better than by listening" (Venez près du feu, et soyez tranquille. Vous ne pouvez me faire un plus grand plaisir que de m'écouter) (*Mauprat*, 19:9/34).

Jean-Luc Nancy recounts the relation between the scene of the mythic narrative and the birth of a "community":

> We know the scene: there are men gathered together and somebody who tells them a story. These gathered men, one does not know yet whether they are an assembly, or a horde, or a tribe. But we call them "brothers," because they are assembled, and because they are listening to the same story. The one who tells the story, one does not know yet if he is one of them, but different from them, because he has the gift, or simply the right—unless it is his duty—to recite. It's the story of their origin: where they come from, or how they come from Origin itself—them, their wives, their names, or the authority among them.[23]

According to Nancy, this ancient scene is indefinitely repeated through time; tribes, cities, peoples are always gathered to hear the story of their origin. The legitimacy or illegitimacy of origin is a problem which preoccupied Sand all her life. Sand is interested here in establishing the myth of origin before telling the story of the Mauprats. Her achievement is to have described the Mauprats' horde in feudal as well as in Freudian terms.

The Mauprat family is organized around the grandfather's arbitrary leadership, and his sons live without wives at La Roche-Mauprat:

> From that time, Mauprat and his sons defied the civil laws, just as they defied the moral laws. They became a band of adventurers. While their well-beloved and trusty poachers supplied the house with game, they levied illegal taxes on the neighboring farms. No province of France has preserved so many old traditions and suffered longer the abuses of feudalism.

Depuis ce jour, Mauprat et ses fils rompirent avec les lois civiles comme ils avaient rompu avec les lois morales. Ils s'organisèrent en bande d'aventuriers. Tandis que leurs aimés et féaux braconniers pourvoyaient la maison de gibier, ils levaient des taxes illégales sur les métairies environnantes. Aucune province de France n'a conservé plus de vieilles traditions et souffert plus longtemps les abus de la féodalité). (*Mauprat*, 19:16/38–39)

As a historical novel, *Mauprat* describes the radical transformation of a feudal period into a postrevolutionary era influenced by Rousseau's *Social Contract*. The destruction of the Mauprats' feudal system historically replays the parricide in the Freudian scene of the primal horde: "One day the brothers who had been driven out came together, killed and devoured the father and so made an end of the patriarchal horde."[24] Whereas in Freud's *Totem and Taboo* "the dead father became stronger than the living one had been," in Sand's novel the grandfather's death coincides with the destruction of the Mauprat horde: "I was fifteen years old when my grandfather died. After his death, the glory which his audacity had gained for us vanished. His sons, who had up to that time been well disciplined, became more and more addicted to drunkenness and disoluteness" (J'avais quinze ans quand mon grand-père mourut. Après lui, l'espèce de gloire que son audace nous avait acquise s'éclipsa. Ses enfants, jusque-là bien disciplinés, devinrent de plus en plus ivrognes et débauchés) (*Mauprat*, 19:50/67). Thus, Freud continues, the murder and incest taboos were created out of the sons' sense of guilt. These two taboos, which constitute the two repressed wishes of the Oedipus complex, were finally, according to Freud, the only two crimes which primitive society concerned itself with. For Sand, the horde represents Bernard's criminal model of education, which will be corrected by Rousseau's *Emile* and implemented by Bernard's cousin Edmée. The grandfather's savage horde can then be replaced by an enlightened matriarchal model subject to the restrictions of Rousseau's own teaching.

Early in the narrative, Bernard establishes the family genealogy by distinguishing two branches: "I belong to the older branch. The younger branch was extinct when I came into the world, except in the person of Hubert de Mauprat, who was called the knight, because he belonged to the Order of Malta, and who was as good as his cousin was bad" (Je suis de la branche aînée. La branche cadette n'existait plus, lorsque je vins au monde, que dans la personne de M. Hubert de Mauprat, qu'on appelait *le chevalier* parce qu'il était dans l'ordre de Malte, et qui était aussi bon que son cousin l'était peu) (*Mauprat*, 19:11/35). Hubert de Mauprat then determines to get married, since he finds no heir worthy of his fortune in the older branch. His daughter Edmée will be born and become Bernard's wife, uniting the two family branches together and closing Bernard's narrative on the absolute bond of marriage: "She was the only woman I ever loved in all my life; never did another attract my attention or feel the pressure of my hand. I am so constituted; when I love any one, I love eternally, in the past, in the present, and in the future" (Elle fut la seule femme que j'aimai; jamais aucune autre n'attira mon regard et ne connut l'étreinte de ma main. Je suis ainsi fait; ce que j'aime, je l'aime éternellement, dans le passé, dans le présent, dans l'avenir) (*Mauprat*, 19:380–81/312). Edmée's fertility provides the basis for a strong matriarchy: "She bore me six children, four of whom are still living, and are advantageously and prudently established. I have continued to live for their sakes, as Edmée, on her dying bed, commanded me to do" (Elle me donna six enfants, dont quatre vivent encore et sont avantageusement et sagement établis. J'ai vécu pour eux, par l'ordre d'Edmée à son lit de mort) (*Mauprat*, 19:380/312).

Patriarchy in the nineteenth century was firmly based on symbolical representations of power. Fatherhood was endowed, as Kristeva remarks, with a unique social status: "The father *represents* reproduction which is really assumed by the mother; as a consequence, the paternal function seems symbolical, even relative, and yet limiting."[25] Women were not so totally deprived of symbolical value as mothers were: "Women in general are not entirely denied any symbolical activity and social representation.

The privileged object of this repression is the spouse, a sexual partner who could be said to be 'genital,' and who can no longer represent your good and almighty mother since she has explicitly become your children's mother."[26] In attributing instability to the Western family in the nineteenth century, Kristeva describes paternal law as undergoing a series of changes. Among them is the father's symbolical power, which is increasingly threatened and forced to seek new roles in order to survive. The position of women is also transformed: "But once it is represented, the famous second sex *jouissance* is weakened: the bourgeoisie's value, at the end of the century, is coextensive to 'women's sexual crisis,' the myth of which is still alive nowadays."[27] It is in part because Sand was legally separated from her husband in 1836 that she was free to give new interpretations in *Mauprat* to women's place in eighteenth-century society. Whereas in the nineteenth century paternal power assumed the functions of the earlier maternal familial authority, in *Mauprat* Sand asserts the primacy of the maternal.

The exclusivity of the mother's role has the effect of limiting women to the sphere of domesticity. In *Mauprat*, the importance given to Edmée as mother and educator is underlined by Bernard himself: "As for me, I can say that my education was accomplished by her; during my whole life, I surrendered myself entirely to her judgment and integrity" (Pour moi, je puis dire que mon éducation fut faite par elle; pendant tout le cours de ma vie je m'abandonnai entièrement à sa raison et à sa droiture) (*Mauprat*, 19:381/313). The shift from the Mauprat horde to Edmée's matriarchy constitutes Sand's most pressing wish. In Sand's writing, the myth of the domestic, maternal power is strongly linked to the family scenarios and to Rousseau's *Emile*.

Joan Landes's analysis of Rousseau's attitude toward the role of women is highly relevant here: "Rousseau's argument for the creation of separate sexual spheres is the basis of women's subjection to a rule of silence and to their political quiescence within a reformed republican polity."[28] Rousseau is not, however, simply an eighteenth-century misogynist. Although he denied women a formal public position, he offered them the opportunity to perform a cultural role on which the moral strength of the entire state depended. As Landes points out, Rousseau's gender politics has stimulated heated discussions among political theorists: "The central paradox is easily identified: that the theorist of democratic liberty and the general will has a profound mistrust of women such that he would deny them the most elementary political rights."[29] Rousseau proposes that the woman/wife be confined to the domestic sphere and controlled by the gaze of just one man, her husband. The institution of the family is absolutely essential to achieving order and legitimacy and to eliminating the risk of chaos and uncertain paternity. In this respect, Sand's vision of the family is in the end surprisingly close to Rousseau's.

When her grandmother revealed to her that her mother had resumed being a libertine in Paris, Sand was assailed with terrible doubts:

> "Will I blush to be my mother's daughter? Oh, if it were only that! they know quite well that I'll have no part of such cowardly shame." I then imagined, without blaming anything in particular, some mysterious connection between my mother and someone else who might exercise unjust or illegitimate power over me.

> "Rougirai-je d'être la fille de ma mère? Oh! si ce n'était que cela! on sait bien que je n'aurai pas cette lâche honte." Je supposais alors, sans rien incriminer, quelque lien mystérieux entre ma mère et quelqu'un qui me ferait sentir une domination injuste et illégitime. (*Story of My Life*, 635/OA, 1:859)

Within Sand's family structure the threat of illegitimacy weighs heavily upon her. Like Rousseau, Sand is quite certain about the need for boundaries between men and women. What Landes says of Rousseau is true of Sand as well: "Rousseau's preferred female figure is the beneficent mother or desexualized bestower of Good, the utopian Maman, Mme de Warrens of his *Confessions*. He insists over and over again on the importance of woman's reproductive role. This is the basis, of course, of one of his most searing indictments of the 'libertine' women of Paris, those who refuse to bear and rear children in an appropriate fashion."[30] In *Mauprat*, Sand advocates a strong family community, believing that without it men would lose their morals and women their virtue. Moreover, traditional ties which can be found in the family or the state require a natural base. In this case the dispersion of the Mauprats' unnatural horde (feudalism) is replaced by the legal declaration of the republic, to the principles of which Edmée adheres entirely.

In *Mauprat*, Sand follows Rousseau's teaching consistently: "Edmée—and believe that I am speaking impartially of her—was, amid the modest obscurity of her surroundings, one of the most perfect women in France. Edmée had illuminated her great intellect by the ardent eloquence of Jean-Jacques"; and later: "But in this she was imbued with the spirit of *Emile*, and put in practice the systematic ideas of her dear philosopher" (Edmée, et croyez bien que ce n'est pas le langage de la prévention, était, au sein de sa modeste obscurité, une des femmes les plus parfaites qu'il y eût en France. Edmée avait allumé sa vaste intelligence aux brûlantes déclamations de Jean-Jacques. . . . Mais en ceci elle était imbue de l'*Emile*, et mettait en pratique les idées systématiques de son cher philosophe) (*Mauprat*, 19:119/116 and 19:169/152). Edmée représents Rousseau's ideas as he expressed them in the figure of Sophie in *Emile*. Let us not forget that Rousseau's carefully elaborated romance of Sophie and Emile fully illustrates his theory: "For according to Rousseau the pressing point of fixing the object of desire is to transcend satyriasis for fatherhood, and female licence for domesticity."[31]

In *Mauprat*, Sand's patiently constructed romance of Edmée and Bernard illustrates the shift from uncontrollable male passion to marriage:

> There can be no one more rough, more touchy, more sly, and more ill-natured, than Bernard; he is a brute who can scarcely sign his name; he is a coarse man who thinks he can break me

in like a Varennes nag. He is much mistaken; I [Edmée] would rather die than ever be his, unless he should become civilized for the sake of marrying me.

Il n'est rien de plus hérissé, de plus épineux, de plus sournois, de plus méchant que Bernard; c'est une brute qui sait à peine signer son nom; c'est un homme grossier, qui croit me dompter comme une haquenée de Varennes. Il se trompe beaucoup; je mourrai plutôt que de lui apartenir jamais, à moins que, pour m'épouser, il ne se civilise. (*Mauprat*, 19:377/309)

We still must keep in mind that Sand's mother and Rousseau's heroine bear the same name: Sophie. The hidden presence of Sophie marks, in effect, the presencing/absencing of the maternal in the Sandean text. Left in Nohant with her grandmother, Sand grieved to be reunited with her mother while feeling abandoned by her. As Landes stresses, Rousseau is very attentive to having Emile meet Sophie in her father's house: "She is in her place, the metaphoric position in which she prepares to assume her 'naturally ordained' role as mistress of a virtuous household."[32] Sand's reconstruction of Rousseau's narrative consists of snatching Bernard away from the gloomy castle of La Roche-Mauprat, the bandits' hideout, to take him to Hubert and Edmée de Mauprat's residence at Sainte-Sévère. Sand clearly demonstrates the need for a strong and good maternal figure to correct Bernard's bad habits and to civilize him. The condensation of the figures of mother and spouse in Edmée manifests Sand's filial and conjugal disappointments and her desire to find a fulfilling solution. Sand's feminism is here interested in the social and familial causes of inequality and the means of its eradication.

From the very beginning, Sand's creative genius seems to be linked to the mother's power. As early as 1829, in *Le Voyage en Auvergne*, Sand seeks a reason to start writing. She begins by writing to her mother:

Here I am! if I were to write to somebody? yes, to my mother for instance! to my mother, Oh God! "Mother, what did I do to you? why don't you love me? I am nevertheless good. A word

from you destroyed all my determination. I told you everything which by keeping secret, I could have used to soften my
fate. How much I could have loved you, mother, if you had
wanted it! But you betrayed me, you lied to me, my mother, is
it possible that you lied to me? How guilty you are! You broke
my heart. You inflicted on me a wound which will bleed all my
life. And when I see another daughter in her mother's arms,
happy, cherished, protected, I am wringing my hands and
thinking of you who abandoned me."

Me voilà bien! si j'écrivais à quelqu'un? oui, à ma mère, par
exemple! à ma mère, ah Dieu! "ô ma mère, que vous ai-je fait?
pourquoi ne m'aimez-vous pas? Je suis bonne pourtant. Un mot
de vous détruisait toutes mes résolutions. Je vous avouais tout
ce qu'en tenant caché j'aurais pu faire servir à adoucir mon sort.
O que je vous aurais aimée, ma mère, si vous l'aviez voulu! Mais
vous m'avez trahie, vous m'avez menti, ma mère, est-il possible, vous m'avez menti? Oh que vous êtes coupable! Vous avez
brisé mon coeur. Vous avez fait une blessure qui saignera toute
la vie. Et quand je vois une autre fille dans les bras de sa mère,
heureuse, adorée, protégée, je me tords les mains et je pense à
vous qui m'avez abandonnée." (OA, 2:504)

In this letter, which would never be sent to Sophie Dupin, Sand
repeats the catastrophic aspect of the family dissolution and
particularly the mother's abandonment.

From the maternal break-up l'écriture féminine is born: "The one
who leaves me is my mother. My father dies, thus father you are
my mother."[33] For Cixous the challenge to self-identity posed
by the mother figure offers a challenge to writing. Writing is
thus constantly governed and unsettled by parental relationships:
"Writing is my father, my mother, and my threatened nurse."[34] Le
Voyage en Auvergne signals the absence of the mother in Sand's
writing and reveals its disastrous effects: "My God, to whom shall
I write? I am going to write to Zoé. No, rather to Jane. Well, I
won't write, but what am I doing now?" (Mais mon Dieu à qui
écrirai-je donc? Je vais écrire à Zoé. A Jane plutôt. Décidément, je
n'écrirai pas, mais qu'est-ce que je fais donc à présent?) (OA,

2:505). The figure of the mother as betrayer causes Sand to waver and to reproduce the split that runs through her texts, separating the image of the good mother from the bad. Sand's *écriture féminine* explicitly confronts maternal love and suicide: "If I killed myself? But no, I can't. Maurice is here! Oh my son, don't be afraid that I [will] leave you. Come, your mother will love you" (Si je me tuais? Mais non je ne peux pas. Maurice qui est là! O mon fils, n'aye pas peur que je te quitte. Va, ta mère t'aimera!) (*OA*, 2:505). In this ceaseless questioning, Sand retrieves the moment when her mother left her. Instead, she will remain with her son and be a good mother.

The concept of maternal plenitude which Sand evokes here is first made impossible by Sophie's absence, whereas Sand's presence guarantees her son of her love. Madelon Sprengnether describes "the spectral mother" as being the Freudian preoedipal mother: "Never a major figure in Freud's theory, which revolves around the drama of the father-son relationship, she has a ghost-like function, creating a presence out of absence."[35] The mother is the object of Sand's fascinated and yet disenchanted gaze. Moreover, the mother evades and frustrates Sand's attempts at understanding. The "spectral" quality of Sophie Dupin exercises a kind of fatal attraction that inspires in Sand a multitude of defensive strategies. Rousseau's *Emile* offers a powerful counterpart to the deceitful mother in declaring that the greatest crime in the family is woman's infidelity.

Just as Sand's autobiography is constituted around the mother's "guilt," so are *Indiana* and *Mauprat* both organized around the construction of the family and the commune. The two novels present, respectively, colonial and revolutionary experiences that liberated the couple from nineteenth-century strictures. In *Indiana*, Sir Ralph declares: "All our days resemble one another; they pass by as swiftly and pure as those of our childhood. The greater part of our income is devoted to the redemption of poor and infirm blacks. That is the principle cause of the evil that the colonists say of us" (Tous nos jours se ressemblent; ils sont tous calmes et beaux; ils passent rapides et purs comme ceux de notre enfance. La majeure portion de nos revenus est consacrée à racheter de pauvres noirs infirmes. C'est la principale cause du mal que les colons disent de nous) (*Indiana,* 4:326/352); while Bernard concludes in *Mauprat:* "The storms of the Revolution did not destroy our well-being, and the passions it aroused did not disturb our domestic happiness. We gave willingly, and considered the relinquishment of a great part of our property under the laws of the Republic a reasonable sacrifice" (Les orages de la révolution ne détruisirent point notre existence, et les passions qu'elle souleva ne troublèrent pas l'union de notre intérieur. Nous fîmes de grand coeur, et en les considérant comme de justes sacrifices, l'abandon d'une grande partie de nos biens aux lois de la république) (*Mauprat,* 19:381/312).

As minimal as these domestic communities are, they offer a *combinatoire* which is no longer blocked in the unilateral daughter-mother relation. The abolition of slavery and the French Revolution momentarily force the family issues to occupy a secondary role. Sand also establishes the dependence of family life on the political life of France.

Mauprat signals the passage from male oral storytelling to women's writing. The myth of the origin is used only to signal the passage from patriarchy to matriarchy. The birth of the republican community shows that another "end" is possible.

In *Narrative and its Discontents,* D. A. Miller says that "what discontents the traditional novel is its own condition of possibility. Less simplistically, one might say that the traditional novelist gives play to his discontent only to assuage it in the end, much as the child in Freud makes his toy temporarily disappear, the better to enjoy its reinstated presence."[36] The apparent opposition between the narratable and closure is not accountable for the subversion of the latter. In addressing the problem of closure in Stendhal's *Le Rouge et le noir,* Miller shows that "the appealingly libertarian ways in which Stendhal resists coming to closure, far from breaking this opposition down, may be the most subtle and persuasive means of keeping it in place."[37] The deliberate "double ending" of *Indiana* might indicate that closure is no longer an act of "make-believe" but that it betrays self-inadequacy. As Miller says: "Just as the child's toy does not answer to what has really been lost, so too, closure, though it implies resolution, never really resolves the dilemmas raised by the narratable."[38] Sand's novel may be a game of fort/da which reproduces the absence/presence of the mother, although it goes beyond this binary opposition. Stendhal's notorious resistance to closure proves his dislike of ending the narratable as if the maternal figure could come back to life only under this condition. Sand seems to display the same kind of dislike at ending *Indiana* while curiously avoiding any definite closure to *The Sin of Monsieur Antoine* (1845).

"Open" Ending: *Le Péché de Monsieur Antoine*

> Weary of contemplating the barrenness and vanity of the intellects of the men of this age, I have felt the need of strengthening my compassionate heart in communion with simple-minded or unhappy mortals.
>
> GEORGE SAND, *Consuelo*

Not surprisingly, Sand gave the name of Emile to the hero of *Le Péché de Monsieur Antoine* (*The Sin of M. Antoine*) endowing him with all the Rousseauistic qualities. Opposed to his father's capitalistic views, Emile is constantly at odds with him: "But, Father, to interfere with personal liberty! you can't" (Mais, mon père, attenter à la liberté individuelle . . . Vous ne le pouvez pas).[39] The antagonism between father and son which is replayed by the opposition communism/capitalism first diverts our attention from the mystery posed by the title. Antoine de Châteaubrun is a poor nobleman who lives with his daughter Gilberte and his housekeeper Dame Janille in a castle half in ruins. Gilberte's mother, who died long ago, seems to be surrounded by a secret which the text will never clearly reveal. Monsieur Antoine's portrait, a "noble and commanding figure, broad-shouldered, with a neck like a bull, the limbs of an athlete" (*Monsieur Antoine*, 5:21), is opposed to

SAND

that of Monsieur de Boisguibault's: "He had not originally a bad figure nor an ugly face. His features were quite regular. But excessive thinness had done away with all pretence of shape, and his clothes seemed to be hung upon a man of wood" (*Monsieur Antoine*, 5:137).

Monsieur de Boisguibault is a wealthy and solitary old nobleman who befriends Emile and becomes a surrogate father figure to him. By stressing the differences between the ruined Antoine and the wealthy M. de Boisguibault, Sand thickens the mystery of these two men, once best friends. The secret which separates them seems to point to the dead Marquise de Boisguibault's adultery. Emile's discovery of the striking resemblance between Gilberte and Madame de Boisguibault's portrait forces him to admit the evidence and to hide it at once:

> The white flesh and golden hair, standing forth from the shadow, produced so powerful an illusion upon him, that he thought that he had a portrait of Gilberte before him, and when he could no longer see anything but a sort of mist filled with dancing sparks, he had to make a strong effort of his will to remember that in his first impression, the only reliable one under such circumstances, there had been no thought of resemblance between Madame de Boisguibault's face and Mademoiselle de Châteaubrun's.

> La peau fraîche et les cheveux dorés qui ressortaient encore lui firent bientôt une illusion si forte, qu'il crut avoir devant les yeux le portrait de Gilberte, et que, quand il n'eut plus dans la vue qu'un brouillard rempli d'étincelles fugitives, il eut besoin de faire un effort de volonté pour se rappeler que sa première impression, la seule juste en pareil cas, ne lui avait offert aucun trait précis de ressemblance entre la figure de madame de Boisguibault et celle de mademoiselle de Châteaubrun. (*Monsieur Antoine*, 5:258/1:254)

Seen in a sort of mist, the spectral resemblance between the portrait and Gilberte induces daydreaming and inconclusive evidence. Moreover, in keeping Madame de Boisguibault's portrait in his bedroom, the marquis ensures that the family secret will not be seen or known. Far from revealing Antoine's sin, the end of the novel will avoid the issue totally. As we will see, Sand's fear of illegitimacy is too overwhelming for her to assume it openly in *Monsieur Antoine*.

In suspecting "some mysterious link between her mother and somebody," Sand is addressing the problem of adultery and procreation. Sand's concern with openly resolving M. Antoine's sin can be illuminated with reference to Freud's *Family Romances* (1909), where the child's daydreams "are found to serve as the fulfilment of wishes and as a correction of actual life."[40] When Sand learned of her mother's numerous sexual relations, she realized that "pater semper incertus est," while the mother is "certissima."[41] Although Sand's paternity was never seriously questioned, illegitimacy is a recurrent theme in Sand's fiction.

A year before *Monsieur Antoine*, Sand still gave another variant of "the neurotic family romance" in *Consuelo* (1842–44). In this novel, the heroine, Consuelo, fully assumes the illegitimacy of her name. Here Sand seems to give illegitimacy a more positive meaning. It is under the pseudonym of Porporina that Consuelo is introduced at the Castle of Giants, which she enters as a governess. Asked by her employer, Christian of Rudolstadt, if she has been legally adopted by her music master, Porpora, she answers: "No, monsignor; among artists such things are not done, and are not necessary. As for his name, it makes no difference, so far as my position in society goes, whether I bear it by virtue of a custom or a contract" (Non, monseigneur. Entre artistes, ces choses-là ne se font pas, et ne sont pas nécessaires. Quant à son nom, il est fort inutile à ma position dans le monde que je le porte en vertu d'un usage ou d'un contrat).[42] There is, in addition, a particular reason which forces Consuelo to adopt her *nom de plume* while she is employed by the Rudolstadts: "'I have no name,' Consuelo replied unhesitatingly; 'my mother bore no other name than Rosmunda. At my baptism, I was christened Maria Consuelo; I never knew my father'" ("Je n'ai pas de nom," répondit Consuelo sans hésiter; "ma mère n'en portait pas d'autre que celui de Rosmunda. Au baptême, je fus appelée Marie de Consolation; je n'ai jamais connu mon père") (*Consuelo*, 2:191/2:53).

One might wonder why Consuelo's avowal of her unknown paternal origin is in complete opposition to Emile's decision to hide the secret of Gilberte's illegitimacy. In her study of the "Enfants de Bohême," Michèle Hecquet argues that illegitimacy was the sign of emancipation and freedom for women and artists. She remarks that "Sand's uniqueness is to have transformed the vague and dubious distinction between legitimate and illegitimate birth into symbolic configurations (and not only sentimental ones) which make the division secondary."[43] In shifting to a larger debate—the fate of the illegitimate child—Hecquet demonstrates that these children constituted a countersociety in opposition to civil law. Henceforth Sand reinvents, through Consuelo, identities which are free of the father's domination. In this sense, Hecquet is right to stress illegitimacy as a means of preserving identity outside the limits of patriarchal society.

We should recall here the role that illegitimacy played in Sand's family. Her great-grandfather, Maurice de Saxe, was the illegitimate son of Frédéric-Auguste de Saxe, King of Poland, and Marie-Aurore de Koenigsmarck. Marie-Aurore de Saxe, Maurice de Saxe's daughter and Sand's grandmother, was likewise an illegitimate child and could not be presented at court because of her birth. It is within the context of illegitimate births in Sand's family that we must understand her uncertainties. The glorious military destiny of Maurice de Saxe makes his illegitimate birth irrelevant to his brilliant career and rather enhances the destiny of the king's bastard son. However, Sand's fear of not being her father's child makes her want to hide her mother's adultery. This is probably why she prefers to cast a veil on uncertain motherhood in *Monsieur Antoine*. For Freud, the child's two principal fantasies (getting free of his or her parents and replacing them with others) are erotic and egocentric. The child's fabricated illegitimacy is in that case a means of occupying a higher social station. The technique used by Sand in carrying out these fantasies is obviously very different from the limited material at the

DOUBLE IDENTITY

child's disposal. Both *Consuelo* and *Monsieur Antoine* finally eliminate the "family romance" fantasies so that the future birth of the commune can occupy the "end" of the fiction.

For Jean-Luc Nancy, "myth is the unique language of people who recognize themselves therein, who communicate and commune in the myth."[44] The mythical ending of *Monsieur Antoine* is in keeping with the sort of mythical vision that Sand tried to capture in her myth of Corambé. While Corambé could not go beyond replaying Sand's familial dissensions, the end of this novel invents a totalizing myth that gives birth to M. de Boisguibault's dreamed-of commune:

> "My children," he said to them, "I have made you rich, because it was necessary to do it in order to overcome the obstacles that separated you. My purpose remains what it was: I believe that Emile knows it and that Gilberte will respect it. I have determined that, in the future, this great estate shall be used to found a *commune*, and in my first will I tried to provide a plan for it, and to lay its foundations."

> "Mes enfants," leur dit-il, "je vous ai faits riches, puisque c'était une nécessité pour vaincre les obstacles qui vous séparaient. Mes intentions demeurent; je crois qu'Emile les connaît, et que Gilberte les respectera. J'ai voulu que, dans l'avenir, cette vaste propriété fût destinée à fonder une *commune*, et dans mon premier acte, j'essayais d'en tracer le plan et d'en poser les bases." (*Monsieur Antoine*, 6:172/2:164)

The myth of the commune also subverts the traditional ending of the nineteenth-century novel and incorporates the union of Emile and Gilberte within its utopian scheme. M. de Boisguibault's mythical commune gives mankind its unifying fiction. The impossible reattachment to the mother, which in the early fiction is represented by the suicide temptation, is here replaced by the myth of the commune, which gives Sand a fulfilling, political solution to her life dilemma. The children's illegitimacy remains the adults' secret, and Sand refuses to conclude *Monsieur Antoine*.

The myth of communal and communist societies makes equality possible between men and women. If, as Engels said, "the degree of women's emancipation is the natural measurement of the general emancipation," Sand's vision of emancipation extends from Sir Ralph's "As for me, I have Indiana" (*Indiana*, 4:327) to the Marquis de Boisguibault's strong political engagement: "'And if my spirit is able to return, a few centuries hence, it will see men free, equal, united, that is to say just and wise! This will be the *garden of the commune*, that is to say, its gynaeceum, its festal and banqueting hall, its theatre and its church'" (Et si mon ombre peut revenir, dans quelques siècles, elle y verra des hommes libres, heureux, égaux, c'est-à-dire justes et sages! Ceci sera le *jardin de la commune*, c'est-à-dire aussi son gynécée, sa salle de fête et de banquet, son théâtre et son église) (*Monsieur Antoine*, 6, 2:175/2:166). M. de Boisguibault's statement extends the limit of the fiction instead of closing it. Indeed, it corresponds to Sand's political views of the transformation of society. In the preface to *Monsieur Antoine*, she says that centuries might be needed to transform the present society into a "community by association." In Naginski's terms, "If the utopian imagination can be defined above all as the capacity to look into the future, we are tempted to speculate on the powerfully antinostalgic vision of Sand's novelistic eye."[45] By leaving the endings of *Indiana* and *Monsieur Antoine* on the threshold of a utopian society, Sand is able to proceed to the new social order. The political engagement described in *Monsieur Antoine* repeats the retroprojective motion of Sandean fiction: the constant oscillation between the aristocratic grandmother, imbued with the values of the past, and the plebeian mother coincide respectively with the constant return to the literature of the ancien régime (Rousseau, Bernardin de Saint Pierre) and the socialist vision of a different world projected into the future.

In *Monsieur Antoine*, Madame de Boisguibault's adultery and M. Antoine's sin are superseded by M. de Boisguibault's communist dream of a better society to come. The individual's fate is absorbed in the destiny of the commune; it is an attempt, on

Sand's part, to establish a rational system of relations that comprehends the totality of men and women and makes their communication possible. M. de Boisguibault's declaration amplifies Sand's statement in *Story of My Life* about the need to live for people or ideas:

> In order for me to live I have always had to have a fixed resolve to live for someone or something, people or ideas. This need has come to me naturally as it were, from childhood on, by force of circumstance, out of frustrated affection.
>
> Il m'a toujours fallu, pour vivre, une résolution arrêtée de vivre pour quelqu'un ou pour quelque chose, pour des personnes ou des idées. Ce besoin m'était venu naturellement dès l'enfance, par la force des circonstances, par l'affection contrariée. (*Story of My Life*, 635/OA, 1:859)

M. de Boisguibault's frustrated affection repeats Sand's experience and reinforces the founding myth of the community. In this sense, the Sandean myth is an autofiguration of the maternal. It must close in on the past in order to be able to formulate the illusions of the future. The destiny of the community is never certain and depends on the power of its myth.

In *Indiana* and *Mauprat*, the Sandean community is shaped according to old models legitimated by the "literary community." In breaking away from both Rousseau's and Bernardin de Saint Pierre's myths, Sand introduces another model of thinking which disrupts them. For Nancy, the individual (the poet, the priest, or their listener) does not invent the myth. Quite the contrary: the individual is invented through the myth itself. The "absence of the community" and its interruption are themselves a myth for Georges Bataille. This Bataillean "headless" community, "Acéphale," that Maurice Blanchot describes as being "still bound to its mystery. Those who participated in it are not certain that they had a part in it,"[46] resembles Indiana's and Ralph's communal life on the island. Perhaps the marginal community of the Sandean fiction is born from this uncertain participation. It is in the lacuna of the old myths that Sand chooses these problematic and vulnerable communities which are yet to be born. Sand's abandonment of past models will become in Bataillean terms "the exigency of a community in relation to inner experience," which we will analyze in our last chapter. It is this "inner experience" that Sand describes as the exile of the community in *Indiana*.

In *India Song* (1972), Marguerite Duras[47] also represented woman alienated and exiled in the colonies. *India Song*, which is contained in *India[na]*, tells the tragic destiny of the wife of the French ambassador to India, Anne-Marie Stretter. Unlike Sand's *Indiana*, Duras's Anne-Marie commits suicide, revealing her despair. Woman's experience is here described as nothingness, as being already death: "It is neither painful nor pleasant living in India. Neither easy nor difficult. It's nothing, really . . . nothing."[48] Anne-Marie's nothingness anticipates her suicide, which leaves nothing behind: "She must have stayed there a long while, till daylight, and then she must have gone along the path . . . they found the wrap on the beach."[49] We still can dream about her death and wonder about these communities which ended as fortuitously as they began. Anne-Marie's suicide in the *mer/mère* homophony constitutes the "oceanic" maternal union which both Sand and Kristeva describe as lethal and joyful. While *Indiana* marked Sand's efforts to reestablish woman's desire at the expense of the death drive, Duras's *India Song* is "uncovering the insane, criminal secret that lies beneath the surface of our diplomatic behavior, of which the sadness of a number of women bears discreet witness."[50] The myth of the maternal is thus replayed in these different communal and colonial forms. Anne-Marie's disappearance foregoes the end of the colonial community. As Duras relives and recounts the trauma and depression of the French ambassador's wife, she also recalls the colonial collapse in her suicide. On the contrary, Sand keeps Indiana's suicide at bay by reinventing the communal myth and by the liberation of the black slaves.

The loss of her mother's love is for Duras the catastrophic event of her childhood. Her mother's preference for Duras's oldest brother is experienced by Duras as sinful, and she will have

Anne-Marie Stretter, the mother of two daughters, kill herself in an attempt to finish off the maternal figure and erase the guilt that goes with it. In Kristeva's terms, "Fear of maternal madness leads the novelist to have the mother disappear, to free herself from her."[51]

For Sand and Duras, the wound inflicted by the mother's detachment is characterized above all by the breaking of the narcissistic barrier between mother and daughter. In *Voyage en Auvergne*, Sand's imaginary letter to her absent mother is a call for forgiveness: "My mother, may God forgive you! He will forgive you. God is perfect. But you hurt me a lot" (Ma mère, Dieu vous pardonne! Il vous pardonnera. Dieu est parfait. Mais vous m'avez fait bien du mal) (*OA*, 2:504). If, for Sand, losing the will to live led to frequent withdrawals from the world, she was nonetheless able to break away from her fits of melancholia and depression and to engage in socialist projects and issues. The resistance to the mother is that formidable act of self-creation that substitutes for the absent maternal figure. *Indiana*'s two endings and *Le Péché de Monsieur Antoine*'s open-endedness affirm the limitlessness of writing. Marquis de Boisguibault's commune, like Fourier's phalanstery, invents itself beyond the fiction.

This quest for a commune can be once again linked to the mother's power. I certainly agree with Jurgrau when she says that Sand owes the creation of "George Sand" to the death of the father. Nevertheless, the bedrock of Sand's nature lies in the two mothers whose reconciliation remained impossible. Sand's attempt to turn toward a utopian prolepsis in some of her novels reveals a persistent effort to reconcile and to achieve, if not personal fulfillment, then a sort of collective happiness in the future. Finally, in evading the maternal dilemma, Sand nonetheless remains a prisoner of her childhood trauma.

Chapter Three

"MADEMOISELLE BAUDELAIRE":
RACHILDE AND THE SEXUAL DIFFERENCE

Je crois que j'ai déjà écrit dans mes notes que l'amour res-
semblait fort à une torture ou à une opération chirurgicale.
Mais cette idée peut être développée de la manière la plus
amère.

I think that I already wrote in my notes that love strongly
resembled torture or surgery. But this idea can be painfully
developed.

CHARLES BAUDELAIRE, *Fusées*

Female Fantasy: Rachilde's *Monsieur Vénus*

The writings of the novelist Rachilde (Marguerite Eymery Vallette) fully embody the values and fantasies of the epoch in which
she wrote. Rachilde (1860–1953) is usually described as "con-
sciously perverse" and as the quintessential writer of the Decadence. Perhaps more important, her novels are highly critical of
the socially accepted forms of love between men and women.
While Rachilde's writing can be read as an act of protest against
women's plight in fin-de-siècle France, her thinking can by no
means be readily assimilated to a feminist perspective. In fact, in

the pamphlet *Pourquoi je ne suis pas féministe* (1927), she explicitly distinguishes her position from that of feminism:

> I never trusted women since I was first deceived by the eternal feminine under the maternal mask and I don't trust myself anymore. I always regretted not being a man, not so much because I value more the other half of mankind but because, since I was forced by duty or by taste to live like a man, to carry alone the heavy burden of life during my childhood, it would have been preferable to have had at least the privileges if not the appearances.

> Je n'ai jamais eu confiance dans les femmes, l'éternel féminin m'ayant trompé d'abord sous le masque maternel et je n'ai pas plus confiance en moi. J'ai toujours regretté de ne pas être un homme, non point que je prise davantage l'autre moitié de l'humanité mais parce qu'obligée, par devoir ou par goût de vivre comme un homme, de porter seule tout le plus lourd fardeau de la vie pendant ma jeunesse, il eût été préférable d'en avoir au moins les privilèges sinon les apparences.[1]

Rachilde exposes the inner workings of a phallocentric culture to a devastating critique precisely by virtue of her strong identification with it. As we will see, the sincerity of her effort to appropriate patriarchal attributes enables her to penetrate their innermost structure.

Rachilde's father was a career army officer and her mother, Gabrielle, the daughter of a successful newspaper editor. Her father had desperately wanted a son, and because she remained an only child, she tried very hard to gain his approval by learning to ride when she was four years old and by participating in the hunt later on. Her ambivalent feelings for her mother can be explained by the latter's coldness. In *Souvenirs sur Madame Rachilde*, Auriant, who was a friend of Rachilde's, describes the relationship between mother and daughter:

> You ask me what I was doing when I was a little girl? I tried to walk straight, to stand up, to be well, that is to say not to fall. Why? Because I was limping. On seeing me crawl at the

bottom of her dress, my mother, the beautiful lady of the epoch of Napoleon III, used to say "little slug."

Vous me demandez ce que je faisais quand j'étais petite fille? Je m'efforçais de marcher droit, à me tenir debout, à me porter bien, c'est-à-dire à ne pas tomber. Pourquoi? Mais parce que je suis boiteuse. Petite limace, disait ma mère, la belle dame très Napoléon III, en me voyant ramper au bas de sa robe.[2]

Furthermore, Rachilde's poor relationship with her mother was worsened by Gabrielle's madness. Rachilde's distrust for the mother who finished her life in Charenton asylum partly explains her reluctance to be assimilated with the feminists. Rachilde regarded her mother's betrayal as characteristic of women in general. In *Pourquoi je ne suis pas féministe*, Rachilde remembers her mother in the following terms: "Frightfully beautiful . . . a talented musician, always head in the clouds, haughty, cold although capricious" (Belle . . . à faire peur, grande musicienne, toujours dans les nuages, dédaigneuse, froide quoique fantasque) (*Pourquoi*, 15). The mother remains remote, icily beyond feeling and identification. Rachilde extends her instinctual distrust of her mother to women in general, whom she generally regards as being unreliable creatures. At the same time, she identifies strongly with masculine desire and tries to reinvent femininity after this model. Unlike Sand, who became a loving mother to compensate for the absence of maternal love she suffered in her childhood, Rachilde never manifested a deep attachment to her own daughter. As a "femme supérieure," Rachilde never devoted much time to motherhood.

In Rachilde's fiction, the place of the mother is occupied by a series of female figures of power: the queen, the mother superior, and imperiously sadistic women who "unsex" weak men and thus reverse the patriarchal order. All of Rachilde's writing seeks to establish the irreversibility and incontrovertibility of the power of the mother, for it is maternal power that she reinvests with the force and resilience of conventional patriarchal attributes. Thus the paradox of Rachildean writing: her apparent iconoclasm belies the most conventional bourgeois values. Although at first glance she appears to be a radical feminist, closer inspection reveals that the return, and indeed the reinvention, of maternal power in her writing is in surprising complicity with patriarchal hegemony. Rachilde relocates women's victimization in connection not with male power but rather with maternal tyranny; but the tyranny of the mother is itself a cipher for a realm of masculine values and attributes. Over and over again, Rachilde depicts young female rebels who try to overcome the tyrannical power of despotic maternal figures, and every time the rebels fail in their revolt. Rachilde feels that she is a superior woman, a successful rebel, the only woman to have emerged victorious in her struggle against maternal power. But—and here lies the essential paradox of her life and writing—she repeatedly denies to other women the ability to emerge victorious from their comparable struggles. She thus places herself outside the maternal genealogy in which other women remain trapped.

Let us begin with Rachilde's reinvention of her own genealogy, which begins with the invention of her pseudonym. Rachilde's defiance of her family took its most radical turn when at age twenty-two she came to live in Paris and assumed the pseudonym she came to be known by for the rest of her life. She first claimed that Rachilde was the name of a Swedish knight who had contacted her through a seance, but she later admitted that this fabrication had been for her parents' benefit, adding that the name was her own invention. Her business cards read "Rachilde, homme de lettres." This "token woman" (femme-alibi) hidden behind a masculine identity was celebrated by Maurice Barrès as "Mademoiselle Baudelaire."

The question of the name that obliterates gender difference anticipates numerous plots which openly play on sexual inversions: Monsieur Vénus, Madame Adonis, La Marquise de Sade. Each title provokes a literary displacement which allows Rachilde to replay her fantasms as if she were a man. It was in 1884 that Rachilde asked the prefect of police to permit her legally to wear man's clothes: "Dear Sir, please authorize me to wear men's clothing.

Please read the following attestation, I beg you: and do not confuse my inquiry with other classless women who seek scandal under the above costume" (Monsieur le Préfet, j'ai l'honneur de vous demander l'autorisation de porter le costume d'homme. Veuillez lire l'attestation suivante, je vous en supplie: et ne confondez pas ma demande avec celle de certaines femmes déclassées qui cherchent le scandale sous le costume en question).[3] This authorization had already been granted to Madame Dieulafoy, an archaeologist, and to Sarah Bernhardt, who wanted to escape formal inconveniences on the stage as well as in the street. If wearing men's clothes is the trope which brings us back to Sand, it also anticipates the 1900s, when fashionable women would have their hair cut "à la garçonne" and wear cycling outfits inspired by English sportsmen.

The character of Missie in *La Jongleuse* (*The Juggler*, 1900) embodies this "new woman," whom Rachilde mocks relentlessly. Rachilde wants to persuade the prefect of police that her eagerness to wear male attire has nothing to do with the women's movement or the current fashion. Her satire of "Missie dressed in an ideal cycling outfit for *the modern fiancée*"[4] offers the kind of double standard that is characteristic of Rachilde. Rachilde's eagerness to wear male clothing must not be confused with feminist positions. In *Pourquoi je ne suis pas féministe*, Rachilde maintains the political status quo by restating her lack of interest in the right to vote: "This tendency to look masculine never prompted me to snatch some rights which were not mine. I always acted as an *individual*, not thinking to found a society or to upset the present one" (Cette tendance à des allures masculines ne m'a nullement inspiré le désir de m'emparer de droits qui n'étaient pas les miens. J'ai toujours agi en *individu* ne songeant pas à fonder une société ou à bouleverser celle qui existait) (*Pourquoi*, 6). Rachilde's masculine clothing thus signals her incorporation of the appearance of the professional man and her realization of her unfulfilled wish to be (like) a man. In *Pourquoi je ne suis pas féministe*, she recalls telling her tutor: "I wish God would change me into a boy since my parents will never love me as long as I am a girl!" (Je demande au bon Dieu qu'il me change en garçon puisque mes parents ne m'aimeront jamais tant que je serai une fille!) (*Pourquoi*, 40). What Rachilde finally asks from the prefect is to be granted sexual anonymity: "I hope, dear sir, that you will allow me to wear the most disgraceful clothes in the world, to travel in Paris" (J'ose espérer, Monsieur le Préfet, que vous me permettrez de prendre pour voyager dans Paris, les vêtements les plus disgracieux qui soient au monde).[5]

Monsieur Vénus (1884) fully expresses Rachilde's early attempt to describe female fantasms of masculinity that efface sexual difference. It provoked a scandal in Belgium, where it was first published. In his preface, Maurice Barrès declared: "This book is quite abominable and yet, I can't say that I am shocked" (Ce livre-ci est assez abominable, pourtant je ne puis dire qu'il me choque).[6] Nevertheless, in France *Monsieur Vénus* was a *succès de scandale*. In calling Rachilde "Mademoiselle Baudelaire," Barrès offers at once a sexual and a critical evaluation of Rachilde's relation to Baudelaire.

Barrès's suggestion recalls Baudelaire's numerous declarations about the poet's androgynous nature. As Michel Butor has argued, it is precisely Baudelaire's "androgynous dream" which is the sign of the power of creation: "Thus, *mundus muliebris* is the necessary theatre for the birth of genius. The thicker women's clothes are, the more decisive the victory of the poet who tears them apart. . . . One understands then why the lesbian is the very symbol of the apprentice poet who has not yet published. Publication will unveil the superior man hidden behind a dress and a woman's role."[7] If, for Baudelaire, poetical inspiration is symbolically equivalent to a woman's strip-tease, it is not surprising that his blatant misogyny in *Mon coeur mis à nu* reveals that the androgynous poet must rid himself of his feminine side in order to find his creative, virile power. Far from being exclusive of each other, femininity and supervirility are linked together. Virility must be willingly conquered by the poet in order to be long lasting: "Virility must have been called into question and must spring from femininity which threatens to engulf it."[8] Baudelaire and Rachilde will describe femininity as a deadly threat; Baudelaire's lesbians and Rachilde's castrating women are both haunting and destructive figures in their works. The sadism of both Baudelaire and Rachilde is conjured up by the nickname "Mademoiselle Baudelaire."[9]

In the fifth section of "Salon de 1846," Baudelaire describes a lithograph he saw, a lithograph which could just as well sum up Rachilde's perverted representation of love:

> I still remember a lithograph which expresses,—but unfortunately it lacks delicacy,—one of the great truths of libertine love. A young man dressed up as a woman and his mistress dressed as a man are seated together on a couch,—the couch that you know so well, the couch that is in furnished hotel or private rooms. The young woman wants to lift up her lover's dress.

> Je me rappelle pourtant une lithographie qui exprime,—sans trop de délicatesse malheureusement,—une des grandes vérités de l'amour libertin. Un jeune homme déguisé en femme et sa maîtresse habillée en homme sont assis l'un à côté de l'autre sur un *sopha*,—le sopha que vous savez, le sopha de l'hôtel garni et du cabinet particulier. La jeune femme veut relever les jupes de son amant.[10]

Baudelaire's brief portrait of what an erotic drawing should be at best offers an exact description of Rachilde's *Monsieur Vénus*.

Unwilling to surrender to men of her own class, Raoule de Vénérande turns instead to Jacques Silver, an untalented painter who earns his living by making artificial flowers. Raoule enjoys seeing how much humiliation Jacques will bear. He becomes, in effect, her kept "mistress"; he is referred to as "she," and Raoule visits "her" in men's clothing. Raoule confides her affair to de Raittolbe, one of her suitors, declaring that modern women have no intention of reproducing a dying aristocracy. Raoule marries Jacques as much to keep him entirely at her disposal as to flout social convention. Jacques tries to seduce de Raittolbe and a day later is killed by de Raittolbe in a duel. In the last chapter, Raoule has transformed her bedroom into a shrine containing a wax figure of Jacques:

> On the shell-shaped bed, guarded by a marble Eros, lies a wax figure covered with transparent rubber. His red hair, his fair eyebrows and the golden down of his chest are natural; the teeth in his mouth, the nails of the hands and feet have been cut from a corpse. This mannequin, a masterpiece of anatomy, was made by a German.

> Sur la couche en forme de conque, gardée par un Eros de marbre, repose un mannequin de cire revêtu d'un épiderme de caoutchouc transparent. Les cheveux roux, les cils blonds, le duvet d'or de la poitrine sont naturels; les dents qui ornent la bouche, les ongles des mains et des pieds ont été arrachés à un cadavre. Ce mannequin, chef-d'oeuvre d'anatomie, a été fabriqué par un Allemand.[11]

The German craftsman's masterpiece recalls Hoffmann's "The Sandman," in which the beautiful Olympia is only an automaton and not a woman, as Nathaniel believed. The inanimate figures of Olympia and Jacques awaken uncanny sensations by upsetting the relation of life and death. In his preface, Barrès declared: "*Monsieur Vénus* describes a young woman's strange soul. I am asking you to consider this work as an anatomy" (*Monsieur Vénus* décrit l'âme d'une jeune fille très singulière. Je prie qu'on regarde cet ouvrage comme une anatomie).[12]

In dissecting Jacques's body, one can see that Raoule is out to discover the secrets of the male body. Sexuality is described in terms of scientific knowledge and social instability. For Rachilde, argues Jennifer Birkett, "class is the insurmountable barrier which must always prevent change in women's condition. With Jacques, Raoule came closest to disrupting her world, first by asking a paid lover to challenge the sanctity of family order, and secondly in marrying him, to bring disorder inside the closed circle."[13] Birkett's point is well taken, for while Rachilde may appear to dismantle the family order, she nevertheless remains circumscribed by it. We will see how, in *Monsieur Vénus*, the *femme froide* is at once a psychological and a social construction through which Rachilde, in the very effort to exorcise the figure of the mother, only succeeds in reinventing her in a fantastic form.

Let us return for a moment to Baudelaire, whose experience of isolation from the mother makes him Rachilde's paradigmatic point of reference. In *Mon coeur mis à nu*, Baudelaire expresses a feeling of loneliness and alienation that stems from his separation from his mother: "Feeling of loneliness in my childhood. In spite of the family—and above all with my friends—feeling of a fate eternally lonely" (Sentiment de *solitude*, dès mon enfance. Malgrè la famille,—et au milieu des camarades surtout,—sentiment de destinée éternellement solitaire).[14] *Spleen et Idéal (Spleen and Ideal)* is poetically organized around Baudelaire's autobiographical acknowledgment of loneliness and replays endlessly his agonized relation to his mother. In *Le Pervers et la femme*, Paul-Laurent Assoun argues that "what is called Baudelairean 'symbolism' could very well be an intense activity to repair something which precisely cannot be symbolized and which is called *symptom*."[15] The loneliness that Baudelaire experiences as fate constitutes retrospectively the maternal abandonment he suffered in his childhood. Baudelaire's demand for maternal love is constantly thwarted. On the contrary, Rachilde completely disassociates herself from the maternal figure by creating an anarchic, imaginary power that at once sublates maternity and places it under erasure. *La Marquise de Sade* (1887) performs this function, as we will see later on. While the figure of the angel is Baudelaire's metaphor for the battle against the mother *within* the mother, Rachilde's feminine figures demand an absolute detachment from the mother or any maternal surrogate. The founding image of *Fleurs du mal (Flowers of Evil)* is that of a mother hysterically bemoaning the birth of "a shrunken monster" (*un monstre rabougri*), whereas the first image of *La Marquise de Sade* is the daughter's horror at discovering that her anemic mother is drinking fresh blood.

Because procreation is always under the potential threat of birth defects or of producing a deformed and mutilated life, Baudelaire regards poetic creation as similarly beleaguered by the malaise that is immanent in the essence of the maternal. As Assoun remarks:

> The subject has one solution: He uses the maternal language to lift it up to its highest level of power: it is there that the poetical Verb in the Baudelairean concept takes its whole meaning. Baudelaire has no choice: he writes under the mother's threat (fantasm). The passage to writing originates from rejection. In doing so, it lifts up the maternal language—the language of suffering—to the poetical word. The beauty of the ideal is a recourse against Misery inflicted by the primitive, lethal Mother: it's literally self-defense.[16]

If eroticism is so strongly connected with death in Baudelaire's work, it is precisely because the maternal power is pervasive and evil.

Rachilde's decadent writing aptly describes the mother as a negative force which must be kept away. Rachilde's masculinization is the ultimate strategy to distance herself from both the mother and the feminists. In declaring that "motherhood is the supreme deceit," Rachilde comes very close to Baudelaire's statement in *Mon coeur mis à nu*: "Woman is the contrary of the dandy. Therefore she must provoke horror" (La femme est le contraire du dandy. Donc elle doit faire horreur).[17] The suppression of maternity puts the problem of a "biological limit" aside once and for all. Women's willed sterility becomes the manifestation of a new discourse which puts women's reproductive role under erasure. Maternity is thus bracketed, but at the expense of a dependency on perverse drives.

Jennifer Birkett describes Rachilde as having been, "almost alone of women writers of her period, accepted into the Club des Hydropathes and Le Chat Noir patronized by Victor Hugo and Barbey d'Aurevilly, approved by the misogynists Huysmans and Léon Bloy, and befriended by Verlaine, Jean Lorrain, Catulle Mendès, Laurent Tailhade and Camille Lemonnier[,] this has had much to do with her willingness to play and play up to the decadent stereotypes."[18] I believe that Birkett's notion of the essential misogyny of Rachilde's thinking is mistaken and that something else is going on.

In *Pourquoi je ne suis pas féministe,* Rachilde points to another aspect of her mother's influence: "My mother, who taught me how to respect one's parents at least in appearance, made me understand very young that my father was a negligible quantity" (Ma mère, en m'enseignant le respect que l'on doit à ses parents, au moins dans la forme, me fit comprendre, de bonne heure, que mon père était une quantité négligeable) (*Pourquoi,* 16). *Monsieur Vénus* is a composite of Rachilde's search for sexual and intellectual identity. Rachilde's novel thematizes its own fictionality as Raoule declares that she needs to create her own work of art:

> "It's true, sir," resumed Raoule, shrugging her shoulders, "that I had lovers in my life as I have books in my library in order to know, to study. . . . But I never felt passion; I have not yet written my book!"

> "Il est certain, monsieur," reprit Raoule haussant les épaules, "que j'ai eu des amants. Des amants dans ma vie comme j'ai des livres dans ma bibliothèque, pour savoir, pour étudier. . . . Mais je n'ai pas eu de passion, je n'ai pas écrit mon livre, moi!"[19]

Woman's exclusion from desire is a figure of her exclusion from language, and it forces Rachilde to invent what Verlaine called "a new sin." Within the violent clichés of fin-de-siècle literature, Rachilde/Raoule transforms creation into a model that corresponds to the masculine other, that is, it eliminates procreation. Feminine desire is so monstrously perverted in *Monsieur Vénus* that it finally becomes the passion to kill.

Moreover, Rachilde calls into question the slow agony of an aristocracy attached to the dying forms of tradition. From the very beginning, Raoule de Vénérande is critical of her class, while spreading the contamination to Jacques, who has already died for her: "I will love Jacques like a fiancé hopelessly in love with his dead fiancée" (J'aimerai Jacques comme un fiancé aime sans espoir la fiancée morte) (*Monsieur Vénus,* 90). Jacques is transformed by turns into a "dead fiancée," a still life, and a wax doll. When

Raoule first meets Jacques, he appears to her at once feminine and strangely unreal, like an object rather than a human being:

> Around his chest, on top of the loose blouse, ran a spiral garland of roses. Those roses were big skin-like satin flowers with a touch of crimson velvet which glided along between his legs, rushed to his shoulders and came around his neck.

> Autour de son torse, sur la blouse flottante, courait en spirale une guirlande de roses, des roses fort larges de satin chair velouté de grenat, qui lui passaient entre les jambes, filaient jusqu'aux épaules et venaient s'enrouler au col. (*Monsieur Vénus*, 24)

Although Jacques's androgynous beauty is compared to paintings of both Venus and Cupid, his final transformation into "Monsieur Vénus" assumes the mode of representation traditionally attributed to women. The scandal of the transformation of Jacques into a "flower-woman" (*une femme-fleur*) suggests that gender roles can be exchanged and upset the social equilibrium on which they are based. Rachilde's implicit criticism of the abuse of women that takes place "normally" in the name of love is more blatant since the victim is a feminized man in the hands of a masculine woman. As one critic has recently remarked: "Each is learning to understand the other by becoming that other in the love relationship. Jacques learns to be observed, admired, decorated, made love to."[20] He is also taught how to be beaten. The gender role inversion stresses how ludicrous and cruel women's victimization is. The inverted sexual relations of Jacques and Raoule reveal the horror of male domination.

Rachilde's depiction of Jacques is an effort to disturb the traditional representation of masculinity, as Barrès stressed: "One would see with terror some people come to be disgusted by feminine grace while at the same time *Monsieur Vénus* proclaims its hate of masculine strength" (On verrait avec effroi quelques-uns arriver au dégoût de la grâce féminine, en même temps que *Monsieur Vénus* proclame la haine de la force mâle).[21] Rachilde's indictments of both masculine and feminine conventions make

Monsieur Vénus characteristic of her most essential thinking. She does not fundamentally believe that sexual relations can be rid of violence, and she replays the story of the sadistic woman within the context of fin-de-siècle France.

In *Fictional Genders*, Dorothy Kelly analyzes how Raoule first feminizes Jacques before transforming him into a work of art, into a poem: "Jacques, whose body was a poem, knew that this poem would always be read more carefully than the letter of an ordinary writer like him" (Jacques, dont le corps était un poème, savait que ce poème serait toujours lu avec plus d'attention que la lettre d'un vulgaire écrivain comme lui) (*Monsieur Vénus*, 139). Kelly's argument consists of showing how "both Raoule's and Rachilde's writing does not imitate nature but points out its own invention (it turns reality into the mannequin), as it plays with conventions."[22] Her point is that "even though this text is written by a woman, woman's writing is monstrous here; it is a deformation of the natural."[23] The ambiguity lies precisely in the deformation of the "natural."

Rachilde retrieves myths of male primacy in theological, scientific, and above all artistic creativity in order to turn them around and establish female mastery. Writers such as Hugo and Balzac described the artist as priest, seer, warrior, and legislator, all the while reinforcing the idea that masculinity is the essential creative gift. Within this literary tradition, Susan Gubar considers the story of Pygmalion a paradigm for reading woman as an object in literature: "Woman is not simply an object, however. If we think in terms of the production of culture, she is an art object: she is the ivory carving or mud replica, an icon or doll, but she is not the sculptor. Lest this seem fanciful, we should remember that until very recently women have been barred from art schools as students yet have always been acceptable as models."[24] The long literary tradition identifying the author as a male who is primary and the female as his passive creation, a secondary object lacking autonomy, is subverted and reversed in *Monsieur Vénus*. Jacques is the deformation of the "natural" insofar as Raoule's desire inverts masculine and feminine roles. In excluding Jacques from language, Rachilde asserts the possibility of female creativity. Clearly, Rachilde reinstalls man as an artifact within culture. As Gubar notes, it is "particularly problematic for those women who want to appropriate the pen by becoming writers. Especially in the nineteenth century, women writers, who feared their attempts at the pen were presumptuous, castrating or even monstrous, engaged in a variety of strategies to deal with their anxiety about authorship."[25] This anxiety is expressed in *Monsieur Vénus* by the attack on maternity.

The attack on maternity in *Monsieur Vénus* proceeds through an opposition of childbearing to the art of dueling. Since Jacques cannot give birth to a child, he must learn to duel: "She ['she' designates Jacques on the wedding night] must ask to kill somebody since she is absolutely forbidden to give birth" (Il faut bien qu'elle demande à tuer quelqu'un puisque le moyen de mettre quelqu'un au monde lui est absolument refusé) (*Monsieur Vénus*, 194). Dueling is here construed as a surrogate of maternity; Jacques's death in a duel with de Raittolbe is very much similar to the death in childbirth of Mary Barbe's mother in *La Marquise de Sade*. Besides, Jacques's desire to learn dueling is just as impossible as his desire to be impregnated by Raoule. Dueling is the privilege of the aristocracy, and de Raittolbe himself confronts Jacques with his absurd wishes: "You did not know how to fight, you gave yourself up to death" (Vous ne saviez pas vous battre, vous vous êtes offert vous-même à la mort) (*Monsieur Vénus*, 223). Jacques's elimination signals the suppression of sexual ambivalence, which is dangerous in a society built on rigorous gender as well as class distinctions.

For Jennifer Birkett, Jacques's death is unavoidable: "With Jacques, Raoule came closest to disrupting her world, first by taking a paid lover to challenge the sanctity of family order, and secondly in marrying him, to bring disorder in the closed circle. The aristocratic de Raittolbe's response—to kill the destructive element—was a logical one."[26] The sexual and social subversions of *Monsieur Vénus* may indicate Rachilde's sense of the seriousness of the social crisis she faced. The discovery, during the wed-

ding night, that she is after all a woman results in Jacques's out-
cry: " 'Raoule,' Jacques exclaimed, his face contracted, his teeth
clenched on his lip, his arms opened as if he had just been
crucified, 'Raoule, aren't you a man? Can't you be really a man?' "
("Raoule," s'écria Jacques, la face convulsée, les dents crispées sur
la lèvre, les bras étendus comme s'il venait d'être crucifié, "Raoule,
tu n'es donc pas un homme? Tu ne peux donc pas être un
homme?") (*Monsieur Vénus*, 198). At that moment, Raoule cannot
take over the man's role and is forced to switch back to her
anatomical one. Raoule's impotence finally reveals her sexual
shortcomings.

Raoule's mourning for Jacques is associated with her undecidable gender identification at the end of the novel. Instead of providing a solution to the sexual impasse she has repeatedly confronted, Raoule's mourning ritual simply reinscribes it at a more
explicit, exaggerated, and indeed hysterical level. She mourns for
what she herself has just destroyed, like a child who mourns for
the doll she has broken:

> At night, a woman in mourning dress, sometimes a young man
> in black clothing, open the door. They come and kneel near
> the bed, and when they have for a long time contemplated the
> wonderful shape of the wax statue, they embrace it, kiss its
> lips. A spring, set inside the body, corresponds with the mouth
> and animates it.

> La nuit, une femme vêtue de deuil, quelquefois un jeune
> homme en habit noir, ouvrent cette porte. Ils viennent s'age-
> nouiller près du lit, et, lorsqu'ils ont contemplé longtemps les
> formes merveilleuses de la statue de cire, ils l'enlacent, la
> baisent aux lèvres. Un ressort, disposé à l'intérieur des flancs,
> correspond à la bouche et l'anime. (*Monsieur Vénus*, 227–28)

It is as though this uncanny pretense of mourning was Raoule's
objective all along. Remember that here she is mourning not over
a dead body but over a wax dummy. Having failed to maintain
her transformed world of gender reversals, Raoule is forced to
replay the scenario in the privacy of her artificial world. There

need not be an end to such artificial mourning. Could we say that Raoule's waxen ritual is in effect an allegory for Rachilde's own experience of artistic creation? Perhaps. What is more certain is that Raoule's performance does appear to replay a trauma in Rachilde's own life.

Just prior to writing *Monsieur Vénus*, Rachilde fell madly in love with the writer Catulle Mendès, who did not respond to her infatuation. She fell ill as a result, and her illness was marked by a hysterical paralysis of both legs. Rachilde's biographer, Claude Dauphiné, says that the idea for *Monsieur Vénus* came to Rachilde during her paralysis: "Writing was to play the compensatory element, and Mademoiselle de Vénérande would avenge Marguerite Eymery."[27] Writing was thus also a cure. By symbolically slaying the would-be lover and reinventing him in the more malleable form of Jacques, Rachilde found her way, in this, her first novel, to the fundamental narrative pattern that would characterize all her writing. The "woman in mourning" who is "sometimes a young man," this dual being whom Rachilde speaks of as "they" ("they embrace the wax statue, they kiss its lips"), embraces the artwork which it has itself created. Raoule can give birth only to this bizarre ritual, this doubleness within herself, in conjunction with the work of art that is the very symbol of the underlying unity of this doubleness. The fetish that substitutes for the corpse reveals the fundamental form of what Raoule was all the while trying to invent through her manipulation of Jacques's gender and appearance. Between them, Raoule and the German craftsman forge the perfect work of art, one that henceforth stands as Rachilde's consummate symbol of the attack on maternity.

For Rachilde, sexual difference is like a surgical dissection which draws an equivalence between woman's "penis envy" and man's inability to become pregnant. But why does Rachilde still see the feminine as being incomplete? Like Raoule, Rachilde's subsequent creations, such as the juggler Eliante and the Marquise de Sade, all refuse maternity. My thesis is that Rachilde's writing turns the violence that is already at work within the bourgeois family against the family itself, against all the conventions and norms of her time. Rachilde's work remains, however, totally given over to this self-destructive work of negation; there is no utopian element to her thinking. Any effort to redeem Rachilde's writing for either an idealist or a materialist feminism would therefore be beside the point. The double strategy of the Rachildean text inheres in its paradoxical commitment to precisely those values it is otherwise intent on destroying. Her assault on maternity would thus reveal that the bourgeois family was itself constituted in part by a certain violence against maternity. What is unique about Rachilde is her ability to reveal the deep-seated complicity between bourgeois culture and the violent spirit of anarchism. Her version of decadence relies upon their fundamental collusion.

A dialectical reading of the relationship of the late nineteenth-century family to the anarchistic social upheavals characteristic of the 1890s is not our direct objective here, though it is one of the implications of the reading of Rachilde that we have undertaken. Let us at least observe, however, that Rachilde's writing is a kind of terrorism; it is an apparatus that seeks to provoke sensational responses from precisely those readers who are most committed or implicated by the very conventions it seeks to undermine. The violence of *Monsieur Vénus* (1884) would thus have anticipated the period of terrorism unprecedented in the history of the Third Republic, in particular the mid-1890s.

In his recent study of this historical period, Richard Sonn analyzes the transformation of anarchistic philosophies from a mystical ideology into a literary style:

> Terrorists may have resented the more elite practitioners of anarchist culture, but they also relied upon them. The inchoate act of the bomb thrower demanded interpretation by purveyors of words, ideas, and images, and the dissemination of these interpretations in various forms of media. Terrorists needed intellectuals, intellectuals fawned on terrorists; this symbiotic, highly symbolic form of activity typified fin de siècle anarchism.[28]

"MADEMOISELLE BAUDELAIRE"

Rachilde's writing belongs somewhere in this transformation. Her plots and characters open imaginative vistas of counter-cultural experimentation that become increasingly literalized as the century draws to a close.

The feminized Jacques, "born of a prostitute and an alcoholic father," is a degenerate, decadent being, incapable of effecting social change. Raoule claims that privilege for herself: "You must see," she said ironically, "that I don't have florist's hands like you, and that I am always the more virile of the two?" ("Tu dois t'apercevoir," dit-elle ironiquement, "que je n'ai pas, comme toi, des mains de fleuriste et que, de nous deux, le plus homme c'est toujours moi?") (*Monsieur Vénus*, 99). And, as we have seen, Raoule's instrument of anarchy is ultimately her wax dummy and her macabre work of mourning. As Birkett observes: "Raoule, who shares Rachilde's own faith in hierarchy, was never more than half-hearted in her challenge to order."[29] The conclusion of *Monsieur Vénus* conjures up images of gloom, perversions, and rebellion against social codes and taboos.

The gruesome ritual of Raoule's artifice of mourning corresponds to the widespread nineteenth-century eagerness on the part of physicians and the general public to dissect female corpses and put them on display. In *Sexual Anarchy*, Elaine Showalter shows how this passion for observation and analysis was first manifested in the development of medical and gynecological instruments: "While male novelists describe their journeys into Kôr, Kafiristan, or the heart of darkness as sexual expeditions into a primordial female body, doctors describe their invasions of the female body as adventurous quests for treasure and power."[30] Rachilde leaves it up to her readers to surmise how Raoule garnered bits and pieces of Jacques's dead body and attached them to the wax dummy. All that is said is that on the night of Jacques's death, Raoule is seen with a scalpel in hand. It is left to us to imagine what ghastly use she makes of it. Like the archetypal late-Victorian physician performing an autopsy on the body of a drowned prostitute, and not unlike a domesticated Jack the Ripper, Rachilde views the ill-fated Jacques as "ce mannequin, chef-d'oeuvre d'anatomie" (*Monsieur Vénus*, 228). Though one could say that Rachilde appears to displace a morbid anatomical interest from the woman's body to the man's, we must not forget that the gender of Jacques's body is highly unstable, even more so in light of Raoule's uncertain surgical intervention.

Finally, the title itself, *Monsieur Vénus*, is a reminder of what were known as "anatomical Venuses": "In the eighteenth century, European medical students studied the internal organs with the aid of 'Anatomical Venuses,' elaborate wax models of women, naturally colored, physically detailed down to the eyebrows and eyelashes, and opened up to display the reproductive organs, sometimes including a fetus."[31] These Venuses, displayed in glass cases, simultaneously evoked an abstract femininity and women's reproductive destiny. *Monsieur Vénus* uses this anatomical tradition in order to create a range of distressing, and slightly terroristic, effects.

The Blood Cure and the Typography of Effraction in *La Marquise de Sade*

Is this the age of vampires? The slaughtermen, it is known, drink the blood of the beast as it pours from the carotid; the aristocratic lady-friends of the count of Orgel come to drink blood from bowls alongside the slaughtermen, in the scalding rooms.

MARGUERITE DURAS, *Outside*

In *La Marquise de Sade* (1887), Rachilde reinvents a crucial figure in the history of patriarchal violence, namely the Marquis de Sade, and appropriates that violence into a female register. Mary Barbe (whose name derives from *barbe*, beard) is the "Marquise de Sade," who turns to violence in order to revenge herself against her family, her lovers, and finally against the entire social order that has poisoned every meaningful experience for her. She is the very figure of women's exclusion from society. She is neglected by her anemic, dying mother and brutalized by her father, a colonel in the French army. When her mother dies giving birth to a son, Mary competes unsuccessfully with her little brother and with her father's new mistress. Mary's sadistic education begins when she witnesses the agony and death of her little brother after her drunken nurse has inadvertently crushed him. After her father's death in the Franco-Prussian War, she becomes the ward of a misogynist uncle who wants to send her to a convent. Mary's rebellion begins when she resists his command:

> "I am listening, Uncle! . . . I am in the way because I am not a boy!" It was precisely the reason, he could not have said it better himself. A boy could have been a doctor or a botanist, whereas Mary's sex prevented this dream from happening.

> "Mon oncle, je vous écoute! . . . je vous gêne parce que je ne suis pas un garçon." En effet, c'était cela, lui-même ne le pouvait mieux définir. Un garçon il en aurait fait un médecin ou un botaniste, tandis que le sexe de Mary empêchait ce rêve.[32]

Piqued by her resistance, her uncle takes an interest and begins to educate her. Her introduction to anatomy becomes an initiation into debauchery. She pretends to submit to her uncle's sexual embrace and somehow manages to remain a virgin. Marriage to a rich, aging libertine, Baron Louis de Caumont, enables her to escape into a lesser domestic dependence. From here on, Mary de Caumont stops at nothing.[33] Maddened by her perversity, poisoned by the aphrodisiacs she feeds him, Baron Louis de Caumont dies of what the doctor calls "a strange case of satyriasis" (*Marquise de Sade*, 284). Mary, the silent victim, has become the true mistress of all circumstances, the "Marquise de Sade" who finally defeats her "family's everlasting passion for males!" (*Marquise de Sade*, 182).

Mary's acquired taste for blood is deeply rooted in nineteenth-century medical practices and in the way the physicians of the time coped with the anemia which plagued and weakened so many middle-class women. Rachilde carefully describes Mary's first horror at seeing her mother Caroline drink the blood of freshly killed oxen: " 'Be quiet!' Caroline said, while sipping the sinister drink with her palid lips. Now, her mother's mouth had become crimson" ("Tais-toi!" dit une seconde fois Caroline en trempant ses lèvres pâlies dans le sinistre breuvage. Maintenant, la mère avait la bouche d'un rouge ardent) (*Marquise de Sade*, 21–22). Mary's formative trauma is the accidental sight of the slaughtered ox:

> For the little girl, this scent took formidable proportions; she imagined that the whole slaughterhouse was a unique, horned head, smashed, gnawing its teeth and splashing her white dress with bloody spurts.

> Il sembla à la petite fille que cette scène prenait des proportions phénoménales; elle s'imagina que tout le bâtiment de l'abattoir était une seule tête cornue, fracassée, grinçant des dents et lui lançant des fusées de sang sur sa robe blanche. (*Marquise de Sade*, 14)

La Marquise de Sade comes full circle: its last scene is set in a bar at La Villette, near the slaughterhouse, where Mary mingles with the butchers' apprentices, pretending to be anemic like her mother in order to mix her wine with blood.

In *Idols of Perversity*, Bram Dijkstra shows how the "metamorphoses of the vampire" in fin-de-siècle literature are deeply embedded in the deluded medical solutions to the problem of anemia: "The supposed invigorating nutritive qualities of blood made it particularly easy for men to suspect women, with their generally anemic constitution, and their inevitable periodic blood loss, of having a constitutional yearning for this tonic."[34] In "La Buveuse de sang" ("The Blood Drinker," 1894), Rachilde embraces "the psychological fascination of her contemporaries for the notion of the bestial vampire woman."[35] For Dijkstra, Rachilde's "The Blood Drinker" is an amazing document of the level of self-hatred felt by some turn-of-the-century women: "As a result of the relentless, strident indoctrination by the men around them, many had developed a fierce distaste for the mere fact of being a

woman, and of having to cope with what men were loudly pro-
claiming the 'inherent' physical disabilities and 'animal require-
ments' of women."[36] There can be no doubt that Rachilde was
misogynist only insofar as she does not hesitate to use the negative stereotypes that were applied to women of her time. However, if Rachilde uses her contemporaries' fascination for the bestial vampire woman in "The Blood Drinker," she again reverts to
the predatory nature of the male vampire in *Le Grand Saigneur*
(1922). The French homophony between *saigneur* (bleeder) and
seigneur (lord) establishes a pun that suggests a pervasive parallel
between vampirism and nobility.

Le Grand Saigneur is ultimately the representation of women's
victimization in marriage. In the Marquis de Pontcroix's strength,
Rachilde recognizes the manifestations of male-female power
relations: "He often took his wife's hand and rolled, under his
impatient finger, the heavy wedding ring which made her his
prisoner" (Il prenait souvent la main de sa femme et roulait, sous
son index impatient, l'anneau d'or, très lourd, qui la faisait sa
prisonnière).[37] Rachilde's indictment against marriage takes on
the gruesome guise of a vampire story. For Rachilde, vampirism is
the most extreme expression of the violent male sexuality and
domination that have oppressed women over the centuries. In *Le
Grand Saigneur*, Rachilde questions the masculine position of mastery. However, her critique is never penetrating, since it is firmly
situated in the decadent mode. In succumbing to the Marquis de
Pontcroix's desire to drink her blood, his fiancée yields unconditionally to his vampiristic nature. The "blood cure," which consists of emptying his healthy fiancée of her blood to restore his
health, is paralleled in *La Marquise de Sade* by Mary's dream of
killing one of the transvestites she sees. The destructive instinct
in the Marquis de Pontcroix and the "Marquise de Sade" is linked
to the abandonment of normal libidinal cathexes. If "neurosis is
based upon a struggle of the ego against the demands of the
sexual function,"[38] then *La Marquise de Sade* describes the perverse
victory of the egocentric trends that have succeeded in rendering
the sexual instincts fatally pathological.

In "Français, encore un effort . . ." Sade elaborates an entire legal system based on women's generalized prostitution, while Luce Irigaray's parody, "Françaises, ne faites plus un effort . . . ," turns the tables on the male pornographers. For Sade, "it is certain, in a state of Nature, that women are born *vulguivaguous*, that is to say, are born enjoying the advantages of female animals and belonging, like them, to all males."[39] Women are all the more in the foreground of the Sadean scene because their fate is already decided and controlled by men's discourse. This apparent paradox brings about the function of woman's *jouissance* in the theoretical and legal power of the libertine's language. For Irigaray, "the pornographic scene can be viewed paradigmatically as the initiation and training of a woman who is and continues to be virginal with respect to the pleasure that some man purports to be teaching her."[40] Women's virginity, their ignorance, is finally a prerequisite for both the vampire and the pornographer. Furthermore, Irigaray argues, woman's pleasure is not even an issue— women's orgasms are necessary as a demonstration of masculine power: "Their [women's] training is designed to subject them to an exclusively phallocratic sexual economy."[41] Mary de Caumont's "liberation" consists in denying herself any distinct female identity. Like Raoule de Vénérande, she resists the maternal model which is naturally attributed to her: "I cynically tell you: I don't want to be a mother, first because I don't want to suffer, second, because I don't want the child to suffer. I know no human power capable to make me change." (Je vous dis cyniquement: je ne veux pas être mère, d'abord parce que je ne veux pas souffrir, ensuite parce que je ne veux pas faire souffrir. Je ne connais pas de puissance humaine capable de me faire fléchir) (*Marquise de Sade*, 215). Mary's abandonment of maternity operates in the same way as the Marquis de Sade's professed victimization of mothers. But as a full-fledged libertine, Mary speaks and acts like the phallocrats: she seduces, strikes, dominates men weaker than herself. "Token women, they're called. For the techniques for pleasure applied in pornography have hardly been suited for women's pleasure."[42] Mary's sexual knowledge is never explicitly established like that of the Sadean male. However, Mary loves blood: "The libertine loves blood. At least the blood that flows according to his own techniques."[43] In acquiring a taste for blood, Mary puts herself under the influence of the anemic mother. Her initial repulsion is transformed into an insatiable thirst for blood in an effort to transform pain into pleasure.

In *La Marquise de Sade*, the traditional couple of male executioner and female victim has been inverted. Mary bleeds her lover, Paul de Caumont, her husband's bastard son, according to typical Sadean methods: "Docile, mocking his own revolts, he used to give her his arms to plow with a hairpin, a very bad copper pin with which she tattooed her initials, first poking softly, then writing the letter in the burning skin" (Docile, se moquant avec elle de ses révoltes, il lui tendait ses bras pour qu'elle s'amusât à les labourer d'une épingle à cheveux, une pointe de métal cuivrée très mauvaise, elle le tatouait de ses initiales, appuyant d'abord doucement, puis écrivant la lettre dans la chair vive) (*Marquise de Sade*, 272). The effraction of the skin is the result of an inscription, but this time it is the marquise who writes her name in her lover's arms. Irigaray asks, "What fantasy of a closed, solid, virginal body to be forced open underlies such a representation, and such a practice, of sexuality?"[44] The marquise's act of inscribing an effraction thus becomes the symbolic equivalent of penetrating a virgin womb. Paul tolerates this apparent abuse for the simple reason that he feels guilty for having raped her in the first place: "Didn't he rape her during their first date?" (Ne l'avait-il pas violée lors de leur premier rendez-vous?) (*Marquise de Sade*, 272). Her symbolic imposition of will is thus finally only a kind of getting even. Rachilde's concern with Mary's neurotic etiology leaves the memory of rape dormant, for Mary does not remember it at all. It is, in fact, Paul who silently recalls the rape. The bloody inscription thus marks the trace of her unconscious memory, which she repeats precisely in order to keep it out of consciousness. Repressed traumatic memories are indefinitely repeated in Mary's pornographic scenes: "It never stops. It always has to start over. One more time. And another. The alibi of pleasure covers the need for endless reiteration."[45]

Mary's repetition compulsion becomes increasingly more tyrannical. The pursuit of pleasure is finally left to fantasies. She sees transvestites, but her pleasure inheres in her memory of her visions. Her capacity for pleasure grows increasingly remote from reality:

> She would take an ideal pleasure in the death agony of one of these men [transvestites], incapable of defending himself against a woman. A good plan . . . that she wouldn't, perhaps, carry out, but would brighten her thoughts during many grim days.

> Ce serait une idéale volupté que lui fournirait l'agonie d'un de ces hommes, peu capable de se défendre d'une femme. Un fin projet . . . qu'elle ne mettrait pas à exécution, mais qui lui aurait illuminé la pensée durant bien des jours sombres. (*Marquise de Sade*, 295)

In assuming man's indefensible claim to privilege and strength, the Marquise de Sade refuses women's subservience and traditional gender relations. But the important point is that she does so at a terrible cost. Her turn to sexual fantasy as an adequate means of seeking *jouissance* reveals the depth of her dilemma. Like Baudelaire's poet, her desire is excited only by the delusive trappings of gender: "Which poet would dare, in describing the pleasure caused by a beautiful woman, to separate the woman from her costume?" (Quel poète oserait, dans la peinture du plaisir causé par l'apparition d'une beauté, séparer la femme de son costume?).[46] So too Rachilde's transvestite puts on "the mask of womanliness": "That one, discreetly made up like a lady imitating a whore, wearing bracelets under his man's sleeve" (Celui-là, fardé discrétement comme une femme du monde qui imite une fille publique, laissant deviner des bracelets sous sa manchette masculine) (*Marquise de Sade*, 294). Mary's hatred of the transvestite remains one of the most troubling aspects of this novel.

"MADEMOISELLE BAUDELAIRE"

Her fantasy of achieving sexual *jouissance* by killing the transvestite is an effort to murder the masculine complex in whose grip she remains; it is thus also a suicidal fantasy insofar as she too is (psychically) a man who dresses like a woman. Following a classic psychoanalytic paradigm, let us assume that the transvestite becomes a woman so that he might become the mother he never had, so that he might, disguised, love another man who, psychically, will be a figure of himself; he dresses like a woman so that he can love another man the way his mother should have (but didn't) love him. This familiar paradigm of transvestite homosexuality helps us to understand why Mary finds the transvestite so repugnant and hateful, why all her rage and passion are predicated on fantasies of his annihilation. As we shall soon see, Mary's final fantasy, like the transvestite's, is of becoming her own mother. She hates the transvestite for two reasons: he is a version of herself, but inverted, a version in which she sees the instability of her own identifications; and he is a figure for her thus far foreclosed identification with her mother, the very lack in her desire that has thus far silently organized her desire. In her final, fatal fantasy, the form of this foreclosed identification becomes unmistakable. The purely visual and fantasmatic experience with the transvestite comes to no apparent conclusion in the text. It remains enigmatic and unreadable—that is, unless we fail to see that the concluding fantasy of maternal identification is in fact the denouement and explication of the entire transvestite sequence.

But before turning to the psychoanalytic deep structure of the transvestite's relation to Mary, let us consider the more obvious, but no less important, social text. To the extent that Mary has always struggled to achieve a feminine identity that is markedly dominating and nonsubmissive, the transvestite would appear to her only as wearing what Joan Riviere calls "the mask of womanly subservience." In her article "Womanliness as a Masquerade" (1929), Riviere describes womanliness as mimicry; to be a woman is to dissimulate a fundamental masculinity. At times Riviere seems to be critical of the masquerade, which she describes as "compulsive ogling and coquetting" and as an inappropriate betrayal of true ability; at other times she seems to see it as answering to "the essential nature of fully developed femininity."[47] The discrepancy between the masquerade and womanliness is represented in *La Marquise de Sade* by the figure of the transvestite. The masquerade entails the coexistence and the negation of both woman and the transvestite. The transvestite reflects the form of Mary's desire. For Riviere, the overachievement of the phallic woman is necessarily compensated by her mask of womanliness, whereas for Rachilde, Mary appears to want to kill the transvestite precisely because he embodies her own feminine otherness. Her masculine supremacy can be fully attained only on the condition of destroying the feminine other.

We might speculate that this is how Rachilde intended us to read Mary's contempt for the transvestite. But we are after something more than that. The enigmatic maternal identification with which the text concludes turns our attention onto Rachilde herself, for at this point we may be witness to the unconscious form of Rachilde's own sexual fantasy.

What I want to suggest is that the form of Rachildean fantasy ultimately depends upon the foreclosure of maternal identification, and that, despite this foreclosure, the image of the fantastically strong and dominant mother takes precedence in each of her texts. The male pseudonym thus becomes the cipher for the uncanny return of the power of the mother.

In spite of her mother's efforts, Rachilde identified herself with the father:

> I secretly admired my father without trying to find out his unworthiness. I admired him in spite of the whip blows, for reasons which belonged to typical feminine childishness: because he could stare at the sun like the eagles; because he was an excellent horseback rider and went to war.

> En secret j'admirais mon père sans essayer de me rendre compte de son indignité. Je l'admirais malgrè les coups de cravache, pour des raisons d'une puérilité toute féminine: parce

qu'il pouvait regarder le soleil en face, comme les aigles; parce
qu'il montait très bien à cheval et qu'il avait fait la guerre.
(*Pourquoi je ne suis pas féministe*, 17)

By relegating the mother to the sidelines—the mad Gabrielle or
the dead Caroline—Rachilde/Mary de Caumont makes sure that
no relation with her is possible. Like the mother's mask, the
transvestite's is deceitful. The fantasmatic desire to kill the transvestite is the acknowledgment of the daughter's desire to kill her
mother. In wanting to kill the transvestite, Mary wants to destroy
that which threatens the return of the foreclosed mother. She is
the Marquise de Sade, the cruel dominatrix whose violently
masculine identifications keep identification with the mother at
bay: "She would take him [the transvestite] along home, would
cover him with her jewels, would wrap him up with laces, would
make him drink her best wines, and without trading with him
anything else but his repulsive life, she would kill him with red-
hot pins" (Et elle l'amènerait chez elle, le couvrirait de ses bijoux,
l'entortillerait de ses dentelles, le griserait de ses meilleurs vins, et
sans lui demander en échange autre chose que sa vie répugnante,
elle le tuerait avec des épingles rougies au feu) (*Marquise de Sade*,
295). This fantasy is the key to the self-creation of the phallic
woman.

Parodying a well-known passage in the Marquis de Sade's
"Yet Another Effort, Frenchmen," Rachilde describes the Marquise's excesses as proceeding precisely from the act of matricide:

> Her life blossomed in excess through what has been called by
> the philosophers *decadence*, the end of everything. After the
> Morgue; naturalist novels; wax museums on the boulevard; the
> deeds of the poisoning spiritualists, there were brothels where
> old men with decorations are whipped; literary cabarets where
> young boys, nearly children, discuss the possibility of killing
> their mother as soon as they have raped her.

> Sa vie s'épanouit en des exagérations à travers ce que les
> philosophes du siècle appellent la *décadence*, la fin de tout. Après
> la Morgue; les romans naturalistes; les musées de cire de boule-

vard; les exploits des empoisonneurs spirituels, il restait encore
les maisons capitonnées bien closes, où l'on fustige des vieil-
lards décorés; les cabarets de lettres où de jeunes garçons,
presque des enfants, causent de la possibilité de tuer leur mère
dès qu'ils l'auront violée. (*Marquise de Sade*, 285)

The parodic tone defends against the more disturbing echoes
that link Mary's experience to the injunctions of the divine
Marquis and cannot be laughed away. This passage recalls, of
course, the famous injunction: "O you who wish to venture upon
this difficult and thorny career, bear in mind that the novelist is
the child of Nature, that she has created him to be her painter; if
he does not become his mother's lover the moment she gives
birth to him, let him never write, for we shall never read him."[48]
La Marquise de Sade takes this very seriously indeed.

The relation between beginning a career as a writer and the
murder of mothers should not be taken lightly, for Gabrielle
Eymery herself spread rumors that her daughter's writings were
plagiarized. The elimination of the mother in, of all places,
Charenton asylum bears a Sadean-oedipal resonance that is far
from merely fortuitous.

At the end of the novel, Mary's fantasy takes the form of an
imaginary invalid; she decides, in other words, to seek her pleasure in feigning illness, in seeking her pleasure in the place of the
mother. Her mother was actually an invalid and sought, as we
saw, alleviation from her anemia by drinking blood. Now, Mary
finds her pleasure in the maternal act that she once found most
repugnant and in the place she found most detestable. In her final
performance, Mary becomes her anemic, blood-drinking mother.
I am arguing that this concluding and conclusive identification
provides the missing closure and the actualization to the transvestite fantasy: "She slipped in among those people, held out her
cup like them, drank with a delicate enjoyment concealed by a
tubercular mask" (Elle se glissa parmi ces gens, tendit son gobelet
comme eux, but avec une jouissance délicate qu'elle dissimula
sous des aspects de poitrinaire) (*Marquise de Sade*, 296). Once
again, the fantasmatic mother returns, and the foreclosed figure

who cannot be remembered is literally repeated, brought back to life.

Nothing could be further from the Rachildean text than the celebration of mother-daughter relations in the writings of Luce Irigaray. But, strangely, they meet at the point where they seem most distant, for the ghost of the mother invariably returns in Rachilde. Try as she may, Rachilde can never exorcise the gender difference that is inscribed in language.

In *Parler n'est jamais neutre*, Irigaray maintains that language is constructed on a mother-based relation:

> We must add that this language [*langue*], neutral in dictionaries or theories, was first conceived as maternal language [*langue maternelle*] or "mother's tongue," with its sexual, social determinants to which overdetermined, plural economies have to be added.

> Il faut cependant ajouter que cette langue, neutre dans les dictionnaires ou les théories, s'est trouvée d'abord imputée en tant que *langue maternelle*, ou en tant que *langage de la mère*, avec ses déterminants sexuels, sociaux, aux économies plurielles, surdéterminées.[49]

In rejecting both motherhood and social determinants, Rachilde's heroines are perfectly aware of being anarchist rebels who are doomed to death. Women cannot emerge from the relation to the maternal body in Rachilde's texts, and they fail tragically in their rebellion against it.

The return to a Sadean model is unsatisfactory because there the mother is still the site of privileged victimization. Unable to find a way to return to the mother, Rachilde invents a genealogy that short-circuits procreation. Once again, her self-creation is not without a dose of self-parody. Nevertheless, the insistence with which she proffers this imaginary genealogy belies the grave issues underlying it. Rachilde writes under an aporetic interdiction, an irresolvable double bind: the very barriers she builds against the mother-daughter relation invariably turn into the means by which that relation reasserts its spectral presence.

RACHILDE

Rachilde's imaginary genealogy is an effort to stand outside human as well as maternal generation. In constructing it, she borrows gothic elements from the werewolf legend and from what she calls her "dreadful atavism." In *Face à la peur,* as on several other occasions, she returns to the family curse which she believes has set her free from humanity itself:

> Because I was born of such a Catholic family, I can truly believe that I belong to the sacred colleges! My great-grandfather was an honorary canon of Perigueux cathedral who got married during the Revolution. Besides, it turns me into a creature cursed by the Church since I come from a sacrilege, *a werewolf.* When I learnt this, I was filled with mad joy; I finally belong to the animal race!

> Or, je suis née d'une famille tellement catholique, que je puis vraiment me croire de la lignée des sacrés collèges! J'ai pour arrière-grand-père un chanoine honoraire de la cathédrale de Périgueux, lequel prince de l'église s'est marié à la Révolution. En outre, cela fait de moi une créature maudite par l'église puisque je proviens d'un sacrilège, *un loup-garou.* Quand j'appris cela, je fus remplie d'une joie folle; j'appartiens enfin à la race animale![50]

Rachilde's identification with that which lies outside human law and society is founded on a conflation of Catholic excommunication and ancient legend. What is most obvious is the eagerness with which she takes this imaginary curse as a very legitimate pretext on which to establish her union with "the animal race."

Her nonhuman origin entails as well the absence of a name: "What does a name mean when it is after all, only a pseudonym?" (Que signifie un nom qui n'est, après tout, qu'un pseudonyme?) (*Face à la peur,* 64). In *L'Animale* (1893), *La Fille du louvetier* (1903), and above all *Le Meneur de louves* (1905), the daughter's revolt takes the form of the violence of the wolf. In *Le Meneur de louves* (*The Leader of the She-Wolves*) Rachilde draws out all the implications of her thinking about the mother-daughter relation and links them to this fantastic genealogy.

"MADEMOISELLE BAUDELAIRE"

The Werewolf Legend Revisited: *Le Meneur de louves*

> Phantasies of being seduced are of particular interest, because
> so often they are not phantasies but real memories.
> SIGMUND FREUD, *Introductory Lectures on Psychoanalysis*

In *Le Meneur de louves*, Rachilde elaborates her family romance in a very particular historical context: against the backdrop of France during the sixth century, she focuses on the revolt of Basine and her cousin Clotild against the abbess Leubovère in Saint Radegund's convent. The historical setting of the novel was inspired by Gregory of Tours's *The History of the Franks*. As Jennifer Birkett aptly observes, *Le Meneur de louves* is "Rachilde's last attempt to play the rebellious young barbarian."[51] As we will see, this historical novel is Rachilde's most searching analysis of the daughter's resistance to maternal power.

Rachilde describes the struggle of King Chilperic's daughter, Princess Basine, whom the abbess Leubovère holds prisoner at Saint Radegund on the order of the princess's stepmother, Queen Fredegund. Clotild, Basine's royal cousin, who is also imprisoned at Saint Radegund, joins Basine in her effort to seek the help of Harog, the titular hero, in their attempt to overthrow the tyrannical abbess. Harog, who is the leader of the royal hunt, usually assembles his pack of hounds in order to chase wolves. Now, allied with Basine and Clotild, he in effect becomes instead "the leader of the she-wolves," that is, of the ferocious and rebellious young women. Moreover, Harog falls in love with Basine. Having witnessed her rape, Harog recognizes from the outset the injustice of her subsequent imprisonment at Saint Radegund. But in spite of his efforts to raise an army in defense of Basine and Clotild, their revolt fails and the power of Leubovère is reestablished. At the end Harog is murdered, Clotild is excommunicated, and Basine enigmatically disappears into the forest with Harog's favorite dog.

Following the text of Gregory of Tours's history, the revolt of the daughters in Rachilde's novel is directed against Queen

Fredegund and Leubovère. What Rachilde found most gripping in *The History of the Franks* was the account of the revolt of Princess Basine. To the historical narrative, Rachilde adds the symbolic transformation of Basine and her cousin Clotild into angry she-wolves. Rachilde's narrative is constructed around Basine's rape, an event to which Gregory devotes only a single sentence: "After having been ill used by the Queen's servants . . . [she] was sent to a convent and took religious orders" (Après avoir servi de jouet aux serviteurs de la reine . . . fut envoyée dans un monastère où elle prit l'habit religieux).[52]

Rachilde develops Basine's ecclesiastical revolt into what can only be compared to the sort of anarchist upheavals that were unfolding in the late 1890s. The link between the mystical Middle Ages and the anarchist movement is a familiar one: "The anarchist madness is perhaps definitely passed; but mysticism, which bore it, has been, is and will be always; only this mysticism will transform itself following the centuries; religious in the Middle Ages, it has shown itself anarchist in our fin-de-siècle."[53]

Gregory himself describes the revolt of Basine and Clotild as a criminal enterprise: "I have told you how Clotild was set upon rebellion and had gathered round her a band of cut-throats, evil-doers, fornicators, fugitives from justice and men guilty of every crime in the calendar."[54] In her fictional elaboration of this incident, Rachilde gives this anonymous "band of cut-throats" a leader, Harog, the wolf hunter. Basine is apotheosized as an "angel lit up by a warrior's vision" (ange illuminée par une vision guerrière). Rachilde's rewriting of Gregory's chronicle expands the daughter's rebellion by making her a tragic symbol of anarchist insurrection.

I want now to turn to the significance of the way in which Rachilde presents the rape. As we have just seen, Rachilde in effect stresses the rape on the basis of what is no more than an enigmatic suggestion in Gregory's text. But this is only the beginning of Rachilde's highly idiomatic way of developing this interpellated incident. What Rachilde wants to emphasize is the demonstrative nature of the crime, and she does so by focusing a great deal of attention on the framing devices in which the rape is witnessed and in which it must be understood. To this end she incorporates in her narrative the equivalent of the pointing hand that appears in the margins of some medieval manuscripts. If a medieval writer anticipated that a reader might question or have doubts about a passage in his text, the writer could choose to include a colophon marker, a hand pointing to a particular passage, which called attention to the text, reinforced its significance, and, by implication, tried to obviate any potential incomprehension or resistance on the part of the reader. Rachilde's equivalent of the marginal device points not only to her own determination to emphasize this event but also to the question of doubt and interpretation itself. As we have seen, Rachilde establishes a central narrative incident on a mere phrase in Gregory's text. There is uncertainty about the legitimacy of her intervention from the outset.

In the narrative itself, Harog, who witnesses the rape, is himself uncertain about what he has seen. His confusion thus doubles Rachilde's own uncertainty about the nature of her invention. The figure of the hand becomes the cipher of the larger question of the authenticity of the event itself. More precisely, Rachilde focuses the reader's interest on the hand behind the curtain that Harog sees during the crime. Harog is uncertain about the reality of the crime he has witnessed, about whether what he has seen was real or imagined. It is not until the mysterious hand behind the curtain reappears in the king's tent that Harog is certain that Basine has been raped by order of the queen; her hand behind the curtain effectively signs the crime with her signature.

Here is Harog's confused vision of the rape: "In the middle of the abominable circle of these drunk armed soldiers, there was a couple lying: the big bearded soldier on top, the white girl underneath" (Au milieu d'une ronde abominable de ces lourds gens d'armes, tous ivres, il y avait un couple renversé: le grand soldat barbu dessus, la fille blanche dessous) (*Meneur de louves*, 18). The scene he witnesses is incomprehensible until he can reconstruct it the next day in the king's tent. The narrator's voice reinforces the significance of the enigmatic hand that appears on the curtain of the king's tent like the typographical hand drawn in the margin of a text: "This hand, seen from Harog's place, seemed to be at the same time very small and powerful, so powerful that it seemed to hold the king's household in the curtain fold" (Cette main, de l'endroit où se trouvait Harog, paraissait à la fois toute petite et fort puissante, si puissante qu'elle avait l'air de tenir toute la maison du roi dans le pli du rideau) (*Meneur de louves*, 17).

Harog's uncertainty about Fredegund's hand doubles Rachilde's uncertainty about the reality of the rape scene. What is important here is that the doubling of the uncertainty from Rachilde's reading of a text to Harog's reading of an event implies the irreducibility of uncertainty; and this is not just any event or any uncertainty, since it surrounds the pivotal scene in which Basine becomes a rebellious daughter. The effect of the frame within a frame sets off a series of displacements that cannot be arrested. No subsequent protestations of certainty can offset the instability that organizes Rachilde's narrative imagination in this novel. Consider further that this is a crime choreographed by a manipulative stepmother, the evil Queen Radegund, who had earlier slain Basine's natural mother. This is indeed the primal scene of *Le Meneur de louves* insofar as it constitutes the crisis of interpretation itself, the irresolvable crisis of interpreting what is real and what is imagined. And the content of this crisis is nothing less than the scene in which the symbolic mother presides over the daughter's violation, which triggers the daughter's rebellion and leads to the daughter's inevitable defeat.

Even after Harog's certainty has been established, he remains silent, and hence Basine's accusation will be invalidated by King Chilperic: "Harog, leave shortly and take away the rebel, this hellish girl who spent the night in my soldiers' arms like the most immodest of my slaves" (Harog, partez sans tarder, en emportant d'ici la rebelle, cette fille d'enfer qui s'est laissée aller cette nuit même aux bras de mes soldats comme la plus impudique de mes esclaves) (*Meneur de louves*, 26). With Basine imprisoned in Saint

Radegund's convent, the queen has rid herself of a dangerous and legitimate rival to Chilperic's throne.

The epistemological status of the rape in this novel opens onto the fundamental cross-currents of Rachilde's thinking. On the one hand, she reads Gregory's history in the way that contemporary theorists and feminists read Freud's renunciation of his "seduction theory"—that is, Gregory's text appears to have inscribed the reality of the rape in the very act of attempting to erase it. The rape remains despite and as this erasure. Likewise Freud, after years of insisting on the reality of sexual seduction as a central factor in the etiology of hysteria, turned finally to a psychical rather than a historical explanation of the victim's symptoms. Rachilde is thus challenging established authority and reinscribing the truth of women's experience despite the efforts of men to place them under erasure. But on the other hand, and we must not forget this "other hand," Rachilde also insists that such efforts at revelation invariably fail. Her narrative denouement ends in complicity with the forces of erasure rather than restitution. Above all, we must insist that there is no way to separate Rachildean textuality from this double bind: on the one hand, revolutionary feminist anarchy, and on the other, the return of conventional bourgeois order.

The inviolability of maternal power is inscribed in *Le Meneur de louves* at a still more profound level. At the very moment when we most suspect that Basine will be redeemed in her rebellion, Rachilde once again reveals the futility of resistance. In her confinement in the convent, Basine discovers what she hopes will be a decisive tool in her struggle for liberation. We might also recall here the violence of the King's condemnation of his daughter to what he regards as well-deserved punishment. It is during her confinement in the convent that Basine discovers one of the most astonishing proofs of the mother superior's cruelty.

What Basine discovers deep within the convent is a recluse who has lived since what appears to be time immemorial in conditions of unspeakable filth and abjection. In the recluse, Basine's fate is taken to unimaginable extremities. The recluse is the ultimate expression of the unfathomable cruelty of maternal tyranny. She lives at the bottom of a pit, her punishment for trying to escape from the convent: "A hole had to be dug, then it had to be filled with a rough mixture of stones and clay. At the level of a man's height, there was a crack big enough to insert a piece of bread" (On avait dû creuser un trou, puis le reboucher avec un grossier mélange de cailloux et de glaise. A hauteur d'homme demeurait une fente: juste la place de glisser un morceau de pain) (*Meneur de louves*, 68). Once again, Rachilde is turning the tables on Gregory of Tours, who regards the recluse's squalid fate as well-deserved treatment for her treachery. For him, the recluse is another figure of the religious revolt which threatens not only the abbess's authority but the power of the fathers of the Church:

> At this time there lived in the nunnery a certain recluse who, a few years before, had lowered herself from the wall and fled to Saint Hilary's church, accusing her Mother Superior of many transgressions. Later on she had herself pulled up into the nunnery from which she had previously lowered herself down. She asked permission to shut herself up in a secret cell. When the revolt started, she broke down the door of her cell, escaped from the nunnery, found the way to Clotild and, as she had done on the previous occasion, made a series of allegations against her Mother Superior. (*History of the Franks*, 532)

For Rachilde, the recluse's self-abjection constitutes in *Le Meneur de louves* the scandal of Saint Radegund. But the irony lies in the fact, which is of course invented by Rachilde, that after years of confinement the recluse has been entirely broken and dehumanized; all she can do is mutter meaningless fragments of prayer. She is thus of no use at all to Basine in her struggle against the mother superior: "Harog heard vague Latin words uttered in an equal clapping of the tongue; without accent or breath, the recluse was speaking as if in a half-sleep state.... She only spoke in fragments of church sentences" (Harog saisit de vagues mots latins prononcés d'un égal clappement de langue; sans accent et sans souffle, la recluse parlait comme dans une sorte de demi-sommeil. . . . Elle ne parlait que par lambeaux de phrases d'église) (*Meneur de louves*, 69, 177).

Rachilde herself suffered two years in a convent: "Between sixteen and eighteen, my parents sent me to a convent in black Perigord where I either had to take the veil or accept a most advantageous marriage according to their wise expectation" (De seize à dix-huit ans, mes parents me mirent dans un couvent du Périgord noir où je devais selon leur sage prévision, prendre le voile ou consentir enfin à un mariage des plus avantageux) (*Face à la peur*, 51). Behind the parental decision to lock her in a convent, we might suspect the lurking presence of Gabrielle, who probably persuaded Rachilde's father to rid himself of a difficult daughter for two years. Rachilde even gives us a retrospective clue that might link Gabrielle to the cruel mother superior. Near the end of her life, she still resents the punishment visited on her by her parents in retribution for her refusal to marry according to their wishes. In the following passage, Rachilde uses the enigmatic pronoun *on* to speak of those who sent her to the convent. But who is this *on*? Is it "they?" "One?" Or might not the mother be silently lingering behind this ambiguous pronoun? I will translate *on*, for reasons that should be clear, as "she": "She [the mother] wishes only one thing, it's her going to the convent" (On ne désire, chez elle, qu'une chose, c'est qu'elle entre au couvent) (*Face à la peur*, 146). Why, above all, does Rachilde speak of herself in the third person? Because, I suggest, she has in such crucial instances become an object of the other's desires; her exclusion becomes the focal point of what the other wants. This is, of course, a speculation, but it points to the fundamental issues underlying *Le Meneur de louves*, to which we will now turn.

Most important here is the question of Rachilde's divided and conflicted identifications both with the oppressive maternal power and with the oppressed victims, the daughters. Her narratives require a double strategy in which to elaborate this double identification. Rachilde is the *only one* to have escaped the ravages of maternal power, and because she has done so, she is in a privileged position from which to diagnose the failure of other women to escape its grasp. It is as though she were saying with every novel: "I, Rachilde, could elude the spectral grasp of maternal power, but you other daughters, you have no chance to circumvent her inexorable tyranny." With one stroke of the pen she indicts the mother, while with the other she shows that maternal oppression is incontrovertible. On the one hand, Rachilde writes as a committed feminist, and indeed at times as a quasi-anarchist. On the other hand, she presumes that she herself stands above the fray and that while she herself managed to find her way to liberation, other women, the protagonists in her fictions, must again and again go down to defeat. In Lacanian terms, we might say that Rachilde herself stands in a privileged relation to the other and that she does so at the price of insisting that the others are incapable of gaining access to it. This is what empowers her as a writer. The difficulty in reading Rachilde is to keep this irreducibly double strategy constantly before one's eyes and not lapse into one or another of its phases.

Rachilde's obvious contempt for religious extremism and for the Catholic mystical tradition is clear and resounding in her depiction of the fate of the recluse. It is with her deeply anticlerical attitude that she rejoins her defrocked great-grandfather's exemplary role. The extremity of the recluse's fate could serve as well as a fitting emblem for all those who are unable to withstand tyrannical power, those who indeed fall fully under its sway:

These people, more naive than guilty, finally saw the reason of their fight against the representation of the divine power stand in front of them. She [the recluse] was there, a living corpse, standing up between the pleasures of earth, and this golden light, too infinite, too imponderable to be able to move them in their flesh.

Ces gens, plus naïfs que coupables, voyaient enfin se dresser la raison de leur lutte contre ce qui était la représentation du pouvoir divin. Elle était bien là, en squelette vivant, debout entre les joies de la terre, et cette lumière d'or, trop infinie, trop impondérable pour arriver à les toucher dans leur chair. (*Meneur de louves*, 218)

Like Basine's imprisonment, the recluse's confinement marks the borderline between the human and the inhuman, and, beyond that, between the living and the dead; she literally becomes "a living corpse." The recluse reveals how devastating, how utterly annihilating, the power of the other can be. It is almost as though Rachilde has here glimpsed an uncanny vision of the power of the mother to determine the fate of the daughter even beyond the grave, as though the daughter, though reduced to a corpse, still remains in the power of the mother superior.

Let us turn to another element of Basine's rebellion. Rachilde makes much of the distinction between Basine's intelligence and the ignorance of the mother superior: "Basine had been raised carefully, studying the sacred manuscripts. She knew since childhood what Leubovère could not even learn at the end of her life" (Basine avait été élevée avec soin dans l'étude des manuscrits sacrés. Depuis son enfance, elle savait ce que Leubovère ne pouvait même pas apprendre au déclin de sa vie) (*Meneur de louves*, 95). This makes Basine's defeat even more painful and unjust. It is characteristic of Rachilde, however, that she distresses her readers, and doubtless herself, with the spectacle of such wasted promise.

Let us turn to the end of the novel. The first of the following two citations is from Gregory's *History of the Franks*, and the second is Rachilde's text, which she explicitly cites from Gregory and which provides the final judgment on which she concludes her most ambitious novel. I leave Rachilde's text untranslated because it differs only negligibly from Gregory's text:

> When we ordered them to beg forgiveness of their Abbess for the wrong which they had done, and to make good the damage caused by their evil behaviour, they had refused to do so. Instead they pressed on with their plan to kill her, as they had now confessed in public. We have opened the canons and we

have consulted them. Our decision is that these two [Basine and Clotild] must in all justice be cut off from communion until they have done proper penance. The Abbess must be restored to her position permanently. (*History of the Franks*, 574–75)

Et nous, ci-dessus nommés, ayant prononcé que les religieuses devaient demander à l'abbesse pardon de leur faute et réparer le mal qu'elles avaient causé: mais elles ayant refusé de le faire et s'étant efforcées au contraire de tuer l'abbesse, ce qu'elles ont publiquement avoué, nous donc, après avoir ouvert et relu les canons, avons jugé de toute équité que les coupables soient privées de la communion jusqu'à ce qu'elles aient fait une pénitence suffisante et que l'abbesse soit rétablie dans sa dignité pour y rester. (*Meneur de louves*, 283)

The text of this ecclesiastical judgment concludes the novel. It is significant because it formally reestablishes the hegemony of the maternal. It provides an almost juridical finality to the ill-fated romantic struggle of the central protagonists, who all perish or are eliminated in one way or another: the recluse dies grotesquely by drowning in wine; Harog is murdered; and Basine disappears from the world of human beings. Rachilde could not make the point more emphatically: the reign of the mothers continues unimpeded.

And our decision was that no charge could be made against the Abbess. We gave her some paternal advice on the small points which had been raised, and we suggested that she take care not to expose herself to such criticism in future. (*History of the Franks*, 573)

N'ayant trouvé aucun crime à l'abesse qui pût la faire renvoyer, nous l'avons exhortée et admonestée paternellement, pour les fautes légères, à ne plus s'exposer à encourir de réprimandes par la suite. (Appendix, *Meneur de louves*, 282).

Basine's disappearance into the forest entails, however, a significant exception to this otherwise almost hermetic closure.

"MADEMOISELLE BAUDELAIRE"

That her fate is only implied, never made clear, is one of the most extraordinary things about this novel. Though she appears to be doomed to extinction in the forest, it must be said that Rachilde leaves open the possibility that Basine and her canine companion will live another life, forever outside human society. The ending is thus irreducibly doubled: the rebellion of the daughters is formally and finally defeated, and the daughter, the unique survivor, goes on to lead another existence, a savage or animal existence. Is not Basine like Rachilde in her determination to stand outside human genealogy? In *Le Meneur de louves* the double strategy of Rachilde's writing reaches its most extreme expression: the mother-daughter relation leads at once to absolute closure and irresolvable paradox.

Rachilde relives her own experience as "femme supérieure" through her heroines and at the same time jealously guards her role as the privileged feminine subject whose experience of masculine identification and maternal resistance endows her with a unique perspective from which she recognizes the impossibility of "liberating" women in general. In *Pourquoi je ne suis pas féministe,* she summarizes her opinion about women when she declares:

> Women are man's inferior brothers, simply because they have physical miseries which prevent them from having *the sort of coherent thinking* that men in general have, even the least intelligent.

> Les femmes sont les frères inférieurs de l'homme, simplement parce qu'elles ont des misères physiques les éloignant de la *suite dans les idées* que peuvent concevoir tous les hommes en général, même les moins intelligents. (*Pourquoi,* 10)

This is a rather virulent misogyny by any reckoning. It is precisely in order to escape this delusive sense of female identity that Rachilde posits her fantasy of the werewolf genealogy. The metaphor of the she-wolf aptly describes Rachilde's lonely heroines. The werewolf myth is expressive of her longing for an impossible genealogy and of her need to believe in her own genealogical superiority.

A Woman's Legend: Don Juan

When Don Juan went down to that last river and had given
Charon his coin, a grim beggar proud as the first Cynic venge-
fully rowed him across.

CHARLES BAUDELAIRE, *Fleurs du Mal*

In concluding this chapter, I want to look at Rachilde's *La Jongleuse*
(1900) as a novelistic parody of feminism in which the contradictions and impasses of Rachildean thinking are fully displayed. In
her preface to the French reprint of *La Jongleuse*, Claude Dauphiné
remarks that the novel "gives a critical view of women's oppression," and it does so, according to Dauphiné, through a "car-
icatural" presentation of woman's fantasms.[55]

The heroine of the novel, Eliante Donalger, a Creole living in
Paris, wants to entice her young suitor, Leon Reille, to marry her
niece Missie. Eliante's resistance to Leon's desire signals her will
to power and her reappropriation of male sexual identification.
Juggling with knives is for Rachilde the means through which
Eliante can create her own language, her own artistic expression.
Juggling is another clever subversion of decadent motifs and can
be read as an experiment in the radical scrambling of definitions.
Instead of developing motifs and themes of cross-dressing and
female dominance, as Rachilde did in *Monsieur Vénus* and *La Marquise de Sade*, respectively, here she seems to adopt gender stereotypes only in order to demonstrate their absurdity. For Leon, the
cynical medical student, Eliante's juggling is incomprehensible:
"He kept for himself the pain of seeing her there, standing and
juggling, separated from her family, from society, from the whole
world, from all of human society by the enigma of her perpetual
comedy."[56] (Il gardait pour lui la douleur de la voir là, debout et
jonglant, séparée de sa famille, de la société, du monde entier, de
toute l'humanité par l'énigme de sa comédie perpétuelle) (*La
Jongleuse*, 143). The comedy, however, ends in tragedy when
Eliante commits suicide while juggling her knives. Her sacrificial
death allows the marriage of Missie and Leon to take place while

assuring that woman's reproductive power continues. Missie's pregnancy is in fact Eliante's legacy, and her sacrifice is ultimately the representation of women's victimization reenacted by her death. Eliante's short-lived independence and refusal of sexuality · are furthermore manifestations of male-female power relations. The end of *The Juggler* constitutes an ironical sexual transgression by having Eliante evade Leon's embrace while marrying off her niece to him.

In the preface to her translation of *La Jongleuse*, Melanie Hawthorne stresses how appropriate it is "that Eliante's blend of sorcery and hysteria should be situated in 1897, the year when Freud recognized the similarities between the behavior of witches and the hysterics he was treating" (*The Juggler*, xxi). Eliante suffers from the characteristic hysteric revulsion with sex: "I'm disgusted by union, which destroys my strength, I find no delightful plenitude in it. For my flesh to be roused and to conceive the infinity of pleasures, I don't need to look for a sex organ in the object of my love!" (*The Juggler*, 22). In *The Juggler*, Rachilde uses Eliante's chastity to attack both phallocentrism and its other.

The most curious thing about the novel is the manner in which Eliante derives sexual pleasure from standing inside an amphora. Rachilde never makes clear just how Eliante achieves satisfaction within the vase: "An alabaster vase the height of a man, so slim, so slender, so deliciously troubling with its ephebe's hips, with such a human appearance, even though it retained the traditional shape of an amphora" (Un vase d'albâtre de la hauteur d'un homme, si svelte, si élancé, si délicieusement troublant avec ses hanches d'éphèbe, d'une apparence tellement humaine, bien qu'il n'eût que la forme traditionnelle de l'amphore) (*The Juggler*, 18/*La Jongleuse*, 44–46). In practicing such eccentric sexual techniques, Eliante is, we are told, still in the grip of her late husband's sexual perversions. On the one hand, Eliante appears to be the liberated woman, free of male dependence, while on the other hand, her strange sexuality appears to be one long work of mourning which belies an inseparable attachment to her dead spouse. As Leon remarks, " 'Here, Eliante, I'm going to confess to you my real curiosity, the idea of a future doctor of medicine. I think you have leprosy, I'm taking exact note of your malady, heart or head' " ("Tenez, Eliante, je vais vous avouer ma véritable curiosité, une idée de futur docteur en médecine. Je crois que vous avez la lèpre, je me rends un compte exact de votre mal, coeur ou cerveau") (*The Juggler*, 17/*La Jongleuse*, 43–44). Like Raoule in *Monsieur Vénus*, Eliante seeks pleasure in the inanimate. Both heroines recall Rachilde's own bout of hysteria. Their difference is far more important, since Eliante perishes while Raoule achieves a kind of artistic self-fulfillment in her mourning charade. Leon's absurd diagnosis indicates how enigmatic the structure of female fantasy remains. Women's sexual resistance to normative behaviour is always seen as a malady which must be cured, whatever the cost. Eliante's tragedy, however parodically it is recounted, is that, despite her best effort, she cannot escape identifying with the very system she rejects.

In *The Female Malady*, Elaine Showalter describes in detail the most extreme and nightmarish efforts undertaken by nineteenth-century British doctors to manage women's minds by regulating their bodies. Because women were accustomed to being ordered to submit to the authority of their fathers, brothers, and husbands, doctors anticipated few problems in managing hysterical women and/or lunatics. Showalter demonstrates that they were wrong in their expectancy, and that rebellion was not infrequent: "Victorian madwomen were not easily silenced, and one often has the impression that their talkativeness, violation of feminine speech, and insistence on self-expression was the kind of behavior that had led to their being labeled 'mad' to begin with." Rachilde shows that men's attitudes toward women are repeatedly negative, and that such attitudes provoke women's rebellion and restlessness. Although it is impossible to reject sex absolutely, the decadents were to some extent pursuing a deliberately pessimistic policy. By exalting the "abnormal," the decadent sensibility accelerated the self-destruction it longed for. In Eliante's suicide, Rachilde seems to reappropriate for her own purposes what Jennifer Waelti-Walters calls an "androcentric taste for per-version into a gynocentric criticism of society."[57] In choosing her subjects, moreover, Rachilde is drawn to those women who seemed to be acting out the very fantasies that their societies condemned as inappropriate for them.

Leon's vision of Eliante comes very close to Dijkstra's description of "women's self-hatred as a result of the relentless indoctrination by the men around them." The figure of the vampire seems to appear here as a mockery of men's castration anxiety: "Eliante Donalger now seemed no more than a beautiful phantom to him, a vampire with a silvery belly, slipping, swaying" (Eliante Donalger ne lui apparaissait plus qu'en beau fantôme, un vampire au ventre argenté glissant, ondulant) (*The Juggler*, 90/*La Jongleuse*, 125). If Rachilde's dream in *Monsieur Vénus* was "to sacrifice the senses, the animal drive," she radicalizes this wish by having Eliante's sexuality manifested only in artistic creations. In killing off the vampire that Leon sees in her, Eliante is subverting the very form by which she is condemned by society. In characteristic Rachildean fashion, *The Juggler* is about the impossibility of discovering an "outside" to the patriarchal system. Eliante's suicide is both an acknowledgment of the impossibility of escape and a heroic act of defiance. Her numerous acts of self-mastery (e.g., juggling, knife-throwing, and self-induced orgasm) seem strangely at odds with her suicide, even though it is, I believe, Rachilde's aim to persuade us to see her suicide as precisely such a life-affirming act.

I want now to focus on one crucial element of Eliante's self-creation: her remarkable transformation of the Don Juan legend. Eliante recounts to her niece and Leon the story of a defrocked Spanish nun whom God transforms into a man in punishment for having challenged him: "She was wearing the altar decorations, and God, to punish her for the sacrilege, had changed her into . . . a man. But she died a *woman* and repentant, in front of My Lady the Virgin, whom she hadn't been able to seduce or wanted to offend" (Elle portait les ornements de l'autel, et Dieu, pour la punir de son sacrilège, l'avait changée en . . . homme. Mais elle mourut *femme* et repentante, devant Mme la Vierge, qu'elle n'avait pas pu séduire ou voulu offenser) (*The Juggler*, 201/*La Jongleuse*, 249). The legend of the female Don Juan enables Rachilde to indicate just how far female Don Juanism is from its male counterpart and to analyze a woman's very un-male need for repentance. Don Juan dies with no sense of guilt or remorse, while the female Don Juan begs the Virgin Mary's pardon. The young Spanish nun's liberation is short-lived and finally contradicted by her repentance. The overpowering portrait of Our Lady coincides with Rachilde's characteristic gesture: while advancing a bold female Don Juan legend, Rachilde is regressing to the most traditional forms of domination. However, Rachilde's insight is to locate power in Our Lady and to foreshadow Kristeva's analysis: "On the side of 'power,' *Maria Regina* appears in imagery as early as the sixth century in the church of Santa Maria Antiqua in Rome. Interestingly enough, it is she, woman and mother, who is called upon to represent supreme earthly power."[58] Mary's function as guardian of power keeps the young nun's sins in check. The function of this "Virginal Maternal" may thus offer an impossible alternative to motherhood. Rachilde's rejection of motherhood goes against the entire philosophic tradition according to which woman's existence is inscribed only as reproductive mother. The figure of Our Lady conciliates Rachilde's negative vision of motherhood with images of domination and power. The weakened version of the female Don Juan seeking Our Lady's pardon points to the power of the mother in the monopoly of the origin. If, for Eliante and Rachilde, juggling, dancing, and storytelling constitute the means of redeeming at least part of the sexuality that has oppressed them, in the long run these substitutes are invalid. Rachilde's revision of the Don Juan legend provides another instance of the daughter's failed revolt against the almighty mother.

Eliante looks like a liberated woman, who, in the final analysis, takes her own life; and in the Don Juan story she tells, the apparently liberated nun who becomes Don Juan is finally retransformed into a repentant woman. Rachilde's Don Juan could not be more unlike the conventional picture here described by Otto Rank: "Don Juan is the audacious blasphemer, who would deny conscience, guilt feelings, and anxiety with a cynicism that surpasses anything in the heroic tradition."[59] Different from both Eliante's version and the traditional form of the story, Rachilde's reworking of this legend is, as we shall see, more radical than even that of Eliante. The myth of Don Juan and his adversary, the Stone Guest, contains the very elements Rachilde needs in order to reinvent her own genealogy.

In *Pourquoi je ne suis pas féministe*, Rachilde reveals that her father fell in love with her grandmother before marrying her mother:

> Sweet Isoline had been, I learnt this later on, her daughter's very innocent rival. For her, my father, the worst kind of Don Juan (the military kind), entered, let's say: fell into marriage. He first courted tender Isoline who, frightened or perhaps sacrificing herself to duty, offered her only daughter instead of her, an elegant trick. How and why this marble statue accepted or even fell in love with this Don Juan, this I don't know because I was not yet there, but I believe that extremes naturally attract each other and that my mother must have imposed the law of the stronger on the weaker one.

> La douce Isoline avait été, je l'ai su plus tard, la très innocente rivale de sa fille. Pour elle, mon père, Don Juan de la pire espèce (l'espèce militaire), était entré, disons: tombé dans le mariage. Il avait d'abord fait la cour à la tendre Isoline qui s'effarouchant ou peut-être se sacrifiant à son devoir, avait offert sa fille unique à sa place, tour de passe passe élégant. Comment et pourquoi cette statue de marbre accepta ou s'éprit de ce Don Juan qui n'en demandait pas tant au point de vue de la ligne droite, ça je n'en sais rien car je n'y étais pas encore, mais je crois que les extrêmes s'attirent naturellement et que ma mère dût imposer la loi du plus fort au plus faible. (*Pourquoi*, 15–16).

The extraordinary twist that Rachilde brings to the legend is, as we might have expected, to switch genders, somewhat after

Eliante's fashion, and to see the haunting figure of the Stone Guest not as paternal imago but as a figure of the mother. Rachilde's analysis of her family configuration leads her back to an insight into the very form of the legend itself. As Otto Rank reveals in his Freudian reading of the myth: "In the figure of the Stone Guest, who also represents the coffin, the mother herself appears, coming to fetch the son."[60]

There is still another twist to the story that will be important to Rachilde's reinvention of her family romance. It is introduced in Eliante's retelling of the Don Juan story: "Well, once upon a time there was a nun in the heart of a dark Spanish convent. . . . She was so bored that one night she slipped over the convent walls. . . . She roamed the world in this disguise, under the name of *Don Juan*" (Eh bien, il y avait une fois une religieuse tout au fond d'un sombre couvent d'Espagne. . . . Elle s'ennuyait tellement qu'une nuit elle passa par-dessus les murs de ce couvent. . . . Elle courut le monde ainsi déguisée, sous le nom de . . . *Don Juan*) (*The Juggler*, 200/*La Jongleuse*, 248–49). Here, Don Juan is a pseudonym under which the young nun can escape the convent imprisonment; Don Juan has suddenly become the daughter figure, who repeats Rachilde's hatred of convent discipline. The Don Juan *combinatoire* is multifaceted in Rachilde's repertoire, and it always emphasizes the daughter's damnation. Once we have grasped Rachilde's reconception of the Stone Guest as the mother figure and of Don Juan as the daughter, one of the elements in Rank's characterization takes on a new meaning: "Don Juan's fantasy of conquering countless women, which has made the hero into a masculine ideal, is ultimately based on the unattainability of the mother and the compensatory substitute for her."[61]

We might also note that Rachilde's transformation of the legend happens to correspond to Baudelaire's poetical reinvention of Don Juan. Like Rachilde, he has no interest in Don Juan the heartless male seducer; his interest is exclusively in Don Juan as a figure of damnation. Paul-Laurent Assoun describes Don Juan as a diabolical angel in Baudelaire's *Fleurs du mal*: "From this complex myth, Baudelaire chooses the moment when Don Juan is sent to Hell."[62] The daughter's damnation in Rachilde's work echoes the son's damnation in Baudelaire's *Fleurs du mal*.

This is another instance of Rachilde's relentless retelling of the daughter's damnation and expiation. *Le Meneur de louves* stops, significantly, at Basine's excommunication, revealing Rachilde's secret joy at the daughter's defeat. However, Basine's damnation manifests her resistance to the mother superior's omnipotence. In order to be liberated from the mother's domination, daughters must be damned like Don Juan or cursed like the werewolf. Rachilde's triumph is ultimately to transform Eliante's sacrificial death by elevating her desire into a legend comparable to Don Juan's. It is at the intersection of Don Juan and the werewolf that Rachilde's rejection of the mother is deployed in all its vigor. The impenitent Don Juan is the model that both Baudelaire and Rachilde appropriate and reinvent as they come to terms with their own genealogies.

In one of her late autobiographical novels, *Duvet-D'Ange*, subtitled *Confessions d'un jeune homme de lettres* (1943), Rachilde invents a new pseudonym, Bathilde, which seems to condense Rachilde and Basine. Bathilde was a medieval queen who was later canonized, which once again reveals Rachilde's nostalgia for powerful feminine figures. The novel is, with a strange irony, dedicated to her daughter, Gabrielle, who was named after Rachilde's mother. The return of the maternal in the daughter's name surreptitiously contradicts Bathilde's genealogy, which remains entirely independent of the mother's. In the absence of a mother-daughter genealogy, Rachilde seems to create a maternal filiation between grandmother and granddaughter whereby she (Rachilde) belongs to the great-grandfather's side. The young poet Duvet-D'Ange, who represents the young Rachilde, is here thinking of the werewolf legend in connection with Bathilde:

> It is indeed real that I [Duvet-D'Ange] invented the fable of this encounter of a woman changed into a she-wolf with a hunter in love with his prey and it is just as real, in the field

of fables, of course, that she [Bathilde] is a priest's great-granddaughter, and that down to the fifth generation.

Il est bien réel que j'ai moi-même inventé la fable de cette rencontre d'une femme changée en louve avec un chasseur amoureux de son gibier et il est aussi réel, dans le domaine de la fable, bien entendu, qu'elle est l'arrière petite-fille d'un prêtre, et ce jusqu'à la cinquième génération.[63]

The great-grandfather's fault is subversive: it turns away from the observance of religious laws and demands that the descendants bear the curse to the fifth generation. Once again, Rachilde shows that Catholicism condemns sexuality by punishing innocent descendants for an earlier fault. The werewolf legend short-circuits the workings of human genealogy.

By separating sexuality from the reproductive function, Rachilde offers an alternative which disenfranchises women from an inimical social order. Basine's vow of chastity in *Le Meneur de louves* shows the difficulties Rachilde faces in her effort to forge a new model of woman's independence, for what could be more conventional and outmoded than such a vow? Chastity or death seems always to be the price that women must pay for their emancipation from an oppressive system: "My glory will perhaps redeem, in abstinence, the horrible stain which was inflicted on me," declares Basine (Ma gloire sera peut-être de racheter, par l'abstinence de tout amour terrestre, l'horrible souillure qui me fut infligée) (*Meneur de louves*, 205). Basine is Rachilde's anarchic angel who signals a certain movement in Rachilde's thinking from politics to mysticism; Basine, whose political ambition is to become a mother superior, is excommunicated, which leaves open to her, as we have seen, only the impossible solution of a life outside human society.

Read against the backdrop of the politics of the period, Basine's failure may have something to do with Rachilde's response to the collapse in 1905 of clerical support for the anarchists' cause. Richard Sonn sets the scene: "If anarchism functioned as an alternate focus of inspiration for lapsed Catholics, one might expect that when the lure of the revolution waned, they might just as readily turn to more traditional sources of faith. Former anarchists joined a number of literati who returned to the church in the decade from 1905 to the war."[64] Basine, the she-wolf, and Bathilde, the werewolf, may thus be figures of Rachilde's rather despondent response to the collapse of any promise that the anarchist movement may have once offered.

Like the werewolf, the novelist belongs to another race. The young poet Duvet-D'Ange remarks: "I don't need a pseudonym, I don't write novels" (Je n'ai pas à m'orner d'un pseudonyme, je n'écris pas de roman) (*Duvet-D'Ange*, 19). He may not need one, but Rachilde certainly did. The statement is axiomatic: If you want to write novels, you need a pseudonym. And as we have seen throughout this study, the axiom holds regardless of one's gender or of one's subjective or social position. Novel writing in the nineteenth century is always an exercise in pseudonymity. Novelists who write under a pseudonym simply make explicit the project of self-invention and self-creation on which all the great nineteenth-century novelists embarked.

Rachilde believed, however, that her act of self-creation and novel writing was utterly exclusive of politics. "I am no *feminist*," she writes, "I don't want to vote because politics bore me. I detest speeches" (Non, je ne suis pas *féministe*. Je ne veux pas voter parce que cela m'ennuierait de m'occuper de politique. J'ai horreur des discours) (*Pourquoi*, 83). But her work as a novelist is permeated by politics, overwhelmed by the ideologies and counterideologies of feminism, morality, and anarchism.

Chapter Four

DIVINUS DEUS:
BATAILLE'S EROTIC EDUCATION

Knowing nothing about the creature I am or what kind of
thing I am—is there anything I do know?
GEORGES BATAILLE, *Guilty*

Was I even in love with my mother? I *worshipped* my mother, I
did not love her.
GEORGES BATAILLE, *My Mother*

Pierre Angélique, a New Oedipus

It was only in 1961, in an interview with Madeleine Chapsal, that
Georges Bataille (1897–1962) revealed that the insanity of both
his parents had a fundamental influence on his childhood. He
also admitted that the different pseudonyms he had used to sign
his various works were devices designed to keep himself at a safe
distance from the family disease. Lord Auch (*Histoire de l'oeil*
[1928]), Pierre Angélique (*Madame Edwarda* [1941]), and Louis
Trente (*Le Petit* [1943]) were pseudonyms through which, as
Bataille explained to his older brother Martial, he hoped to cure
himself of the familial madness:

But I want to tell you this, what happened nearly fifty years ago makes me still tremble today and I am not surprised if one day I found the means to escape it in writing anonymously. I was treated (my case was serious) by a doctor (the psychoanalyst Adrien Brel) who told me that the means I used in spite of all was the best one I could find.

Mais je veux te dire ceci dès aujourd'hui, ce qui est arrivé il y a près de cinquante ans me fait encore trembler et je ne puis m'étonner si un jour je n'ai pas trouvé d'autre moyen de me sortir de là qu'en m'exprimant anonymement. J'ai été soigné (mon état étant grave) par un médecin (le psychanalyste Adrien Brel) qui m'a dit que le moyen que j'ai employé en dépit de tout était le meilleur que je pouvais trouver).[1]

Bataille's effort to cure himself by using pseudonyms demonstrates a particularly complex relation to both parents. Bataille's concern with insanity and guilt takes a definitive turn in *Ma Mère* (*My Mother*), which was written during the last year of Bataille's life (1962) and published posthumously in 1966. Here the weakness of prohibitions is boldly delineated, in particular the weakness of the interdictions intended to protect the subject from sinking into the abjected maternal body. In this narrative all prohibitions collapse and the son, Pierre, becomes engulfed in the mother's madness.

Bataille intended to publish *Ma Mère* along with a reedition of *Madame Edwarda*, which was first published in 1941. He did not live to complete *Charlotte d'Ingerville* and *Sainte*, which he intended as sequels or elaborations of *Ma Mère* and which remain only in fragmentary form. All four of these works were collectively intended to constitute a magnum opus to be called *Divinus Deus*. *Madame Edwarda* and the three later narratives, though written at different times, and though each is unfinished, were all published (posthumously or not) under the pseudonym of Pierre Angélique.

On the most obvious level, Bataille chose to write under a pseudonym whenever it was a question of a pornographic work that it would be embarrassing to acknowledge under his own name. But his motivation in choosing to write under a pseudonym is in every instance overdetermined, always at once an evasion and a confession, both an escape from responsibility and an effort to respond to the most fundamental questions of his life and his thinking. I am above all concerned with the overdeterminations at work in *Ma Mère*. In this text the pseudonym is a strategy for probing personal secrets and memories, obsessions and illicit feelings, with an honesty that shatters all barriers of decorum, taste, and perhaps even sanity itself.

In *Georges Bataille: la mort à l'oeuvre*, Michel Surya recognizes that Bataille's pseudonymous identities, rather than concealing the self, create for Bataille an unprecedented occasion for self-exposure and self-analysis: "Nothing would any longer separate the authors of *Story of the Eye* (Lord Auch) and *Le Petit* (Louis Trente) from himself; *Story of the Eye* and *Le Petit* are two books where he tried to tell the truth of his memories."[2] In Pierre Angélique's *Ma Mère*, fragments of autobiographical memories are disseminated throughout the narrative.

By transforming his transgression of the incest taboo into a religious experience, Bataille illuminates the relation between the incest prohibition and the sacred:

> For me, only my mother's gentle—and always tragic—phrases were appropriate to a drama, a mystery, which was no less grave, no less dazzling than God himself. It seemed to me that my mother's monstrous impurity, and mine, no less revolting, cried out to heaven and that they bore an affinity to God, inasmuch as only utter darkness can be likened to light.[3]

> Pour moi, le langage tendre—et toujours tragique de ma mère était à la mesure d'un drame—d'un mystère qui n'était pas moins lourd, ni moins aveuglant que Dieu lui-même. Il me semblait que l'impureté monstrueuse de ma mère—et que la mienne, aussi répugnante—criaient au ciel et qu'elles étaient semblables à la lumière. (OC, 4:203)

The orgies staged by Hélène, Pierre's mother, become the occasion for the son's experience of what is at once a mystical and erotic transcendence. Son and mother enjoy one incestuous embrace, and Hélène kills herself immediately afterward. En route to this catastrophe, she in effect panders her lesbian lovers, Rhea, Hansi, and Loulou, to her own son so that his sexual awakening will come more to resemble her own. After this sexual education, which culminates in incest and the mother's suicide, Pierre is at last capable of becoming a writer. The life of the writer is the destined goal of all the initiations and transgressions.

By his own account, Pierre's involvement with his mother, his progressive understanding of her "crimes," and his transformation into a debauchee all take place in the aftermath of his father's death. Before his father's death, Pierre believed that he, not his mother, was the debauchee of the family. Hélène soon reveals that she herself is the locus of unbridled desire. *Ma Mère* is, we must remember, an unfinished text with many inconsistencies and irregularities. Rather than try to make it conform to a linear pattern of causality and meaningful narrative, we must recall that it is a textual experiment whose contradictions and ambivalences embody the deepest conflicts of Bataille's own existence. What may appear to be narrative contradiction will often in fact be the expression of deep-seated unconscious complexes.

The pseudonym Pierre Angélique, which Bataille had earlier used to sign *Madame Edwarda,* signals a clear link between this text and *Ma Mère.* Furthermore, both texts are linked to *L'Expérience intérieure,* the second part of his *Somme athéologique,* which applies mystical states to "states of ecstasy, of rapture, at least of medi-tated emotion"[4] ([on nomme *expérience mystique*] les états d'extase, de ravissement, au moins d'émotion méditée) (*OC,* 5:15). *Madame Edwarda* and *Inner Experience* both explore the link between mysti-cal and erotic experience. Why, we wonder, is *Inner Experience* signed by Bataille, while *Madame Edwarda* is pseudonymous?

> I wrote this short book in September–October 1941, just before *The Torment,* which constitutes the second part of *Inner Experience.* In my opinion, the two texts are closely related to each other, and they cannot be understood separately. If *Madame Edwarda* did not remain united to *The Torment,* it is partly due to regrettable reasons of decency. Of course, *Madame*

Edwarda expresses me more truly; I could not have written *The Torment* if I had not first given the lewd meaning of it.

J'écrivis ce petit livre en septembre–octobre 1941, juste avant *Le Supplice*, qui forme la seconde partie de *L'Expérience intérieure*. Les deux textes, à mon sens, sont étroitement solidaires et l'on ne peut comprendre l'un sans l'autre. Si *Madame Edwarda* n'est pas demeurée unie au *Supplice*, c'est en partie pour des raisons de convenance regrettables. Bien entendu, *Madame Edwarda* m'exprime avec plus de vérité efficace; je n'aurais pu écrire *Le Supplice* si je n'en avais d'abord donné la clé lubrique. (OC, 3:491, notes)

Despite Bataille's insistence on the relation between these two texts, the fact that he signs one of them with a pseudonym still suggests an underlying difference. Bataille's *Somme athéologique* evokes the *Summa theologiae* of Thomas Aquinas, while of course removing God, or at least holding him at a distance. It is important to recall that Thomas Aquinas was known as Père Angélique, the angelic father. Bataille's work of erotic atheology to some extent reinvents Aquinas's mystical theology. Aquinas as the angelic father provided Bataille with a figuration for the paternal function. After the death of the father of the narrator of *Ma Mère*, the mother forces her son into his father's role. Pierre Angélique, the angelic "stone," takes the place of the deceased angelic father. By enmeshing Aquinas in this grotesque oedipal scenario, Bataille is not only punning on the play of "père" and "pierre," he is also, and more importantly, monumentalizing the paternal function by dramatizing the father's return, *in* the son and *as* the son.

The father's monumentalization recalls the Don Juan legend at the point where the impenitent sinner defies the stone statue of the Commander. Rachilde reinvents the Don Juan legend in order to define her experience of the structure of maternal power. The Don Juan figure is likewise reinvented in Bataille's work, and in quite a radical fashion. In *Story of the Eye*, for example, we meet with Don Juan in just those instances where we would expect to meet with the Commander. Denis Hollier has remarked on this situation at length:

An odd jamming effect, a strange role confusion, makes it generally difficult to single out in Bataille's work the attributes assigned by the traditional legend to Don Juan and the Comendador. At decisive moments the characters even seem to change roles. Don Juan appears when we might have expected the Comendador. In *Story of the Eye* the scene in La Caridad is the rigorous, but inverted, equivalent of the scene that, in canonical versions of the legend, occurs in the cemetery: here, however, the grave is not that of the Comendador; Don Juan has taken the cadaver's place.[5]

Just as Don Juan occupies "the cadaver's place" in Bataille's work, I will demonstrate that Pierre takes the place of the dead father in *Ma Mère*. Pierre's name is itself a kind of crypt, but a failed one. On the one hand, Pierre hopes to seal the family crypt, to put an end to the unreadable desires and imbroglios between his mother and father. But on the other hand, Pierre himself, by virtue of his name and his own obsessions, keeps the unholy family secret alive in the stone crypt, in the angelic stone, alias Georges Bataille.

In *Ma Mère*, it is Hélène who plays the Don Juan role, for it is she who dares to transgress all prohibitions and conventions. Hélène's sexuality not only lures Pierre back onto the terrain of preoedipal desire, it is utterly without limits, which means that it includes a wide variety of so-called perversions like exhibitionism and masochism. In the absence of oedipal law, Pierre regresses into the preoedipal domain of the mother. The lack of any libidinal limits makes her look for all intents and purposes like a psychotic, a schizophrenic who has lost all contact with the external world. This is Julia Kristeva's reading of this novel, which she sees as an effort to exhaust the sum total of possible excesses and perversions to which a mother might lend herself in her sexual liaison with her own son.[6] Hélène's sexual reality exists entirely outside of any external stimuli or constraint. What Kristeva calls the "psychotizing" mother can be glimpsed in a passage like the following: "My mother destined me for that violence over which she reigned. There was in her and for me a love like the one that, so mystics tell, God reserves for His creature, a love appealing to violence, excluding peace from the heart for ever" (Ma mère me destinait à cette violence, sur laquelle elle régnait. Il y avait en elle et pour moi un amour semblable à celui qu'au dire des mystiques, Dieu réserve à la créature, un amour appelant à la violence, jamais ne laissant de place au repos) (*My Mother*, 88/OC, 4:236). The appeal to violence, to transgression, to overcoming all restraints and limitations, stands, for Bataille, at the center of erotic *and* of mystical experience. The uncontrollably libidinal female Don Juan becomes, paradoxically, the locus of a certain sacred truth for Bataille, the truth that invariably must be found outside all social and moral laws.

In his essay "Attraction and Repulsion," Bataille describes the relation between the incest taboo and the sacred:

> Everything about the institution of the taboo is generally rather well known, and I shall remind you that it consists essentially in the institution of certain objects into a region that is impossible to penetrate. It is, in essence, not a case of objects consecrated by beliefs or fixed rituals, it is corpses, blood, especially menstrual blood. There is, additionally, the fact that certain persons in particular are taboo for certain others from the limited standpoint of sexual relations, which is what is called the incest taboo. These objects at any rate, are impure and untouchable, and they are sacred.[7]

The logic of prohibition determines the abject, the "impure and untouchable" objects that are, as the double meaning of the word *sacer* implies, at once "defiled" and "sacred." This has been a commonplace at least since Freud's *Totem and Taboo;* what is unique to Bataille is his relentless concern with exposing his readers to the horrors onto which this irreducible duplicity of the sacred opens, the horrors that sustain the social order but are always rigorously excluded from it as being filthy, disgusting, and intolerable.

Pierre's initiation into his mother's sexual life begins with the elimination of the paternal function:

Pierre, you are not his son, but the fruit of the torment that would possess me in the wild. You came from the terror I mated with when I was naked in the woods, naked like the beasts that live there; terror was my joy. That joy, Pierre, would be with me for hours on end as I lay squirming upon the leaf-mould; that ecstasy bred you.

Pierre! tu n'es pas son fils mais le fruit de l'angoisse que j'avais dans les bois. Tu viens de la terreur que j'éprouvais quand j'étais nue dans les bois, nue comme les bêtes, et que je jouissais de trembler. Pierre, je jouissais pendant des heures, vautrée dans la pourriture des feuilles: tu naissais de cette jouissance. (*My Mother,* 72–73/OC, 4:222)

Hélène's claim that Pierre was engendered parthenogenetically, that is, through an enigmatic act of autoreproduction, reflects of course a fantasized suppression of the father's role. It is precisely because she regards her reproductive powers as self-contained that there need be no incest taboo: since heterosexual contact would have no instrumentality in any case, it need not be prohibited. She in effect absorbs the father into her own sexuality, even, as she remarks, transforming him into a woman and a victim: "I would beat your father. I never tired of humiliating him, I put him in women's clothes, I dressed him up like a clown and we would have dinner" (Puis je battis ton père. Je l'habillais en femme, je l'habillais en pitre et nous dînions) (*My Mother,* 74/OC, 4:223). Bataille's oedipal scenario is unlike Freud's, since here it is the mother who wants to "kill" the father. The mother's violence prevents the separation between mother and son from taking place; the father's demise leaves the son enmeshed in a preoedipal bondage from which there is no exit.

At the same time, however, and apparently contradicting the parthenogenetic thesis, Hélène also accuses her husband of having raped her. In this scenario the father appears as the victimizer. The mother's rape transforms her into a victim in her son's eyes and makes their incestuous alliance even stronger: "You issued from the foliage of the forest, from the damp forest dews that gave me joy, but your father—I didn't want him, I didn't want that, I was bad-tempered. When he found me naked he raped me, but I got my nails into him, I tried to claw his eyes out. I wasn't able to" (Tu viens des feuillages des bois, de l'humidité dont je jouissais, mais ton père, je n'en voulais pas, j'étais mauvaise. Quand il m'a trouvée nue, il m'a violée, je voulais arracher les yeux. Je n'ai pas pu) (*My Mother*, 71/OC, 4:221). We are somewhere between rape and parthenogenesis. The mother responds to her rape by trying, unsuccessfully, to blind her rapist. The question of blindness is a crucial one, and we will return to it in detail later in this chapter. Here we need note only that the son's conception is associated with paternal aggression.

Pierre Angélique wants to explore what has been repressed, or, as Bataille writes in the preface of *Madame Edwarda*: "Pierre Angélique is careful to explain it. We know nothing and we are in the depths of darkness. But at least we can see what it is that deceives us, what it is that hinders us from knowing our own distress, or more accurately from knowing that joy is the same thing as death."[8] The knowledge that enables Pierre to reach the sacred through thought is a strange sexual knowledge. The invitation to divine perfection is thus an invitation to sin. Mother and son are caught in the ambiguity of holy abjection: "He violated you, and I am nothing but the resulting horror. When you told me you had bloodied his face it hurt me to hear it, but I would have aided you, Mother, I would have ripped his face too" (Il t'a violée, je ne suis que l'horreur qui en résulte! Quand tu m'as dit: j'ai mis son visage en sang, j'étais malheureux, mais j'aurais déchiré le visage avec toi, maman!) (*My Mother*, 72/OC, 4:222). Though abjection lifts the taboo, it does not radically release the subject from what threatens it—on the contrary, abjection only acknowledges the continuing menace.

In *Essais de Sociologie*, Bataille writes that the "word 'miserable,' which once meant 'to be worthy of pity,' has become synonymous with 'abject'" (OC, 2:218). Bataille thus asserts the link between the sacred and the abject. Pierre's mother is miserable in this sense, and his narrative in effect transforms the mother's abjection into a kind of holy catharsis where purification proceeds only through increasing defilement. Furthermore, Hélène's ascent/descent involves a regression to animality. This is reported to Pierre by Charlotte in *Charlotte d'Ingerville*: "A kind of trembling seized her [Hélène] as if she were becoming one with the animals of the forest. She was naked except for her boots, and while trembling, she urinated. Her face was no longer human. She was entering a crisis which transfigured her" (Une sorte de tremblement s'était emparée d'elle comme si elle était tout à coup à l'unisson des bêtes des bois. Ainsi nue et bottée, frissonnante, elle pissa. Son visage n'était plus humain. Elle entrait dans une crise qui la transfigurait) (*OC*, 4:289). The mother's metaphoric dehumanization is what fascinates Bataille. Unlike Kristeva, who argues that the differentiation of proper/improper and clean/dirty is expressive of a maternal authority, Bataille maintains that there is no separation between these oppositions and that the mother's authority proceeds not through such injunctions but rather through its own incessant self-abjection.

In *Ma Mère*, Bataille questions the authority of both parents by revealing their essential violence and madness. The mother's abjection repeats the father's and transforms it into a willful act of revolt. The nondifferentiation of purity and impurity turns the body into a borderless territory closer to the animal than to the human, a territory that can no longer be mapped out as Kristeva would insist. Hélène's abjected *jouissance* and her excremental defilement develop themes and elements that are already familiar to readers of Bataille's *Le Bleu du ciel* (1957), where the prostitute Dirty undergoes almost every conceivable abjection. Likewise, Hélène is both prostitute and animal.

In *Death and Sensuality*, Bataille traces the difference between animal sexuality and human eroticism: "Human eroticism differs from animal sexuality precisely in this, that it calls inner life into play. In human consciousness eroticism is that within man which calls his being into question. Animal sexuality does make for disequilibrium and this disequilibrium is a threat to life, but the animal does not know that" (*Death and Sensuality*, 23). According to Bataille, the birth of human eroticism emerges by moving from unashamed sexuality to sexuality with shame. This also entails the specifically human attitude toward death: Bataille argues that sexual restrictions derive from taboos concerned with the dead. The connection between eroticism and death is complicated by elementary organisms which reproduce themselves through asexual reproduction. Asexual reproduction establishes the continuity of beings, whereas sexual reproduction "implies the existence of *discontinuous* beings" (*Death and Sensuality*, 6). Hélène's parthenogenesis names this asexual reproduction which so fascinated Bataille:

> In asexual reproduction, the organism, a single cell, divides at a certain point in its growth. Two nuclei are formed and from one single being two new beings are derived. But we cannot say that one being has given birth to a second being. The two new beings are equally products of the first. The first being has disappeared. It is to all intents and purposes dead, in that it does not survive in either of the two beings it has produced. But at one stage of the reproductive process there was continuity. There is a point at which the original *one becomes two*. (*Death and Sensuality*, 8)

Might we not consider Pierre's own act of narrative reproduction a kind of asexual reproduction, a deathly return to the one? And perhaps in this sense Bataille regards the life of the writer as only another version of the fatal regression on which Hélène has embarked. The mother's abjection opens the pathway back to extinction and death. Instead of seeing discontinuity between sexuality and death, Bataille stressed a continuity between them. We might say along these lines that the book has itself become Pierre's creation. From the deadly copulation with the mother, the book is born. Hélène, in Pierre's sexual imaginings, is only a more or less obliging mother for the enactment of his fantasies. However, not knowing what she wants, Pierre's eroticism takes shape in the aftermath of her demise. We might say that Bataille thus reappropriates the strange generative power of the psychotic mother for himself. Pseudonymous writing is the quintessential strategy for such appropriations. It may be that, for Bataille, the life of the work seemed strangely enhanced under a pseudonym, as though it enabled one to risk writing deeper truths, truths that one would shy away from under one's own name, truths that might ensure a longer life for the work itself.

Lord Auch and the Father's Name

Each of us is incomplete compared to someone else—an animal's incomplete compared to a person . . . and a person compared to God, who is complete only to be imaginary.

GEORGES BATAILLE, *Guilty*

L'expérience intérieure (1943), *Le Coupable* (1944), and *Sur Nietzsche* (1945) were supposed to be collected in *Somme athéologique*, but only the first two texts were actually reedited for inclusion under this title. These three books constitute a kind of war triptych that examines the nature of thought during that period. *Guilty* was begun under very peculiar conditions: "The date I start (5 September 1939) is no coincidence. I'm starting because of what's happening, though I don't want to go into it. I'm writing it down because of being unable *not* to"[9] (La date à laquelle je commence d'écrire [5 septembre 1939] n'est pas une coïncidence. Je commence en raison des événements, mais ce n'est pas pour en parler. J'écris ces notes incapable d'autre chose) (OC, 5:245). It started the day World War II began. For Bataille, "completeness should be the basis of human knowledge. If it isn't complete, it's not *knowledge*—it's only an inevitable, giddy product of the will to know" (*Guilty*, 24). But at the beginning of the war there is only incompleteness and anxiety. Bataille's intellectual uneasiness at writing *Guilty* during World War II is linked to his personal memories of World War I, which were triggered by the new hostilities.[10]

Guilty also commemorates a traumatic event in Bataille's life: the death of his lover, Laure, in 1938. Because Laure's death greatly affected Bataille, it brought back to his mind the death of his own father, whose face looked very much like Laure's. The father's death in 1915 is thus recalled in 1938. The incredible resemblance between his lover's and his father's dead faces brings about Bataille's guilt:

> What terrified me also is that Laure's face looked obscurantly like this man so tragically fated: a face of a hollow and half-insane Oedipus. Her resemblance increased with him as she was agonizing, while she was eaten by the fever, perhaps when she particularly had her fits of anger and hatred against me. I tried to escape what I finally met: I escaped my father (twenty-five years ago, I abandoned him during the German invasion, escaping with my mother). He remained alone in Rheims under a cleaning woman's care; he was blind and paralysed.[11]

> Ce qui m'a également terrifié: le visage de Laure avait une obscure ressemblance avec celui de cet homme si affreusement tragique: un visage d'Oedipe vide et à demi dément. Cette ressemblance s'accrut au cours de sa longue agonie, pendant que la fièvre la rongeait, peut-être en particulier pendant ses terribles colères et ses accès de haine contre moi. J'ai essayé de fuir ce que j'avais ainsi rencontré: j'ai fui mon père il y a vingt-cinq ans, je l'ai abandonné à son sort pendant l'invasion alle-mande, fuyant avec ma mère: il demeura seul à Reims, confié aux soins d'une femme de ménage; il était aveugle et paralysé. (OC, 5:504).

The figure of the blind Oedipus is evoked by Bataille's father's hollow-eyed face. The guilt felt by Bataille at having abandoned his father when France was occupied by the Germans was re-awakened when Laure died a year before World War II started. The apparent disappearance of the father figure in *Ma Mère* seems to be another reenactment of the son's (and also the mother's) guilt. When Bataille threatened to return to Rheims to be with his father, his mother feigned insanity to prevent him from going. In *Ma Mère*, Hélène is described as being completely insane and thus reenacts Bataille's own mother's madness. Bataille's treatment of the maternal figure is always situated at the intersection of the pornographic text and personal memories.

If one has a feeling of discomfort at what the mother wants in *Ma Mère*, it is because she advocates the trespassing of all erotic limits. The will to know is, for her, the will to die, and her position is a movement toward every possible excess. When Bataille recognizes "Hegel's greatness to see that knowledge depends on completeness" (as if there could be knowledge worthy of the name while still in process!) (C'est la grandeur de Hegel d'avoir fait dépendre la science de son achèvement [comme s'il pouvait y avoir une connaissance digne de ce nom tant qu'on l'élabore!]) (*Guilty*, 24/OC, 5:259), he is already expressing the all-encompassing, mad knowledge of the mother who threatens Pierre. In treating the father as a non-father, we should consider what is *not* solved in Bataille's Oedipus complex. In his blindness, Bataille's father himself assumes the role of Oedipus, which enables Bataille to proceed even further than Oedipus. As Bataille writes in *W.-C. Preface to Story of the Eye*: "Since my father conceived me blind (absolutely blind), I cannot put out my own eyes like Oedipus. Like Oedipus I guessed the riddle: nobody guessed further than me" (Mon père m'ayant conçu aveugle [aveugle absolument], je ne puis m'arracher les yeux comme Oedipe. J'ai comme Oedipe deviné l'énigme: personne n'a deviné plus loin que moi) (*OC*, 3:60).

It is in this same preface that Bataille explains the meaning of "Lord Auch," the pseudonym he used to sign *Story of the Eye*, and which reveals further connections to the return of the repressed figure of the father:

> There is in *Story of the Eye* another reminiscence of "W.-C."
> [water closet], which in its title page already inscribes what
> follows under the sign of the worst. The name of Lord Auch
> describes the habit of one of my friends: angry, he could no
> longer say "aux chiottes!" [to the john!], shortened it and said
> "aux ch'." In English "Lord" means God in the holy scriptures:
> Lord Auch is God defecating.

Il est dans "L'Histoire de l'Oeil" une autre réminiscence de "W.-C.," qui, dès la page de titre, inscrit ce qui suit sous le signe du pire. Le nom de Lord Auch se rapporte à l'habitude d'un de mes amis: irrité, il ne disait plus "aux chiottes!," abrégeait, disait "aux ch'." Lord en anglais veut dire Dieu (dans les textes saints): Lord Auch est Dieu se soulageant. (OC, 3:59).

Why is Bataille's work so deeply obsessed by defecation? Words are excrement; this is the fundamental Bataillean equation. What we see in the pseudonym of Lord Auch is the sliding (*glissement*) of the notion of transgression from the realm of experience to the realm of words. The excremental name of Lord Auch signifies Bataille's linguistically scandalous combinations. Behind Lord Auch, there is also the blind, paternal figure whom Bataille remembers as a haunting vision:

> What strikes me more: to have seen my father shit many times. He would get out his bed, blind and paralyzed (my father was both a blind and crippled man). He would get out painfully (I helped him), sit on the chamber pot, in his nightshirt, often wearing a cotton hat (he had a grey unkempt goatee, an eagle's long nose and huge, hollow, fixed eyes staring at emptiness).

> Ce qui m'abat davantage: avoir vu, un grand nombre de fois, chier mon père. Il descendait péniblement (je l'aidais), s'asseyait sur un vase, en chemise, coiffé, le plus souvent, d'un bonnet de coton (il avait une barbe grise en pointe, mal soignée, un grand nez d'aigle et d'immenses yeux caves, regardant fixement à vide). (OC, 3:60)

If the pseudonym is a means by which the father's name is put under erasure, it also contains his powerful presence. For Bataille, guilt is an "inner experience" in which he endlessly relives the abandonment and death of his father. The father's victimization is associated with the sacred; God and the father are undifferentiated in the ludicrous and irreverent image of defecation. There is an ambiguous oscillation in Bataille's work between the father as a victim and as a victimizer. Bataille feels both guilt for his betrayal and hatred of the father and love for the father as victim: "Nevertheless, unlike the majority of the male babies who are in love with their mother, I, for my part, was in love with this father" (*OC*, 1:75). This statement is later on denied: "I was about fourteen years old when my affection for my father became a deep and unconscious hatred" (*OC*, 1:76). At the beginning of *Ma Mère*, Pierre replays this oscillation between love and hate for the father: "Later she was to borrow a phrase from my father, 'Just lay the blame for everything on me.' That was his wish, understanding that in my eyes my mother was beyond reproach and must at all costs remain that way. But perpetuating that convention became intolerable after his death" (Plus tard, elle devait me dire ce mot de mon père: "Mets tout sur mon dos." Ce fut le souhait de mon père, comprenant qu'à mes yeux, ma mère était inattaquable, qu'elle dût à tout prix le rester. Sa mort rendait la convention intolérable) (*My Mother*, 33/*OC*, 4:185). The victim/victimizer role might be the result of the unusual physical proximity of father and son. The attraction/repulsion Bataille felt for his father is contained in the name Lord Auch and explicitly expressed in *Guilty:* "Others resist their anguish. They laugh, sing. They're *innocent*—and I'm *guilty*" (D'autres sont rebelles à l'angoisse. Ils rient et chantent. Ils sont *innocents* et je suis *coupable*) (*Guilty*, 57/*OC*, 5:295).

In *Subversive Intent*, Susan Suleiman questions the Western model of textuality that plays out the eternal oedipal drama: "But the insight provided by Bataille's text about itself has its own limits. Among the questions that Bataille's text cannot ask about itself—are these: Is there a model of sexuality possible in our culture that would not necessarily pass through the son's anguished and fascinated perception of the duplicity of the mother's body? Is there a model of *textuality* that would not necessarily play out, in discourse, the eternal Oedipal drama of transgression and the Law—a drama which always, ultimately, ends by maintaining the latter?"[12] If Bataille stages too clearly the confrontation over the body of the mother between an all-powerful dead father and a traumatized son, it is because he still carries the incest taboo beyond the traditional limit. The incest between mother and son is finally a pretext to a more fundamental interrogation of birth and death:

> I exist, I remain blind, in anguish: other individuals are completely different from me, I feel nothing of what they feel. If I envisage my coming into the world—linked to the birth then to the union of a man and a woman, and even, at the moment of their union . . . a single chance decided the possibility of this *self* which I am.

> J'existe, je demeure aveugle, dans l'angoisse: chacun des autres est tout autre que moi, je ne sens rien de ce qu'il sent. Si j'envisage ma venue au monde—liée à la naissance puis à la conjonction d'un homme et d'une femme, et même, à l'instant de la conjonction—une chance unique décida de la possibilité de ce *moi* que je suis. (*Inner Experience*, 69/OC, 5:83)

Bataille's *Inner Experience* excludes the female imaginary and provides for only a male-governed one, which is how Bataille deals with sexual difference. In Bataille's autobiographical scenario, procreation was the result of a chance encounter. This is the origin of his metaphysical anguish of being.

We come here to an important juncture in our argument. Bataille's pseudonymous ruminations about his own origins led him beyond a phallogocentric regime and toward an interrogation of the powers of the mother that has no analogue in contemporary theory. Bereft of a symbolic order, having dismantled all conventions and all modes of instinctual renunciation that organize the super-ego, Bataille plunges back into the miasma of maternality. He risks everything on this leap into the irresistible maternal site of death.

In *This Sex Which Is Not One*, Luce Irigaray has "another look" at psychoanalytic theory. She begins with the Freudian theory that "the little girl is a little man during the phallic phase." This statement leads Freud to conclude that the little girl's sexual drives and pleasures are in fact "masculine." The parallel drawn between the little girl and the little boy stops when Freud recognizes the specificity of the feminine castration complex. When the little girl recognizes that her clitoris cannot be compared to the boy's sex organ, she recognizes that her amputation has already been performed. Freud insists on the dread that the little boy has of losing his penis, whereas the little girl recognizes her loss as a "fait accompli." Penis envy and the desire "to have a child" can be summed up in Freud by the importance of the reproductive function. In "becoming the *mother of a son*, the woman will be able to transfer to her son all the ambition which she has been obliged to suppress in herself."[13] In order to achieve her femininity, women must become mothers. However, the woman's masculine claims would never be entirely solved, according to Freud, and "penis envy" would seek to compensate for her "inferiority complex." What Irigaray does is to link the differential development of the little girl and the little boy in the structure of the castration complex. The aggression which both boys and girls are said to exhibit at the anal stage is turned, in the case of girls, into masochism; their aggression is turned against themselves, while men protect themselves against self-aggression through castration and the "normal" structure of masculinity. In this scenario, as long as it functions effectively, the male subject is protected from his own self-destructive masochism at the expense of woman, who cannot sublimate her own death drives. Bataille is concerned with these violent unsymbolized death drives, which are always present in female sexuality. By connecting the death drives with the castration complex, Irigaray makes a link between the naturalization of castration and the naturalization of female masochism. Hence the mythological image of Medusa on man's shield. It is his own fears that he turns away from and projects onto woman. The "other of the other" for man is that which is unthinkable. By making death instead of women the "other of the other," and by making women the representatives of death, men attempt to master the unthinkable.

Instead of simply seeking the death of the father, as in the oedipal configuration, Bataille comes to realize that he seeks the death of the mother. Bataille's elimination of the mother describes a sexual deviation, a morbid process, that has traditionally been attributed to women. True, Freud would probably agree that even if masochism is a component of "normal" femininity, the latter cannot be completely reduced to masochism. In Bataille's work the libido is fundamentally necrophilic. It is for this reason that the collapse of the oedipal complex as the guardian of social, moral, cultural, and religious values determines Bataille's sexual aberrations. In one of his posthumous texts, Bataille describes his pathological craving for loving his dead mother:

> I found myself lying down in the apartment of my dead mother: her corpse rested in the next room. I was sleeping poorly and remembered that two years before I participated in an orgy in my mother's absence, exactly in her room and in her bed which was now supporting her corpse. This orgy in the maternal bed took place by chance during my birthday night: my ecstatic motions among my accomplices were interposed between the birth which gave me life and the dead woman for whom I felt then a desperate love. I expressed it several times in terrible, childish sobbings. The extreme voluptuousness of my memories prompted me to go to this orgiastic bedroom to masturbate amorously while looking at the corpse.[14]

> Je me trouvai la nuit couché dans l'appartement de ma mère morte: le cadavre reposait dans une chambre voisine. Je dormais mal et me rappelai que deux ans auparavant je m'étais livré à une longue orgie pendant l'absence de ma mère, précisément dans cette chambre et sur le lit qui servait maintenant de support au cadavre. Cette orgie dans le lit maternel avait eu lieu par hasard la nuit anniversaire de ma naissance: les postures obscènes de mes complices et mes mouvements extasiés au milieu d'eux étaient interposés entre l'accouchement qui m'avait donné la vie et la morte pour laquelle j'éprouvais alors un amour désespéré qui s'était exprimé à plusieurs reprises par de terribles sanglots puérils. La volupté extrême de mes souvenirs me poussa à me rendre dans cette chambre orgiaque pour m'y branler amoureusement en regardant le cadavre. (OC, 2:130)

It is in connection with the most repulsive perversions that the psychological factor must be considered as playing its largest part in the transformation of the sexual instinct. As Freud argues, "The omnipotence of love is perhaps never more strongly proved than in such of its aberrations as these. The highest and the lowest are closest to each other in the sphere of sexuality."[15] In linking abjection to "the inability to assume with sufficient strength the imperative act of excluding" (OC, 2:220), Bataille is also suggesting that necrophilia is the total collapse of the act of excluding. When Kristeva stresses that Bataille was the first to have specified that the plane of abjection is that of the "subject/object relationship (and not subject/other subject) and that this archaism is rooted in anal eroticism rather than sadism,"[16] she is also suggesting that such an archaic relationship to the object interprets the relationship to the mother.

Necrophilia for Bataille means that the mother's dead body becomes the privileged site of desire. For Bataille as for Sade, the mother is nature's privileged victim; Hélène's suicide allows the birth of Pierre's narrative, which is "coupable"—guilty, but also that which can be cut off (*couper*, to cut), that is to say, severed: "When in my sleep I thought I heard my name whispered, my mother had just died, my mother had just killed herself" (Lorsque dans mon sommeil je crus que j'entendais, à voix basse, prononcer mon nom, ma mère venait de mourir, ma mère venait de se tuer) (OC, 4:400, notes). This narrative variant places *Ma Mère* in the aftermath of the mother's death, which leaves Pierre "free" to create his own "family romance." However, Bataille seems unable to assume the separation from the mother. What is *coupable* has not yet been cut (*coupé*), and I will argue that the transgressive relationship with the mother occults the father's place: "My piety is an attempt to escape at any cost, I wanted to escape destiny, I abandoned my father. Today, I know that I am measurelessly 'blind,' an abandoned man on earth like my father was" (Ma piété n'est qu'une tentative d'élusion: à tout prix, je voulais éluder le destin, j'abandonnai mon père. Aujourd'hui, je me sais "aveugle" sans mesure, l'homme "abandonné" sur le globe comme mon père; OC, 3:61). Blind Oedipus loving dead Jocasta becomes the haunting image which Bataille cannot escape.

Unlike Stendhal's mourning for the mother, which assumes in *Vie de Henry Brulard* the Freudian structure of the fort-da, Bataille's relationship to his mother is a relationship with a dead object (Bataille's mother died in 1930). However, both Stendhal and Bataille experience guilt in their relationship to the mother. For Bataille, the mother's sex is the cause of his anguish. The narrative of *Ma Mère* is an account of this dread which culminates in the unveiling of her sexual fantasies. Bataille's fascination for the maternal corpse, his revolting arousal, completes the total degradation of her body. Desire can be fully assumed in Bataille's work on the condition that the mother has become literally matter (*la matière*). The displacement from *mater* (mother) to matter brings back to mind the maternal metaphor of the book, which in Bataille's writing is the equivalent of the womb.

"Blind Iris" and the Mother's Metamorphoses

> Terror on the edge of the grave is divine and I sink into the terror whose child I am.
>
> GEORGES BATAILLE, *My Mother*

A note in the manuscript of *La Tombe de Louis XXX*, a posthumous volume composed by Bataille around 1942–43, indicates that the photograph of a vulva was to be inserted. Such a photograph was never inserted; instead, we find the final poem, entitled "Le Livre," using the maternal metaphor of the book:

> The Book
> I drink from your slit
> and I spread your naked legs apart
> I open them like a book
> where I read what kills me (OC, 4:161)

At the very core of the pornographic mise-en-scène is the concept of woman as object. A woman's body forms the centerfold of a magazine. She spreads apart her thighs and stares into the camera. Her eyes reflect nothing: she is not human. In her image all the meanings of absence are realized. All the pornographic clichés are condensed in "Le Livre" while transforming woman into matter.

In *Against Achitecture*, Denis Hollier remarks that "for psychoanalysis the book is a maternal symbol." In showing how the metaphor of the mother's body works when displaced into the pages of the book, Hollier argues that transgression takes place. Furthermore, Freud's desire to propose a sort of science of desire is doubly transgressive: "Science (only active on the basis of desire's repression, only as the repression and transposition of desire) is perverted and desire, from which science wrests the secret, is transgressed."[17] Continuing Hollier's argument, I would like to show how the maternal metaphor leads to a complete deconstruction of the mother's function in both Bataille's and Freud's work. In this context, *My Mother* will logically pursue Freud's theoretical *Interpretation of Dreams*.

The writing of a book has always traditionally been compared to the birth process. Freud, for example, linked the writing of *The Interpretation of Dreams* to his desire to father his own immortality. As Freud was writing the book and anxious to have it finished, his friend Wilhelm Fliess wrote to say that he saw Freud's book "finished before him." The letter triggered Freud's so-called "dream of the botanical monograph" in which he sees himself and his sister tearing apart a book their father had given them: "I had been five years old at the time and my sister not yet three; and the picture of the two of us blissfully pulling the book to pieces (leaf by leaf, like an *artichoke*, I found myself saying) was almost the only plastic memory that I retained from that period of my life."[18] Freud's claim of scientific objectivity is negated by this dream. The repressed memory of his childhood separates knowledge from the desire it transposes. Forgetfulness, in Freud's terms, reveals the importance of this "plastic memory."

In his brief analysis of the "dream of the botanical mono-graph," Freud is concerned not with the interpretation of the dream itself but with the direction dream analysis takes. Further-more, Freud's ambiguity consists of giving the "key" to the in-terpretation of dreams in revealing that there exists a "science of desire" although desire is always unconscious. Freud's dream marks his desire to know and to understand the meaning of the tearing of the book. As Hollier argues, "Tearing a book, opening the maternal body; writing a book, wresting away de-sire's secret. These are actions disturbing to bookish metaphor, actions that challenge the economy of science whose primary function is the active forgetting of the maternal body."[19] For Hollier, the joy of tearing up the pages is similar to the awaken-ing of desire. His argument is that the book is closed up by the author's surname—the name of the father separates desire from knowledge. It guarantees the book but kills the desire to know, which is taboo.

Pierre Angélique can risk the viability of the book for the sake of sexual knowledge. The fact that Bataille's death inter-rupted the completion of the book marks the dissolution of knowledge at the point where death and sexuality meet. Consid-ered within the present feminist critique, the experience of fe-male reading is "erotic, dangerous and expressive of the desire to merge with the mother. The book which a woman treats with such care, is the mother's body."[20] This underlies Freud's gesture of opening the mother's body to dissect the child's desire. In Freud's dream, the book's pages are pulled apart leaf by leaf like an artichoke, while Bataille spreads them open like a woman's naked legs. In *La Tombe de Louis XXX*, the picture of the vulva which was to be introduced between "Le Livre" and "La Méditation," so that the mother (the womb) becomes literally the book itself, marks Bataille's intent to penetrate the book (the mother). Sacrificing the mother seems to be the prerequisite for writing the book, as Pierre declares in *My Mother*: "I have no desire to behold my mother again, no, not even by some insidious means to resurrect her elusive image. The place my book allots her, that is the place she still has in my mind" (Je ne désire pas revoir ma mère et pas même en faire apparaître insidieusement l'insaisissable image. Elle a toujours dans mon esprit la place que marque mon livre) (*My Mother*, 89/OC, 4:236). The image of the dead mother is perfectly encrypted in the making of the book and becomes literally matter.

In *Women, Art, and Power,* Linda Nochlin shows a reproduction of Georgia O'Keeffe's "Black Iris" (1927), which is a hallucinatory image of a plant form that has a striking similarity to the female genitalia. As Nochlin argues: "The analogy is based not on a shared abstract quality, but rather a morphological similarity between the physical structure of the flower and that of woman's sexual organs—hence on a visual, concrete similarity rather than an abstract, contextually stipulated relation."[21] There is of course no indication that Bataille knew of O'Keeffe's "Black Iris," but what makes the parallel striking is that through the botanical metaphor of "iris–female genitalia" it provides a visual equivalent of the fantasm of a figure of creative immortality.

Besides being a flower, the iris is also the eye, which recalls a prominent Bataillean metaphor. Bataille's concern is to depict the son's view of both the mother's genitalia and the father's blindness. If the iris image at once desacralizes and reactivates the feminine, it also reveals the absence of the iris in the father's "white eyes." The repetition compulsion at work in Bataille's oedipal father's "hollow-eyed face" signals its regressive tendencies. The regression that Bataille's text outlines conforms to the Freudian paradigm in which the penetration and possession of the mother lead to abject submission before the father's law. The real drama of *Ma Mère* is, ironically enough, between the son and the father, not between son and mother, as it first appears. The botanical metaphor of Freud's dream and O'Keeffe's painting depicts the maternal body as something which is known and perceived (the artichoke, the iris), whereas Bataille's "secret" consists of revealing that behind the apparently monstrous mother lies the more powerful figure of the father. Incest with the mother is what ultimately enables Pierre to separate himself from her and thus retrieve the lost figure of the dead father.

The mother's dissolution in *Ma Mère* traces what Bataille in *Death and Sensuality* calls the dissolution from the normal to the erotic state: "Dissolution—this expression corresponds with *dissolute life*, the familiar phrase linked with erotic activity. In the process of dissolution, the male partner has generally an active role, while the female partner is passive" (*Death and Sensuality*, 11). Having acknowledged our human limits, Bataille gives Hélène a divine nature which transforms reality into a desire to return to the stasis of death. It also gives her an active role in the absence of male partners. Bataille's fascination for complex forms of animality in which birth and death are confused, so that we never can tell when these animals are born or when they die, is rearticulated in *Ma Mère*'s incest and suicide. Hélène's excessive and no longer human desire is valorized in Bataille's pornographic fiction as exceeding the bonds of traditional motherhood. As Bataille says in the notes to "Paradoxe sur l'Erotisme": "If I speak of eroticism, I am speaking of the inner experience men have of it, and I proceed saying that this experience can be only located on the plane where religion is" (Si je parle de l'érotisme, je parle de l'expérience intérieure que les hommes en ont communément, et j'avance que cette expérience ne peut être située que sur le plan où se situe la religion) (*OC*, 4:396). The "horror" in *Ma Mère* consists of transforming the mother's abjection into the sacred. More than a simple reenactment of the Oedipus complex, *Ma Mère* displaces the mother figure to an infinity of figures in an effort to erase her totally.

In *Death and Sensuality*, Bataille writes: "The lowest kind of prostitute has fallen as far as she can go. She might be no less indifferent to the taboo than animals are except that because what she knows about taboos is that others observe them, she cannot attain an absolute indifference; not only has she fallen but she knows she has. She knows she is a human being. Even if she is not ashamed of it, she does know that she lives like a pig" (130).

In scrupulously marking the frontier between prostitution and its prohibition, Bataille underlines the complementarity of prostitution and Christianity: "Conversely, common prostitution as an institution complements the world of Christianity" (*Death and Sensuality*, 130).

In the streets of Cairo, Hélène, as her niece Charlotte tells Pierre in *Charlotte d'Ingerville*, "repaired, perhaps tardily, what she called her fault, in becoming a white prostitute in Cairo" (*OC*, 4:291). The expiation of the mother's "fault" constitutes Hélène's familiarity with abjection and brings her even closer to the sacred: "But what she sought every night, was death" (*OC*, 4:273). The masochistic economy of this *jouissance* is obvious and resembles a variety of mystical descents into abjection. One recalls, of course, Francis of Assisi, who visited leper colonies and left only after having kissed each leper on his mouth. Abjection thus becomes the prerequisite for a reconciliation which can only take place in death, for sin, here subsuming biblical abjection and closely associated with the passion of the flesh, must carry out the fearsome process of interiorization. It is at that moment when, returning from Egypt that the mother becomes her son's lover, only to poison herself shortly afterwards. It is this final act that transforms Bataille's multiform oedipal structure into confrontation with the enigmas that lie within and beyond the maternal.

The mother's total exclusion, her suicide, is the last attempt at warding off opprobrium. Hélène's atonement for her sins is rapidly silenced, and her suicide is transformed into another's death. *Ma Mère* marked the definitive return of the repressed when Bataille himself committed his most amazing Freudian slip, writing "my father" instead of "my mother" in the following passage: "I am able to tell myself that I killed my father; it could be that my mother died from having yielded to the tenderness of the kiss I laid upon her lips" (Je puis me dire que j'ai tué mon père: peut-être mourut-elle d'avoir cédé à la tendresse du baiser sur la bouche que je lui donnais) (*My Mother*, 89/*OC*, 4:236). Incest seems here to have been unconsciously transformed into a parricide that leaves no room for the mother. Bataille here "forgets" the mother.

As Christiane Olivier has recently reminded us, the mother is like Jocasta, whom Sophocles and Freud ignored: "Can she really be forgotten, this Jocasta, embodiment of the ancient androgynous dream all humans have known? She who closes over the unfillable gap in Being, she who does away with lack, who abolishes castration: she can be left in the shadows?"[22] The series of questions Olivier addresses leads to the following conclusion: if Oedipus is considered the universal model of man, Jocasta must be considered the universal woman and mother. What about Jocasta's guilt? Hélène's exclusion repeats that of Jocasta in our cultural tradition. The mother's divine and abjected power is nonetheless registered in the pseudonym Pierre Angélique, behind whom the stone father is also concealed.

As a prostitute, Hélène is associated with *Madame Edwarda* and also provides its sequel. *Madame Edwarda* ends in an interrogation: "God, if He knew, would be a swine. O Thou my Lord (in my distress I call out unto my heart), O deliver me, make them blind! The story—how shall I go on with it?)" (Dieu, s'il savait, serait un porc. Seigneur [j'en appelle, dans ma détresse, à mon coeur] délivrez-moi, aveuglez-les! Le récit, le continuerai-je?) (*Madame Edwarda*, in *My Mother*, 159/OC, 3:31). Here God and Bataille's father are "swine" if they knew. Hollier writes that "the note at the end of *Madame Edwarda* constitutes a transgression of the codes. It inserts a piece borrowed from a foreign code into the development of the narrative."[23] This means that the text has a circular structure. The note refers to this sentence in the narrative: "I said 'God, if He knew, would be a swine.'" In spite of his blindness and repulsive appearance, the powerful and godlike father is omnipresent in Bataille's writing. In the two pseudonyms Lord Auch and Pierre Angélique, Bataille registers, respectively, the abjected and the divine figure of the father in the act of naming God. Abjection becomes the means by which Bataille can retrieve the memory of the father from behind both the mother's madness and the desecration of the divine.

Bataille's concern with the elimination of the subject is particularly unsettling in *Ma Mère*. Hélène, who is assimilated to a book, is something like a still life, a *nature morte*. She reminds us of Manet's *Olympia*, who has lost her humanity. In Bataille's words, "We saw that *the destruction of the subject*, at least that of its meaning, was essential in *L'Exécution de Maximilien*. It is more subtle in *Olympia* where, I imagine, it is even more radical and provoking" (Nous avons vu que la *destruction du sujet*, du moins celle de sa signification, était essentielle à *L'Exécution de Maximilien*. Elle est plus subtile dans l'*Olympia* où, j'imagine, elle est plus essentielle encore, et plus provocante) (*OC*, 9:138). The Manet essay, which Bataille wrote in 1955, foreshadows Bataille's *Ma Mère*. While Rachilde's *Monsieur Vénus* mockingly reverses the gender of the anatomical Venuses, *Olympia* and *Ma Mère* manifest the scandalous death of the female model. Bataille emphasizes the extent to which death problematizes man's relation to sexuality. This constant notion of continuity between death and sexuality leads Bataille to pursue "immor(t)ality" as a means of transcending death. Immortality might thus be gained at that cost; *separare*, to separate, is here constituted around the other Latin verb *se parere*, to engender oneself, which attempts to give continuity to the life-death sequence in the guise of the maternal matrix.

"[La] Bataille, *Ma Mère*"

Death, the fact of death coming towards you, is also a memory. Like the present. It's completely here, like the memory of what has already happened and the thought of what is still to come.
MARGUERITE DURAS, *Practicalities*

The death of the Other: a double death, for the Other is death already, and weighs upon me like an obsession with death.
MAURICE BLANCHOT, *The Writing of the Disaster*

"Prostitutes and organs of pleasure are marked with 'the sign of disaster'" (Les prostituées, les organes du plaisir sont marqués "du signe néfaste") (*Guilty,* 86/*OC,* 5:329). Bataille thus anticipated the tragic destiny of *Ma Mère*. The notion of disaster is common to both Bataille and Blanchot. In *The Writing of the Disaster*, Blanchot writes: "The disaster does not put me into question, but annuls the question, makes it disappear—as if along with the question, 'I' too disappeared in the disaster that never appears."[24] *Ma Mère* explores and elaborates the "horror of being"—birth, the origin, the father's rape, the mother's abjection. That horror of being is the equivalent of what is called in *Inner Experience* a "despicable destiny" (40). If the book is a substitute for the maternal womb, the book is necessarily disastrous, improper, and "guilty" as the mother herself. The mother's elegance, beauty, and above all her laughter are signs for Pierre of her destitution: "When she had left I told myself that her beauty, her laugh, were diabolical" (Je pensai, quand elle fut partie, qu'elle avait une beauté, qu'elle avait un rire diaboliques) (*My Mother*, 29/*OC*, 4:182). Active, provocative coquetry is felt to be an aggression, a diabolical act of transgression. It is interesting to note that Hélène's aggression can constitute a mask for deeply feminine instinctual desires that are dangerous for her. And her laughter is the tragic expression of her fall.

The "absolutely feminine" is also what has been known for centuries as the "fallen woman." Linda Nochlin, quoting a Rose Macaulay novel, makes an interesting remark in this respect about how "'fallen' in the masculine means killed in the war, and in the feminine given over to a particular kind of vice."[25] The sexual asymmetry peculiar to the notion of "fallen" is worth considering, especially if we bring together Bataille's *Ma Mère* and Ernst Jünger's *La Guerre, notre mère* (1933), on which Bataille meditated and wrote extensively. We also could operate a slight change in the titles in order to stress the parallel between the two from Bataille's *Ma Mère* to Pierre Angélique's *La Bataille, ma mère*, since *bataille* means battle. The displacement of the name Bataille to the common noun "battle" not only annuls the father's name but echoes Jünger's *La Guerre, notre mère* in pointing out that the mother is the site where the battle takes place. Bataille's "war" consists of literalizing the mother into the metaphor of the book and reducing her to lifelessness. The son's desire for what is lifeless—the book, the dead mother—is the final image of man's "unity" confronted with woman. The dread derived from the menacing mother's power is finally resolved in her suicide: the son's guilt can momentarily shift from the dead father to the dead mother.

When Bataille declared, "The battlefield and its horror have not been more harshly described than by Jünger. I want to show that there exists an equivalence between *war, ritual sacrifice,* and *mystical life:* it is the same game of 'ecstasies and terrors'" (OC, 7:251), he was calling for the totalizing experience of transgression. Bataille gives special attention to warlike and religious practices that acknowledge death as a force of life rather than its tragic demise. Violence, which is traditionally kept in check by its prohibition, is constantly transgressed by Bataille's writings. *La Guerre, notre mère* is a very vivid description of World War I which depicts war as violence without limit; death becomes inextricably involved with life itself: "When the soldiers dressed in rags, went to the rear lines to get some rest, they marched in long, grey and silent columns. 'They look like they are coming from the grave,' whispered a man to his daughter" (OC, 7:253). The "generalized" violence of war is described here as absolute "horror" by Jünger and transformed into "restricted" violence in *Guilty:* "The torment of orgies is inseparable from the agony of war as Jünger pictured it" (Ce que Jünger a dit de la guerre, est à l'avance donné dans le tourment) (*Guilty,* 13/OC, 5:247). Bataille here marks the decisive passage from World War I and his father's death to *Guilty,* which, as I have already mentioned, was begun the very day World War II was declared. Could then the Oedipus complex be the discourse of mourning for the father's death? Could *Ma Mère* represent the guilt experienced by a son who was forced to take his father's place?

When France was invaded in 1914, the momentary loss of the fatherland replayed Bataille's personal drama: his mother's abandonment of his blind father in Rheims. In his "Reflections on War and Death" (1915), Freud stressed the threat to morality that war represents and the menace of "barbarism" it inevitably revives. Mourning for the father transforms the mother into that unrecognizable ab-ject which is no longer human. According to Freud, an obscure sense of guilt has been common to man since prehistoric times and has been transformed into the doctrine of original sin. It is for Freud the expression of a blood guilt incurred by primitive man: "The primal crime of mankind must have been a parricide, the killing of the primal father of the primitive horde, whose image in memory was later transformed into a deity."[26] While the primal crime of mankind has become the founding myth of religion, we have compensated for it, according to Freud, by inventing "a conception of life after death." Immortality defends against guilt and the fear of death. But guilt comes back in Bataille's writing. Not only do the deaths of his father and of his lover Laure constitute the traumatic events of his life, but they offer a vision of death and sexuality which Bataille mixes with that of death.

In Ecrits de Laure, Bataille collected his lover's writings and a short narrative, Ma Mère diagonale, written by her nephew, Jérôme Peignot.[27] In his narrative, Peignot recounts his innocent love for his aunt, whom he called "ma mère diagonale." It is the knowledge of her political commitment, sexual excesses, and marginal life that makes Peignot desire and worship Laure. This attraction recalls Pierre's infatuation with his mother. Besides, the resemblance between the two titles hints at an "oblique" lover/mother figure which obsesses Bataille's imagination. As her nephew declared, "Laure's premature death installed death in my life forever." Now, if we remember that it is the faces of the lover and the father that Bataille blurred in the same vision, there seems to be a paradox: is Laure like the father, or is she like Hélène in Ma Mère? The confusion between the two calls into question one of Bataille's most psychotic inventions.

Michel Surya shows that Bataille was convinced for a long time that his father tried to rape him in the basement of their house in Rheims. The terror that Bataille feels at the door of the basement first remains vague: "I remember having been terrified at the door" (Je me rappelle avoir tremblé de peur à la porte) (*OC*, 5:555). The fear is explicitly connected with male rape in a nightmare that Bataille retells: "I see him with a malignant and blind smile stretch his obscene hands out to me. This memory appears to be the worst of all. . . . I am perhaps three years old, with naked legs on my father's lap, and my sex in blood like the sun" (Je le vois avec un sourire fielleux et aveugle étendre des mains obscènes sur moi. Ce souvenir me paraît le plus terrible de tous. . . . J'ai comme trois ans les jambes nues sur les genoux de mon père et le sexe en sang comme du soleil) (*OC*, 2:10). The son's deepest desire and fear of being raped in the hands of the father is here expressed in the dream. Is it "a glorious castration" ("my sex in blood") that Bataille stages while dreaming? In arguing that Bataille committed a Freudian slip when he wrote "my mother" for "my father" at the end of *Ma Mère*, one can wonder if instead he was still thinking of his fears in the basement at Rheims. In this sense, *Ma Mère* would not be a matricide but a disguised patricide. Let us not forget that Bataille says: "This kiss, right away, revolted me, and I cannot stop gnashing my teeth" (Ce baiser, dès l'abord, me révolta, et je ne cesse pas d'en grincer des dents) (*OC*, 4:236). It remains undecidable whether or not Bataille was raped by his father. The impossible family constellation, however, repeats Bataille's various scenarios in which by turns the face of the lover is assimilated first with the father, then with *Ma Mère*.

Ma Mère unfolds as a jubilatory, guilty meditation, eliminating both parents. Whence the literally maddening difficulty: in order to unravel the enigma of birth and sexuality, one must destroy at one blow (*coup*) that to which no one has access, the mother's body and the father's blindness. Bataille's unrelenting contemplation of violent sexual abuses, rape, incest, and death call for the unfolding of truth. In *Ma Mère*, both parents are guilty, and the son can find no truth until they are both dead. In *Inner Experience*, Bataille wrote that "despair is simple: it is the absence of hope, of all *enticement*. It is the state of deserted expanses and—I can imagine—of the sun" (le désespoir est simple: c'est l'absence d'espoir, de tout *leurre*. C'est l'état d'étendues désertes et—je puis l'imaginer—du soleil) (*Inner Experience*, 38/OC, 5:51).

Bataille and the Desecrated Mother

> The earth beneath that body open like a grave; her naked cleft
> lay open to me like a freshly dug grave.
> GEORGES BATAILLE, *Blue of Noon*

For both Bataille and Blanchot, writing cannot be separated from the exigency of the community: "Desire, pure impure desire, is the call to bridge the distance, to die in common through separation. Death suddenly powerless, if friendship is the response that one can hear and make heard only by dying ceaselessly."[28] Blanchot's "ceaseless death" is echoed in *Ma Mère* by Hélène's injunction to her son: "I want to lead you into this world of death and corruption where you already sense that I am imprisoned; I always knew you would love it too" (Je veux te faire entrer dans ce monde de mort et de corruption où déjà tu sens bien que je suis enfermée: je savais que tu l'aimerais) (*My Mother*, 133/OC, IV:276). As I pointed out earlier, the moment Pierre begins the narrative of *Ma Mère* coincides with her death in one of the many narrative variants. Hélène's suicide leaves her son free to enter her world of excesses and suffering. If one juxtaposes the exigency of the erotic community in *Ma Mère* with writing, the posthumous text fulfills Bataille's most pressing desire, as expressed in *Guilty*:

> These notes link me to my fellow humans as a guideline, and
> everything else seems empty to me, though I wouldn't have
> wanted friends reading them. The result is I have the impres-
> sion of writing from the grave. I'd like them to be published
> when I'm dead . . . only there's the possibility I'll live a long
> time, and publications will be in my lifetime. The idea makes
> me suffer. I might change. But I have a feeling of anguish
> meantime.

Ces notes me lient comme un fil d'Ariane à mes semblables et le reste me paraît vain. Je ne pourrais cependant les faire lire à aucun de mes amis. Par là, j'ai l'impression d'écrire à l'intérieur de la tombe. Je voudrais qu'on les publie quand je serai mort, mais il se peut que je vive assez longtemps, que la publication ait lieu de mon vivant. Je souffre à cette idée. Je puis changer, mais j'éprouve en attendant de l'angoisse. (*Guilty*, 17/*OC*, 5:251–52)[29]

That Bataille wants to write from the grave suggests that by withdrawing into a symbolical death he can control his destiny. As Hollier remarks: "We might conceive as a matrix or emblem for Bataille's reflections on eroticism a somehow inverted 'plastic pun': it would equate the female sex organs and the tomb in which bodies bereft of life are laid. Deep in the Lascaux caves we realize that man's grave is also the cradle of mankind."[30] The cryptological dimension of *Ma Mère* must be recognized as an echo of *The Tears of Eros*.

The representation of woman's body as man's phallus seems to have fascinated Bataille for a long time. In a series of conferences published in the 1950s, Bataille lectured on a prehistoric figurine called the Venus of Lespugue, an illustration of which was to be inserted in *The Tears of Eros*. The figurine blurs the feminine image into the male genitals, leaving no human features to woman: "This minuscule figure has the breasts, the belly, and the buttocks of a plump woman; but her head, recalling the featureless faces of primitive statues, is relatively bigger and without doubt a phallus" (Cette figure minuscule a les seins, le ventre et les fesses d'une femme corpulente: or, sa tête rappelant en un sens les visages sans traits des statuettes aurignaciennes— mais elle, est relativement plus volumineuse—est sans équivoque un phallus) (*OC*, 9:349). This subversive nondifferentiation between woman's nakedness and man's sex—the figurine can be seen either as a naked female body or as an erect phallus— suggests Bataille's strong phallocentrism. The figurine's ambivalence replays the effacement of the maternal in the phallic paternal figure of *Ma Mère*. The father/mother confusion already noted is the trope by which Bataille radicalized the affinities between reproduction and death.

In response to his erotic fantasms, Bataille creates all throughout his literary work lovers who can't escape his obsessions. In "La Communauté désoeuvrée," Jean-Luc Nancy describes Bataille's lovers in terms of subject and object: the subject is necessarily man, the object always woman. However, claims Nancy, "it is not certain that at another level, in another reading, love and *jouissance* do not essentially belong to woman."[31] Now, it is also true that in Bataille's fiction, the privileged locus of drama is the female body: Simone in *The Story of the Eye*, Hélène in *Ma Mère*, Eponine in *L'Abbé C*, Dirty in *Blue of Noon*, *Madame Edwarda*, and Marie in *The Dead Man*.[32] The question asked by Susan Suleiman is here quite relevant even if left unanswered: "Why is it a woman who embodies most fully the paradoxical combination of pleasure and anguish that characterizes transgression—in whose body the contradictory impulses toward excess on the one hand and respect on the other are played out?[33] As far as *Ma Mère* is concerned, Hélène becomes superfluous, as we just saw. Bernard Sichère indicates also how Bataille empties out *Madame Edwarda*, leaving nothing: "Instead of Being, instead of God, not the primitive and phallic Mother, but Edwarda, a woman, a whore, a woman's sex."[34] For Sichère, *Madame Edwarda* is the triumphant negation of the occult and fetishistic religion of the maternal. *Ma Mère* confirms this notion.

The woman, the erotic object, is thus a paradoxical object in Bataille's writing. Her erotic presence is necessary only for sexual transgression and/or sacrifice. Bataille's morbid attraction to the dead mother encapsulates the dual operation of interdiction and transgression. His obsession with the mother's desecration had already been expressed in an earlier article, "Marcel Proust et la mère profanée" (1946), before it was developed in *Literature and Evil* in 1957. In this essay, called "La Jouissance fondée sur le sens criminel de l'érotisme," Bataille uses André Fretet's theory on criminal sexuality: "Somebody [i.e., Fretet] saw, arbitrarily, the sign of a pathological state in associating murder and profanation with the absolutely sacred image of the mother" (Quelqu'un a vu, arbitrairement, le signe d'un état pathologique dans l'association du meurtre et au sacrilège de l'image absolument sainte de la mère) (OC, 9:265). Bataille notes that Proust's mother disappears from *Remembrance of Things Past* without further detail. However, the grandmother's death is narrated at great length, and Bataille quotes Proust's mysterious comment: "Drawing a parallel between my grandmother's and Albertine's death, it seemed to me that my life was stained by a double murder" (Rapprochant la mort de ma grand-mère et celle d'Albertine, il me semblait que ma vie était souillée d'un double assassinat) (OC, 9:265). Bataille's reading of *Swann's Way* offers an interesting interpretation of Proust's "desecrated mother."

In *Swann's Way*, Bataille chose the episode when Mlle Vinteuil, in mourning for her dead father, lets her lesbian lover spit on the dead man's portrait. Bataille shows that Proust insists on Vinteuil's death and suffering while leaving a blank page for his mother's death in *Remembrance of Things Past*. Bataille effectively replaces one scene with another in his final argument:

> Vinteuil's daughter embodies Marcel and Vinteuil is Marcel's mother. The coming of Mlle Vinteuil's lesbian lover to the father's house is paralleled by Albertine's coming to the narrator's apartment (Albertine is in reality the chauffeur Albert Agostinelli). Nothing is said, which leaves the mother's reaction unknown in the presence of the female (or male) intruder. I imagine that there is no reader who did not see that the narrative was at this point imperfect. On the contrary, Vinteuil's death and suffering are stressed.

> La fille de Vinteuil personnifie Marcel et Vinteuil est la mère de Marcel. L'installation dans la maison, du vivant de son père, de l'amante de Mlle Vinteuil est parallèle à celle d'Albertine dans l'appartement du narrateur (Albertine, en réalité le chauffeur Albert Agostinelli). Rien n'est dit, ce qui laisse dans l'embarras, des réactions de la mère à la présence de l'intruse (ou de l'intrus). Il n'est point de lecteur, j'imagine, qui n'ait vu qu'à ce

point le récit est imparfait. Au contraire, la souffrance et la mort de Vinteuil sont dites avec insistance. (OC, 9:265)

Bataille's reading examines the reasons Marcel did not describe his mother's death in detail. For Bataille, Marcel expressed his guilt in this silence. Madame Proust's death will be in effect the result of her son's homosexuality. Like Vinteuil, she dies of a broken heart. The sadistic son (Marcel) revels in tormenting the mother. Here again, Bataille replaces the mother (Marcel's) with the father (Vinteuil). This obsessive shift in the parental constellation marks Bataille's ambiguity. It also stresses Bataille's sadism toward both mother and father.

To return to *Ma Mère*: Pierre Angélique learns that rape is the introduction to sexual reproduction and death. Henceforth, the undecidability between the different systems produced scissiparity and rape, madness and guilt, *jouissance* and death. Instead of leaving a blank about the mother's death as Proust did, Bataille elaborates a fantasmatic mother/whore who seeks her own desecration. The conspiracy of silence is continued in Bataille's *Ma Mère*, since we finally do not know what the mother wants, and Pierre's numerous narrative variants make it all the more unclear. Dark continent in Bataille or blank space in Proust: the mother, who once appeared to offer a solution to the most profound questions, is herself eclipsed and condemned to death.

AFTERWORD

Even the greatest fame leaves you unsatisfied and one almost
always dies in the uncertainty of one's proper name.

La célébrité la plus complète ne vous assouvit point et l'on
meurt presque toujours dans l'incertitude de son propre nom.

GUSTAVE FLAUBERT, *Correspondance*

"One" is always an impostor because the proper name is nothing
but a pseudonym in the final analysis. Place the emphasis here on
the "one," as in "one is always," or, as in the epigraph from Flaubert's letter to Maxime du Camp, "one dies" (*on meurt*).[1] The lesson
of the pseudonymous identities of Stendhal, Sand, Rachilde, and
Bataille is that beneath the pseudonymity of all naming lies
the irreducible anonymity of the "one," the impersonal pronoun
that hauntingly lingers within the individual idiom and without
which the idiom could never come into being. The "one" is
always there before we begin to match a name and a face; the
anonymity of language, of the "one," has always been there as the
necessary precondition for all our utterances and attributions.

The pseudonym can be either a father's name or a mother's
name or neither. As we have seen, the practice of pseudonymous
signing places the authors we have studied in a highly ex-centric
position, a position from which the invented and imposed char-

acter of names and identities becomes evident and analyzable. What I want to consider here is what becomes of the pseudonym as the moment of death approaches, at the point when the pseudonym recognizes its essential anonymity.

Having analyzed the experience of living with pseudonymity, I want now to turn to an anecdote that gives us a glimpse of what it might mean to die with a pseudonym, what Flaubert calls dying "in the uncertainty of one's proper name."

The anecdote concerns Rachilde at the age of eighty-two; she died in 1953 at the age of ninety-three. She recounts the story in *Face à la peur* (1942).[2] While trying to make her way from Paris to her country estate during the Occupation in 1941, she runs into difficulties that make her reflect on the mystery of her name. She needs money and goes to the bank, where she must establish her identity in order to withdraw funds. The problem, however, is that she has no identification papers. In order to establish her identity she goes to the local bookstore to find a copy of her latest book, which has her picture on the back cover. Luckily, there is one copy left. Proof in hand, she goes to the bank, where she discovers that the banker is acquainted with the name Rachilde but surprised to learn that Rachilde was not, as he thought, a man. This is yet another experience of "facing fear," which is revealed in its essential form as the fear of being an impostor. The inherent instability of identity and the name is radically foregrounded in times of crisis. The threat of anonymity, which we are normally able to elude and cover up, is something we are forced to face up to in wartime.

Pseudonymity is always a response to a crisis, whether it is a question of personal or familial psychology, of political or social repression or censorship, or the ultimate existential dilemma of confronting the essential anonymity of human experience. The "uncertainty of one's proper name" is what makes possible the incessant reinvention and dissolution of the self. The question of pseudonymity will thus always be a question of crisis and of the demand for self-fashioning. The pseudonym, and the name as such, are always the effect of both chance and necessity; the instability of naming is a necessary element of every name, but this necessity is given through a series of chance events and encounters. Pseudonymity is in effect inescapable in precisely the sense that chance is what must happen. In this book I have pursued the relation of pseudonymity to the maternal and to a certain resistance to patriarchal order. The issue of pseudonymity extends, however, far beyond the social and historical crises of modern French literature. Rachilde's anecdotal reflection pushes the question of the pseudonym toward the distant and more troubling horizon of the anonymity of language itself. The more extreme the crisis, the more "one" is pushed from the temporary solace of pseudonymity to the abyss of the anonymous.

Rachilde characteristically uses "one" (the French *on*) when she speaks of her mother and "she" (*elle*) when referring to herself. The replacement of the name by the pronoun signals what is for her a conflict between the *on* and the *elle*. Such usage is also a mockery of the social norms implicit in French grammar. The *elle* (Marguerite Eymery) indicates Rachilde's alienation from her own socially constituted identity. Her parodic use of *elle* constitutes an important chapter in what Luce Irigaray calls the history of "women's speech," which differs from the dominant paradigm of male speech precisely insofar as it sexualizes the neutral and neutered uses to which the masculine pronoun is commonly put: "The impersonal pronoun is the same as the masculine pronoun: *il tonne, il neige, il faut,* and not *elle tonne, elle neige, elle faut.*"[3] The pervasive use of the masculine pronoun in French grammar is for Irigaray a clear indication of masculine dominance. And Rachilde's use of pronouns, if not a subversion, is at least a disruption of our expectations concerning gender difference, since *elle,* the mother, becomes *on,* the neutral pronoun, while *je* (Rachilde) becomes *elle.* Rachilde's *elle* is not, from her point of view, an *elle* spoken by another *elle,* since it is precisely this feminine position that has been contaminated and condemned by the mother, by the *on.* It is Rachilde, "homme de lettres," who speaks of her biographical self as *elle.* As we have seen, in the process of mocking gender difference and inversions,

Rachilde invariably ends up affirming a certain masculinist bias, and she does so as a result of a fundamental and insurmountable distrust of the mother, a distrust of the nevertheless inescapable *on*. It is in the place of the *on* that Rachilde moves beyond the maternal relation to something like the work of language, death, and time. And as we have now seen in her wartime anecdote, the threat of the *on*, the threat of an absolute anonymity, appears as a menace that extends beyond the maternal relation.

And we should not fail to add that *on* too can be a name. In André Gide's *Les Caves du Vatican* (1914), Lafcadio Lwuki (pronounced Luki) is called Lonnesaitpluski, that is, *on ne sait plus qui*, one no longer knows who.[4] This character's bisexuality and illegitimacy are central issues in the narrative. The point is simply that even in the *on*, gender and origin never really disappear but only go momentarily into hiding.

NOTES

Introduction

1 Pierre Citron, "Sur deux zones obscures de la psychologie de Balzac," in *L'Année balzacienne* (1967), 4; my translation.

2 Ibid., 5. Citron here relies on the research of M. Fargeaud and R. Pierrot.

3 Honoré de Balzac, *Autre étude de femme,* in *La Comédie Humaine,* ed. Pierre-Georges Castex et al., 12 vols. (Paris: Gallimard, La Pléiade, 1976–81), 3:727–28.

4 This information is in a letter to Madame Hanska cited in Maurice Allem's introduction to *La Cousine Bette* (Paris: Garnier Frères, 1962), x.

5 In *Dudding: Des noms de Rousseau* (Paris: Galilée, 1991), Geoffrey Bennington analyzes Rousseau's pseudonyms, particularly "Dudding," a name Rousseau took during a trip to recover his physical strength. In Bennington's words, "The word 'dud' means useless, unsatisfactory, futile, something which does not work, which is not complete. The word could be used to mean a firework which cannot be lit up, a machine or a technical device which does not work, and even a bad musical composition" (56; my translation). But even though Dudding named something which does not work, Rousseau used it successfully in recovering his health with Madame de Larnage. The curative function of the pseudonym in Rousseau's life is analogous to Balzac's use of Horace de Saint-

Aubin. Unlike the figures I study in *Maternal Fictions*, Balzac and Rousseau use pseudonymous identities only on a short-term basis.

6 Luce Irigaray, *This Sex Which Is Not One*, trans. Catherine Porter and Carolyn Burke (Ithaca: Cornell University Press, 1985), 86.

7 Ibid., 87.

8 Julia Kristeva, *Tales of Love*, trans. Leon S. Roudiez (New York: Columbia University Press, 1987), 358.

9 Victor Brombert, *Stendhal: Fiction and the Themes of Freedom* (New York: Random House, 1968), 18.

10 This letter is reproduced in *Les Femmes en France*, ed. Marie Collins and Sylvie Weil Sayre (New York: Scribner's, 1974), 141–46.

11 In chapter 3, I give a detailed account of Rachilde's choice of pseud-onym. She kept the name "Rachilde, homme de lettres" all her life, even after marrying Vallette, the director of the *Mercure de France*.

12 Jennifer Birkett, *The Sins of the Fathers: Decadence in France 1870–1914* (London: Quartet Books, 1986), 189.

13 Georges Bataille, *Blue of Noon*, trans. Harry Mathews (New York: Urizen Books, 1978), 46; *Le Bleu du ciel*, in *Oeuvres complètes*, 12 vols. (Paris: Gallimard, 1971), 3:412.

Chapter One
Stendhal: The Oedipal Palimpsest

1 Jean Starobinski, *The Living Eye*, trans. Arthur Goldhammer (Cambridge: Harvard University Press, 1989), 79.

2 Stendhal, *The Life of Henry Brulard*, trans. Jean Stewart and B. C. J. G. Knight (New York: Minerva, 1968), 58; Stendhal, *Vie de Henry Brulard* (Paris: Garnier, 1961), 71. Subsequent references to the English and French editions of this work will be to page numbers of these editions. In every case the English translation will be followed by the French original.

3 Louis Marin, *La Voix excommuniée* (Paris: Galilée, 1981), 37; my translation.

4 Sigmund Freud, "Medusa's Head," in *The Standard Edition of the Complete Psychological Works of Sigmund Freud*, ed. James Strachey et al., 24 vols. (London: Hogarth Press and Institute of Psycho-Analysis, 1953–74), 18:273. All subse-quent references to this edition will be to *SE*.

5 Victor Brombert, *Stendhal: Fiction and the Themes of Freedom* (New York: Random House, 1968), 53. On p. 188, n.12, Brombert gives a historical back-ground to "babilanism": "There was supposedly, in the seventeenth century, one Babilano Pallavicino who suffered from the infirmity that later went by his name."

6 Stendhal, *Correspondance*, 2 vols. (Paris: Pléiade, 1967), 2:96–99. In this

letter to his friend Prosper Mérimée, Stendhal explained why he initially wanted to keep the name Olivier: "I took the name Olivier without thinking, just for the challenge. This name is dear to me because it is self-explanatory and not obscene. If I took Edmund or Paul, many people would not guess then that he is impotent." But later on, Stendhal listened to Mérimée's advice and changed Olivier to Octave.

7 Julia Kristeva, *Tales of Love*, trans. Leon S. Roudiez (New York: Columbia University Press, 1987), 361.

8 Ibid., 356.

9 Starobinski, *The Living Eye*, 79.

10 Stendhal, *Armance*, in *Romans et Nouvelles*, 2 vols. (Paris: Gallimard, La Pléiade, 1952), 1:183; my translation. Subsequent references to *Armance* will be made first to my translation and then to this edition of the French text.

11 Henri de Latouche, *Olivier* (Paris: Société des Médecins Bibliophiles, 1924), 94.

12 Louis Marin, "Un Evénement de lecture: ou un texte de Stendhal est pris à la lettre," *L'Ecrit du temps* 1 (1982): 100; my translation.

13 Voltaire, *Zadig*, in *The Portable Voltaire* (New York: Viking, 1963), 390.

14 Marin, *Voix excommuniée*, 185.

15 Ibid., 103–4.

16 Marin, "Un Evénement de lecture," 109; my translation.

17 Starobinski, *The Living Eye*, 86.

18 Stendhal, *Memoirs of Egotism*, trans. Hannah Josephson and Matthew Josephson (New York: Lear, 1949), 75.

19 Stendhal, *Souvenirs d'egotisme*, in *Oeuvres intimes* (Paris: Bibliothèque de la Pléiade, 1955), 1408.

20 Marin, *Voix excommuniée*, 92.

21 Stendhal, *Les Privilèges*, in *Oeuvres intimes*, 1525; my translation.

22 I am not taking into account Stendhal's numerous pseudonyms, since I am only interested in the name with which he signed his works. My concern is to examine the relationship between authorship and the maternal figure. However, I should mention that under Napoleon, Beyle changed his name to de Beyle. Some French used to mock him by saying "M. de Beyle, the son of M. Beyle," as Victor del Litto reports in his *Vie de Stendhal* (Paris: Editions du Sud, 1965), 189. Because "de Beyle" abandoned his proper name shortly after the fall of Napoleon, I don't see his gesture as marking the return to paternal legitimacy, as in the case of Honoré de Balzac.

23 Jacques Lacan, *Ecrits*, trans. Alan Sheridan (New York: W. W. Norton, 1977), 43.

24 Stendhal, *Red and Black*, trans. Robert Adams (New York: W. W. Norton, 1977), 202. Stendhal, *Le Rouge et le noir: Chronique du XIXe siècle* (Paris: Gallimard, 1972), 298–99. All references to this novel will be made first to Adams's English

NOTES TO CHAPTER ONE

translation (*Red and Black*) and then to the French text, followed by the page numbers of these two editions.

25 Brombert, *Stendhal*, 56.

26 Stendhal, *Armance*, in *Romans et nouvelles*, 2 vols. (Paris: Gallimard, La Pléiade, 1952), 1:39. Hereinafter, my English translations of this novel will be followed by references to this French edition.

27 Luce Irigaray, *Parler n'est jamais neutre* (Paris: Minuit, 1985), 170; my translation. "The forbidden," *l'interdit*, is literally in French what is not said (*entre dit*).

28 Kristeva, *Tales of Love*, 359.

29 Irigaray, *Parler n'est jamais neutre*, 160; my translation.

30 Voltaire, *Zadig*, 331.

31 Marin, "Un Evénement de lecture," 110; my translation.

32 Latouche, *Olivier*, 69.

33 Jacques Derrida, *Parages* (Paris: Galilée, 1986), 234.

34 Ibid., 237.

35 Ibid., 241.

36 Michel Serres, *L'Hermaphrodite* (Paris: Flammarion, 1987), 74. "Sarrasine s'oppose à Zambinella comme le S au Z, certes. Mais le nom de la femme ou de l'homme ou du castrat signifie, ôté le Z, en italien, les deux en elle: homme et non-homme puisque châtré, non-femme donc mais aussi femme en apparence."

37 Ibid., 143.

38 Derrida, *Parages*, 121. Derrida's phrase is "écrire-sur-vivre."

39 Gilbert Lascault, *Le Monstre dans l'art occidental* (Paris: Klincksieck, 1973), 422; my translation.

40 Shoshana Felman, *La "Folie" dans l'oeuvre romanesque de Stendhal* (Paris: José Corti, 1971), 188–90. In this chapter, Felman demonstrates how the counterfeit letter is privileged over Octave's authentic confession.

41 Irigaray, *Parler n'est jamais neutre*, 161; my translation.

42 Peggy Kamuf, *Signature Pieces: On the Institution of Authorship* (Ithaca and London: Cornell University Press, 1988), 3.

43 Antoine Berthet's trial is not the only source of inspiration for Stendhal. In *L'Affaire Lafargue et Le Rouge et le noir* (Lausanne: Editions du Grand Chêne, 1961), Claude Liprandi analyzes Adrien Lafargue's criminal affair as a supplement to *Red and Black*. According to Liprandi, it is thanks to Stendhal's *Red and Black* that the Lafargue affair is not completely forgotten today. In this study I will limit myself to Stendhal's main source of reference.

44 Kamuf, *Signature Pieces*, 4.

45 Stendhal, *Ecrits intimes*, préface et notes de Ernest Abravanel (Lausanne: Edition Rencontre, 1962), 374; my translation. Regarding the probable origin of the name Stend[h]al, Victor del Litto writes: "His pseudonym; he did not invent it. Stendal is a little town in Prussia" (*La Vie de Stendhal*, 159). This hypothesis

about Stendhal's name seems to be the strongest one, since he took the name in 1813, the year when he was the governor of Sagan, near Stendal.

46 Nicholas Rand, *Le Cryptage et la vie des oeuvres* (Paris: Aubier, 1989), 48. "Force nous est d'imaginer que désormais Beyle ne saurait rester étranger à Verrières, ni à la guillotine. Le nom propre Beyle veut dire *hache* en allemand." We should also note that Stendhal contains the five letters of (Madame de) Staël. Both Madame de Staël in *De l'Allemagne* and Stendhal in *Racine and Shakespeare* analyze in their studies the beginning of a romantic school in French literature. If Staël is contained in Stendhal, perhaps it manifests Stendhal's secret admiration for his elder.

47 Nicolas Abraham, *The Wolf-Man's Magic Word*, trans. Nicholas Rand (Minneapolis: University of Minnesota Press, 1986), lxiv.

48 Kristeva, *Tales of Love*, 358.

49 Carol Mossman, *The Narrative Matrix: Stendhal's Le Rouge et le noir* (Lexington, Ky.: French Forum, 1984), 34.

50 Ibid., 76.

51 For a discussion on Madame de Rênal's historicity as "bad" motherhood, see Leslie Rabine, *Reading the Romantic Heroine: Text, History, Ideology* (Ann Arbor: University of Michigan Press, 1985), 81–106.

52 Kristeva, *Tales of Love*, 234.

53 Ibid., 362.

54 Peter Brooks, *Reading for the Plot: Design and Intention in Narrative* (New York: Alfred A. Knopf, 1984), 87.

55 Ibid., 88.

56 Corrado Ricci, preface to *Beatrice Cenci*, trans. Morris Bishop and Henry Longan Stuart, 2 vols. (New York: Boni and Liveright, 1925), 1:v.

57 Sigmund Freud, *New Introductory Lectures on Psychoanalysis*, in *SE*, 22:120.

58 Luce Irigaray, *Speculum of the Other Woman*, trans. Gillian Gill (Ithaca: Cornell University Press, 1985), 38. Several books have been written on Freud's renunciation of the seduction theory; see Marie Balmary, *Psychoanalyzing Psychoanalysis*, trans. Ned Lukacher (Baltimore: Johns Hopkins University Press, 1982); Jeffrey Moussaieff Masson, *The Assault on Truth* (Farrar, Straus and Giroux, 1984); and Marianne Krüll, *Freud and His Father*, trans. Arnold Pomerans (New York: W. W. Norton, 1986).

59 Ibid., 38.

60 Stendhal, *Les Cenci*, in *Romans et nouvelles*, 2 vols. (Paris: Gallimard, La Pléiade, 1952), 2:691. My English translation will henceforth be followed by references to this edition.

61 Marin, *Voix excommuniée*, 80.

62 Percy Bysshe Shelley, *The Cenci*, in *Poetical Works* (London: Oxford University Press, 1967), 315.

63 Irigaray, *Speculum of the Other Woman*, 47.

NOTES TO CHAPTER ONE

64 Sigmund Freud, "The Uncanny," in *SE*, 17:245.

65 Stendhal, *Correspondance* (Paris: Le Divan, 1934), 9:310.

66 Luce Irigaray, *Le Corps-à-corps avec la mère* (Ottawa: Editions de la Pleine Lune, 1981), 19; my translation.

67 Marin, *Voix excommuniée*, 31.

68 Stendhal, *The Last Romance: Earline*, in *Oeuvres intimes*, 1503–1522. It was Henri Martineau who first published *Earline* in 1930.

Chapter Two
Sand: Double Identity

1 George Sand, *Story of My Life*, a group translation, ed. Thelma Jurgrau (Albany: State University of New York Press, 1991), 76; all references to *Story of My Life* will be made to this edition. George Sand, *Oeuvres autobiographiques*, 2 vols. (Paris: Gallimard, La Pléiade, 1970), 1:13. I will refer to the French original as *OA*.

2 *The George Sand–Gustave Flaubert Letters* (Chicago: Academy Chicago, 1979), 49. *Gustave Flaubert–George Sand Correspondance*, texte édité, préfacé par Alphonse Jacobs (Paris: Flammarion, 1981), 121.

3 Helene Deutsch, *The Psychology of Women*, 2 vols. (New York: Grune and Stratton, 1944), 1:304.

4 Ibid., 1:319.

5 Ibid.

6 Phillipe Berthier, "Corambé: Interprétation d'un mythe," in *George Sand*, ed. Simone Vierne (Paris: SEDES et CDU Réunis, 1983), 11; my translation.

7 Ibid., 15.

8 George Sand, preface to *Indiana*, in *Novels*, 20 vols. (Boston and New York: Jefferson Press, 1900–1902), 4:xv; references to *Indiana* will be made to this English translation, followed by the French text. George Sand, *Indiana* (Paris: Garnier, 1983), 14–15.

9 Nancy K. Miller, *Getting Personal* (New York and London: Routledge, 1991), 107.

10 Naomi Schor, "Female Fetishism: The Case of George Sand," in *The Female Body in Western Culture*, ed. Susan Suleiman (Cambridge: Harvard University Press, 1986), 369.

11 Schor, "Female Fetishism," 370.

12 George Sand, *Story of My Life*, 9. The editor, Thelma Jurgrau, devotes most of her introduction to Sand's *Story of My Life* to "gender positioning."

13 Sigmund Freud, "The Uncanny," in *The Standard Edition of the Complete Psychological Works of Sigmund Freud*, ed. James Strachey et al., 24 vols. (London: Hogarth Press and Institute of Psycho-Analysis, 1953–74), 17:220. Hereinafter referred to as *SE*.

14 Ibid., 17:224.

15 Julia Kristeva, *Black Sun: Depression and Melancholia*, trans. Leon S. Roudiez (New York: Columbia University Press, 1989), 26.

16 Nancy K. Miller, "Arachnologies: The Woman, the Text, and the Critic," in *The Poetics of Gender*, ed. Nancy K. Miller (New York: Columbia University Press, 1986), 278.

17 Isabelle Hoog Naginski, *George Sand: Writing for Her Life* (New Brunswick: Rutgers University Press, 1991), 75.

18 Miller, *Poetics of Gender*, 280. Miller has a long discussion in which she demonstrates that *Indiana* offers a representation of the female signature of protest. See particularly Miller, "Arachnologies," 270–81.

19 Kristeva, *Black Sun*, 256.

20 George Sand, *Entretiens journaliers avec le très docte et très habile docteur Piffoël*, in *OA*, 2:1000–1001; my translation.

21 Jean-Luc Nancy, *La Communauté désoeuvrée* (Paris: Christian Bourgeois, 1986), 42; my translation.

22 George Sand, *Mauprat*, in *Novels*, 19:9; all references to this text will be made according to this edition and followed by the French edition. George Sand, *Mauprat* (Paris: Garnier-Flammarion, 1969), 34.

23 Nancy, *Communauté désoeuvrée*, 109–10; my translation.

24 Sigmund Freud, *Totem and Taboo*, in *SE*, 13:141.

25 Julia Kristeva, *La Révolution du langage poétique* (Paris: Seuil, 1974), 452; my translation.

26 Ibid., 453.

27 Ibid.

28 Joan B. Landes, *Women and the Public Sphere in the Age of the French Revolution* (Ithaca and London: Cornell University Press, 1988), 66–67.

29 Ibid., 67.

30 Ibid., 85–86.

31 Ibid., 82.

32 Ibid., 85.

33 Hélène Cixous, *La Venue à l'écriture* (Paris: UGE, 1977), 27; my translation.

34 Ibid.

35 Madelon Sprengnether, *The Spectral Mother: Freud, Feminism, and Psychoanalysis* (Ithaca and London: Cornell University Press, 1990), 5.

36 D. A. Miller, *Narrative and Its Discontents: Problems of Closure in the Traditional Novel* (Princeton: Princeton University Press, 1981), 265.

37 Ibid., 267.

38 Ibid.

39 George Sand, *The Sin of Monsieur Antoine*, in *Novels*, 5:73; all references to this text will be followed by the French edition. George Sand, *Le Péché de Monsieur Antoine*, 2 vols. (Paris: Calmann-Lévy, 1864), 1:74.

40 Sigmund Freud, "Family Romances," in *SE*, 9:239.

41 Ibid.

42 George Sand, *Consuelo*, in *Novels*, 2:191; all references to this edition will be followed by the French edition. George Sand, *Consuelo*, 3 vols. (Paris: Garnier Frères, 1959), 2:53.

43 Michèle Hecquet, "Enfants de Bohême: naissance et légitimation chez Sand," in *Revue des Sciences Humaines* 226 (1992): 112; my translation.

44 Nancy, *Communauté désoeuvrée*, 128.

45 Naginski, *George Sand*, 177.

46 Maurice Blanchot, *The Unavowable Community*, trans. Pierre Joris (Barrytown: Station Hill Press, 1988), 13.

47 Marguerite Duras is the pseudonym that she took when she began writing. Duras is the name of a small town in the southwest of France where her father had a small estate. In an interview, Marguerite Duras comments on her hatred of her family name: "But I've never tried to find out why I've been so horrified by my name that I can hardly manage to pronounce it" (Marguerite Duras and Xavière Gauthier, *Woman to Woman*, trans. Katharine Jensen [Lincoln: University of Nebraska Press, 1987], 10).

48 Marguerite Duras, *India Song*, trans. Barbara Bray (New York: Grove, 1976), 77.

49 Ibid., 143.

50 Kristeva, *Black Sun*, 249.

51 Ibid., 243.

Chapter Three
"Mademoiselle Baudelaire": Rachilde and the Sexual Difference

1 Rachilde, *Pourquoi je ne suis pas féministe* (Paris: Edition de France, 1928), 6.

2 Auriant, *Souvenirs sur Madame Rachilde* (Paris: A l'Ecart, 1989), 26.

3 Auriant, *Souvenirs*, 60. Rachilde's letter is cited by Auriant in his footnotes.

4 Rachilde, *The Juggler*, trans. Melanie Hawthorne (New Brunswick: Rutgers University Press, 1990), 161.

5 Auriant, *Souvenirs*, 61.

6 Maurice Barrès, preface to Rachilde, *Monsieur Vénus* (Paris: Flammarion, 1977), 5.

7 Michel Butor, *Histoire extraordinaire: Essai sur un rêve de Baudelaire* (Paris: Gallimard, 1961), 86; my translation.

8 Ibid., 85.

9 Barbara Johnson has an interesting point concerning sadism versus masochism in Baudelaire. She writes: "When men employ the rhetoric of self-torture, it is *read* as rhetoric. When women employ it, it is confession" (Barbara

Johnson, "Charles Baudelaire and Marceline Desbordes-Valmore," in *Displacements: Women, Tradition, Literatures in French*, ed. Joan Dejean and Nancy K. Miller [Baltimore and London: Johns Hopkins Press, 1991], 176). In the parallel that I am drawing between Baudelaire's and Rachilde's work, both described love as an experience of fragmentation, wounding, and/or loss of psychological control. When Barrès nicknamed Rachilde "Mademoiselle Baudelaire," he certainly intended to read Rachilde's "sadism" as a reinscription of the dominant ideology. In reconsidering masochism and masculinity in Baudelaire's *Fleurs du mal*, Johnson insists that "Baudelaire would seem to have raised the poetics of masochism to new heights. There is certainly no simple correlation here between femininity and passivity, masculinity and action" (175). Rachilde's *Monsieur Vénus* seems indeed to dramatize masculine masochism.

    10 Charles Baudelaire, *Oeuvres complètes*, ed. Yves Dantec (Paris: Gallimard, La Pléiade, 1961), 902.

    11 Rachilde, *Monsieur Vénus*, 227–28; my translation throughout.

    12 Barrès, preface to *Monsieur Vénus*, 5.

    13 Jennifer Birkett, *The Sins of the Fathers: Decadence in France 1870–1914* (London: Quartet Books, 1986), 165.

    14 Charles Baudelaire, *Mon coeur mis à nu*, in *Oeuvres complètes*, 1275.

    15 Paul-Laurent Assoun, *Le Pervers et la femme* (Paris: Anthropos, 1989), 92; my translation.

    16 Ibid., 100.

    17 Baudelaire, *Mon coeur*, 1272.

    18 Birkett, *Sins of the Fathers*, 159.

    19 Rachilde, *Monsieur Vénus*, 85.

    20 Jennifer Waelti-Walters, *Feminist Novelists of the Belle Epoque* (Bloomington: Indiana University Press, 1990), 162.

    21 Barrès, preface to Rachilde, *Monsieur Vénus*, 19.

    22 Dorothy Kelly, *Fictional Genders: Role and Representation in Nineteenth-Century French Narrative* (Lincoln: University of Nebraska Press, 1989), 154.

    23 Ibid.

    24 Susan Gubar, "The Blank Page and the Issues of Female Creativity," in *The New Feminist Criticism*, ed. Elaine Showalter (New York: Pantheon, 1985), 293.

    25 Ibid., 295.

    26 Birkett, *Sins of the Fathers*, 165.

    27 Claude Dauphiné, *Rachilde, femme de lettres 1900* (Périgueux: Pierre Franlac, 1985), 27. Dauphiné's source for her account of Rachilde's paralysis is Rachilde's own *A Mort* (Paris: Monnier, 1886).

    28 Richard Sonn, *Anarchism and Cultural Politics in Fin de Siècle France* (Lincoln: University of Nebraska Press, 1989), 238.

    29 Birkett, *Sins of the Fathers*, 165.

NOTES TO CHAPTER THREE

30 Elaine Showalter, *Sexual Anarchy: Gender and Culture at the Fin de Siècle* (New York: Viking, 1990), 129–30.

31 Ibid., 128.

32 Rachilde, *La Marquise de Sade* (Paris: Mercure de France, 1981), 182. All future references to this work will be to this edition; my translation throughout.

33 It is intriguing that Rachilde chose Mary de Caumont as her heroine's married name, for there was a seventeenth-century woman writer called Charlotte-Rose de Caumont La Force whose works influenced the young Rachilde. She never married. Mary breaks away from all forms of familial tyranny, as Rachilde did when she became a novelist.

34 Bram Dijkstra, *Idols of Perversity: Fantasies of Feminine Evil in Fin-de-Siècle Culture* (New York: Oxford University Press, 1986), 336.

35 Ibid., 338.

36 Ibid., 340.

37 Rachilde, *Le Grand Saigneur* (Paris: Flammarion, 1922), 258; my translation.

38 Sigmund Freud, "Some Psychical Consequences of the Anatomical Distinction between the Sexes," in *The Standard Edition of the Complete Psychological Works of Sigmund Freud*, ed. James Strachey et al., 24 vols. (London: Hogarth Press and Institute of Psycho-Analysis, 1953–74), 19:257.

39 Marquis de Sade, "Yet Another Effort, Frenchmen," in *Philosophy in the Bedroom*, trans. Richard Seaver and Austryn Wainhouse (New York: Grove, 1965), 318.

40 Luce Irigaray, *This Sex Which Is Not One*, trans. Catherine Porter and Carolyn Burke (Ithaca: Cornell University Press, 1985), 199.

41 Ibid.

42 Ibid., 201.

43 Ibid., 200.

44 Ibid., 201.

45 Ibid., 201–2.

46 Charles Baudelaire, *Le Peintre de la vie moderne*, in *Oeuvres complètes*, 1182.

47 Joan Riviere, "Womanliness as a Masquerade," in *Formations of Fantasy*, ed. Victor Burgin, James Donald, and Cora Kaplan (London and New York: Methuen, 1986), 37, 43.

48 Marquis de Sade, "Reflections on the Novel," in *The 120 Days of Sodom and Other Writings* (New York: Grove, 1966), 110.

49 Luce Irigaray, *Parler n'est jamais neutre* (Paris: Minuit, 1985), 172; my translation.

50 Rachilde, *Face à la peur* (Paris: Mercure de France, 1942), 54–55.

51 Birkett, *Sins of the Fathers*, 187.

52 Rachilde, *Le Meneur de louves* (Paris: Mercure de France, 1929), 7, 22; my translation throughout. In one of Rachilde's later autobiographical novels,

Duvet-D'Ange, one of the characters comments proudly on her ability to translate the Latin of Gregory of Tours: "Could you find me a woman of letters capable of translating Gregory of Tours without a dictionary" (Trouvez moi donc une femme, même de lettres qui traduise Grégoire de Tours à livre ouvert) (Rachilde, *Duvet-D'Ange: Confessions d'un jeune homme de lettres* [Paris: Albert Messein, 1943], 146). This character doubtless speaks for Rachilde herself.

In *Rachilde*, Ernest Gaubert mentions Rachilde's translation and transformation of Gregory's text while quoting the Latin in a footnote: "Delusa a pueris reginae" (Ernest Gaubert, *Rachilde* [Paris: Bibliothèque Internationale d'Edition, 1907], 33). In Gregory's chronicle, Rachilde discerns a rape and elaborates it into the traumatic event that transforms Basine into a she-wolf. Lewis Thorpe's English translation renders Gregory's "ill usage" as the even vaguer notion of "trickery": "His sister (Basine) was tricked by Fredegund's servants and persuaded into entering a nunnery, where she has become a religious and where she remains to this day. All their property was purloined by the Queen" (Gregory of Tours, *The History of the Franks*, trans. Lewis Thorpe [New York: Penguin, 1986], 304–5). Rachilde in effect invents rather than translates this tragic event of Basine's life.

53 Sonn, *Anarchism and Cultural Politics*, 272.

54 Gregory of Tours, *History of the Franks*, 567.

55 Rachilde, *La Jongleuse* (Paris: Edition des Femmes, 1982), 7–23. All references to *La Jongleuse* will be to this edition.

56 Rachilde, *The Juggler*, trans. Melanie Hawthorne (New Brunswick: Rutgers University Press, 1990), 108. All references to *The Juggler* will be to this edition.

57 Waelti-Walters, *Feminist Novelists*, 173.

58 Julia Kristeva, *Tales of Love*, trans. Leon S. Roudiez (New York: Columbia University Press, 1987), 244.

59 Otto Rank, *The Don Juan Legend*, trans. David Winter (Princeton: Princeton University Press, 1975), 87.

60 Ibid., 29.

61 Ibid., 95.

62 Assoun, *Le Pervers et la femme*, 109.

63 Rachilde, *Duvet-D'Ange*, 140–41.

64 Sonn, *Anarchism and Cultural Politics*, 280.

Chapter Four
Divinus Deus: Bataille's Erotic Education

1 Georges Bataille, *Oeuvres complètes*, 12 vols. (Paris: Gallimard, 1970–1988), 1:644, notes. All references to OC will be made in the text; my translation throughout.

2 Michel Surya, *Georges Bataille: la mort à l'oeuvre* (Paris: Garamont, 1987), 16; my translation.

3 Georges Bataille, *My Mother*, trans. Austryn Wainhouse (London: Marion Boyars, 1989), 50.

4 Georges Bataille, *Inner Experience*, trans. Leslie Ann Boldt (Albany: State University of New York Press, 1988), 3.

5 Denis Hollier, "Bataille's Tomb: A Halloween Story," in *October* 33 (1985): 82.

6 Cf. Julia Kristeva, *Tales of Love*, trans. Leon S. Roudiez (New York: Columbia University Press, 1987), 365ff.

7 Georges Bataille, *The College of Sociology*, trans. Betsy Wing (Minneapolis: University of Minnesota Press, 1988), 121.

8 Georges Bataille, *Death and Sensuality: A Study of Eroticism and the Taboo* (New York: Ballantine Books, 1962), 264.

9 Georges Bataille, *Guilty*, trans. Bruce Boone, introd. Denis Hollier (Venice: Lapis Press, 1988), 11.

10 Denis Hollier writes that *Somme athéologique*, published during the Second World War, obliterates Bataille's earlier *Notre-Dame de Reims* (1914), "the cathedral that anticipated the Te Deum celebrating the end of World War I" (*Against Architecture: The Writings of Georges Bataille*, trans. Betsy Wing [Cambridge, Mass.: MIT Press, 1989], 152).

11 This long footnote, which illuminates Bataille's complex relationship with his father, was not translated in the English edition of *Guilty* mentioned above.

12 Susan Suleiman, "Transgression and the Avant-Garde: Bataille's *Histoire de l'Oeil*," in *Subversive Intent* (Cambridge: Harvard University Press, 1990), 86.

13 Luce Irigaray, *This Sex Which Is Not One*, trans. Catherine Porter and Carolyn Burke (Ithaca: Cornell University Press, 1985), 42.

14 Necrophilia with the mother is again mentioned in *OC*, 3:60, and *Blue of Noon*, trans. Harry Mathews (New York: Urizen Books, 1978), 76–77.

15 Sigmund Freud, *The Standard Edition of the Complete Psychological Works of Sigmund Freud*, ed. James Strachey et al., 24 vols. (London: Hogarth Press and Institute of Psycho-Analysis, 1953–74), 7:161. Hereinafter referred to as *SE*.

16 Julia Kristeva, *Powers of Horror*, trans. Leon Roudiez (New York: Columbia University Press, 1983), 64.

17 Hollier, *Against Architecture*, 155.

18 Freud, *SE*, 4:172.

19 Hollier, *Against Architecture*, 156.

20 Jane Marcus, *Art and Anger* (Columbus: Ohio State University Press, 1988), 237.

21 Linda Nochlin, *Women, Art, and Power* (New York: Harper and Row, 1988), 92–93.

22 Christiane Olivier, *Jocasta's Children: The Imprint of the Mother*, trans. George Craig (London and New York: Routledge, 1989), 1.

23 Hollier, *Against Architecture*, 160.

24 Maurice Blanchot, *The Writing of the Disaster*, trans. Ann Smock (Lincoln: University of Nebraska Press, 1986), 28.

25 Nochlin, *Women, Art, and Power*, 57.

26 Freud, *SE*, 14:293.

27 Jérôme Peignot, *Ma Mère diagonale*, in *Ecrits de Laure* (Paris: Jean-Jacques Pauvert, 1971).

28 Blanchot, *Writing of the Disaster*, 29.

29 This quotation is accompanied by a footnote explaining that *Guilty* was to be published in 1940 in the magazine *Mesures* under the pseudonym Dianus. The first edition of *Guilty* was finally published in 1944, since it had not been destroyed in the war. The anguish expressed by Bataille at publishing while he was still alive might partly explain his love for pseudonyms. Dianus can be made into *di[t] anus* (said anus), combining guilt with scatological references.

30 Hollier, "Bataille's Tomb," 74.

31 Jean-Luc Nancy, "La Communauté désoeuvrée," in *Alea* 4 (1983): 33.

32 *Le Mort (The Dead Man)* was first published posthumously in 1964. However, the original draft of *The Dead Man* dates back as far as 1943. If one recalls that *Madame Edwarda* was first published in 1941, one is struck by the similarity of the two names: Edwarda the divine prostitute and Edward the dead man. Surely this is no coincidence. Edward is closely related to Bataille's state of being during 1942–43. As he himself said: "There is in any case the narrowest tie between *Le Mort* and my stay in Normandy as the consumptive I then was" (*The Dead Man*, in *My Mother*, 165). The intense sexual excitement which dominates both *The Dead Man* and *Madame Edwarda* replays Bataille's own mad and anguished excitement in nearly complete solitude.

33 Suleiman, *Subversive Intent*, 82–83.

34 Bernard Sichère, "Le Nietzsche de Georges Bataille," in *Stanford French Review* 12 (1988): 26; my translation.

Afterword

1 Gustave Flaubert, *Correspondance*, in *Oeuvres complètes*, 9 vols. (Paris: Louis Conard, 1926–37), 2:442.

2 Rachilde, *Face à la peur* (Paris: Mercure de France, 1942), 64.

3 Luce Irigaray, *Je, tu, nous* (Paris: Grasset, 1990), 37. The English translation cannot, of course, render Irigaray's point, since "il neige, il faut" is translated in English as "it snows" and not "he snows," "you must" and not "he has to."

4 André Gide, *Les Caves du Vatican* (Paris: Gallimard, 1922), 227.

NOTES TO AFTERWORD

INDEX

217

INDEX

About the Author

Maryline Lukacher is Associate Professor of French
at Northern Illinois University. Her articles on nineteenth-
century French literature have appeared in *Romanic
Review, Nineteenth-Century French Studies, George Sand
Studies,* and *George Sand Today.*

Library of Congress Cataloging-in-Publication Data

Lukacher, Maryline
Maternal fictions : Stendhal, Sand, Rachilde, and Bataille /
Maryline Lukacher.
p. cm.
Includes index.
ISBN 0-8223-1432-0 (cloth). — ISBN 0-8223-1436-3 (paper)
1. French fiction—19th century—History and criticism.   2. Stendhal,
1783–1842—Characters—Mothers.   3. Sand, George, 1804–1876—
Characters—Mothers.   4. Rachilde, 1860–1953—Characters—
Mothers.   5. Bataille, Georges, 1897–1962—Characters—Mothers.
6. French fiction—20th century—History and criticism.   7. Mother and
child in literature.   8. Motherhood in literature.   9. Mothers in
literature.   I. Title.
PQ653.L84   1994
843.009'352042—dc20   93-38693
CIP